CONTENTS

ACKNOWLEDGEMENTS
AND SOURCES

George Weidenfeld and I have discussed a memoir on and off for years. I have now decided to write it, after meeting Cate Haste and realizing that her enthusiasm and professionalism could make it possible. I would like to thank Cate for all her sympathetic help.

*　　*　　*

This memoir has drawn on Clarissa Eden's letters to friends and acquaintances and the letters written to her from members of her family, including regular correspondence from her mother, Lady Gwendeline, her brothers and her Uncle Winston and Aunt Clemmie. We have also had the benefit of her appointments diaries, especially during and shortly after the war, and the diaries she kept from 1952 to 1957. The diaries are continuous for the period; most were written on the day or within a day of the events described, with some exceptions when she looks back over a brief period. We have also drawn on her husband Anthony Eden's diaries, his letters to Clarissa and his memoirs.

Letters to Clarissa Eden from friends, colleagues and acquaintances from her early life through her years in politics have been an invaluable source, and in all cases we have appreciated the co-operation of the authors and that of their trustees in reproducing these.

We would like to thank those who have helped us with access to documents and other material, and with advice and the benefit of their expertise during the course of researching and writing this memoir: D.R. Thorpe, Mary Gifford of the Berners Trust, Hugo Vickers for his encyclopaedic knowledge of the period, Vernon Bogdanor, Guy Millard, George Weidenfeld, Henry Hardy, Mark Amory, Michael Mallon, Fionn Morgan for kindly tracing Clarissa's correspondence with Ann Fleming. Also Nicola Rayner and Casie Kesterton for additional research. We have appreciated the assistance and co-operation of Chatham House (Royal Institute of International Affairs); Andrew Riley at the Churchill Archives Centre, Churchill College, Cambridge Philippa Bassett at the Avon Archive, Special Collections, University of Birmingham; Dr Louis Marchesano, Wim de Witt and Jeanne Roberts at the Getty Research Institute, Los Angeles, and the staff of the London Library.

We are particularly grateful to those who generously read the manuscript and offered their invaluable advice, amendments and encouragement: D.R. Thorpe, Vernon Bogdanor, Hugo Vickers, John Gross, Melvyn Bragg, Faith Evans.

We acknowledge the following:
The letters and unpublished diary of Cecil Beaton: © the Literary Executors of the late Sir Cecil Beaton, 2007. Letters of James Pope-Hennessy: Copyright by permission of the estate of James Pope-Hennessy. Quotations from Isaiah Berlin letters: © The Isaiah Berlin Literary Trust 2007, used with the Trustees' permission. Extracts from Lord Berners' letters and from *Far From the Madding War* by permission of the Berners Trust. Extracts from Duff Cooper letters by permission of John Julius Norwich. Clementine Churchill's letter to Lady Gwendeline Churchill by permission of Mary Soames. Ann Fleming's letter by permission of her literary executor, Mark Amory. Extract from Joyce Cary's *Memoir of the*

Bobotes: © Arthur Joyce Lunel Cary. Reprinted by permission of the Trustees of the A.J.L. Cary Estate. Extract from Winston Churchill letter reproduced with permission of Curtis Brown Ltd, London, on behalf of the Estate of Winston Churchill. © Winston S. Churchill. Evelyn Waugh's letters by permission of PFD on behalf of the Estate of Laura Waugh. Extract from Cyril Connolly letter © Cyril Connolly 1956 by permission of the author c/o Rogers, Coleridge & White. Extracts from *Vogue* © Condé Nast. Simon Asquith letters by permission of Vivien Asquith. Extract from John Sparrow letter by permission of the literary executors of John Sparrow. Letters from Julian Oxford reproduced with his permission.

With the following exceptions, all photographs are reproduced from the collection of the Countess of Avon:

Ex-prime ministers' wives, 2004, Camera Press/Jane Hodson

Duff Cooper; Garbo and cat; with Garbo on the terrace; formal tiara portrait; leaning on birdcage; with Radziwill and Freud; with Claudette Colbert; with Anthony Eden on terrace; with Anthony Eden in Rose Bower, Cecil Beaton Archive/Sotheby's

Anthony Eden says goodbye to Winston Churchill at No. 10, Getty Images

Dinner at No. 10 for Winston Churchill; election cover of *Sphere;* with the Queen and others; with Mamie Eisenhower, Geneva; old friends say goodbye, Illustrated London News Picture Library

Wedding reception in garden No. 10; Tilbury departure for New Zealand tour, Mirrorpix

Sir Isaiah Berlin and Lord David Cecil © Norman Parkinson Archive

Clarissa Spencer Churchill working for Korda Publicity; Anthony Eden 1935; leaving No. 10 for wedding; arrival at Caxton Hall;

Anthony Eden with Nasser; Guy Mollet at No 10; Foster Dulles at No. 10; dinner at French Embassy, TopFoto

Beaton, Berners, Ashton, Cecil Beaton/*Vogue* Sept 1946 © The Condé Nast Publications Ltd

INTRODUCTION

Cate Haste

On 18 January 1957 Clarissa Eden and her husband, Anthony, boarded a liner at the Royal Albert Dock bound for New Zealand. Both were under strain. At sixty, Eden was still handsome, but exhaustion and illness were etched on his face. Only nine days before (9 January) he had resigned as Britain's Prime Minister due to ill health. He had served only twenty months in office.

Friends and political colleagues lined the quay in the frozen sunshine to wave the couple off; at the entrance to the covered gangway they were greeted by a round of clapping from dock workers, and messages of support and goodwill flowed in from all over the country. There was deep sadness at the parting. Clarissa's concern was the recovery of her husband's health and spirits. For Eden, it was the end of a political career spanning three decades in which early promise had ripened to distinction as Foreign Secretary and then the prize of the premiership.

Even before they sailed away, the new Prime Minister, Harold Macmillan, had taken over, politics had moved on and the reckoning on Eden's premiership had begun.

The pressures at Downing Street during the previous six months had been intense as the Suez Crisis, one of the major turning points in the twentieth century, had engulfed the couple and the nation.

Eden's decision, backed by a well-nigh unanimous Cabinet, to reclaim the Suez Canal to international control by force was – and remains – controversial, though Eden's personal popularity rating just prior to his resignation was high at 56 per cent.

For Clarissa, much younger at thirty-seven, their departure was another new beginning. Before her marriage and her late entry into politics, she had already crafted a life of her own. Politics had changed all that.

This memoir covers Clarissa's early life and her life in politics. It properly falls into two parts. They are both factually and atmospherically different, though Clarissa entered wholeheartedly into each phase. Her life has spanned several different worlds, and she met and made friends with some of the most colourful and influential figures of the twentieth century. Always clear-sighted and individual, she observes them with a shrewd and perceptive eye.

Happily, Clarissa belongs to a generation who wrote regularly to each other and who preserved their letters, many in their original envelopes, so she could draw on these and her appointment diaries as aides-mémoires for the early part of her life covered in Part One. From 1952 she kept regular diaries recording her own experiences and what her husband told her of the day's events in Cabinet and the interactions of government when he was Foreign Secretary, then Prime Minister. We have quoted from these at length and they form the backbone to Part Two of the memoir. The difference in tone and atmosphere reflects the change in Clarissa's own life.

Though born into the aristocracy, Clarissa Churchill seemed never to have quite identified with that class. When she was old enough to decide on the direction of her life, it was not to a make a 'good' marriage, as was expected, or to become the graceful chatelaine of a country estate. She decided to pursue her own interests.

Her mother, Lady Gwendeline Bertie, known as 'Goonie', was the daughter of the 7th Earl of Abingdon. Renowned for a subtle twilight beauty and alluring charm, she was intelligent and widely read, although untutored, and had a wide-ranging interest in culture and the arts. She seemed a romantic figure, with blue eyes the colour of cornflowers and dark auburn hair, elegant and civilised, with a delicate natural sympathy and perceptive appreciation for other people's qualities. Admirers noted her clear-eyed shrewdness, amused scepticism and the mischievous irony that flickered over her conversation.

In 1908 she married John Strange Spencer-Churchill, a quiet man, courteous and good-looking, the younger brother of Winston Churchill. 'Jack' had become a partner in the City stockbrokers Vickers, da Costa with the help of his Harrow schoolmate, Lionel de Rothschild. He had fought in the Boer War, arriving on a hospital ship equipped by his mother, Jennie Churchill, and then in the First World War, where he served on the staff of General Birdwood, Commander of the ANZAC Corps, at Gallipoli then the Western Front. He was mentioned in dispatches and awarded the DSO.

Within a month of Jack marrying Goonie, Winston married Clementine Hozier and the two families spent much of their early married lives together. The brothers were close, with Jack playing the supportive role to the more ambitious, flamboyant Winston. It was one of Winston's dictums that blood was thicker than water, Clarissa recalls, and that was how he behaved towards the family, whatever idiocies the younger members got up to. Goonie, with her sympathetic nature, got on well with the more highly strung Clemmie, who found in her sister-in-law a safety valve and confidante.

Though Jack and Goonie were not well off, they were well connected. Goonie already had an extensive network of friends including those from the Liberal world and the more interesting figures from the Conservative aristocracy, and her admirers included people from the world of the arts who paid her regular visits. Clarissa found her mother's friends from this varied social tapestry sympathetic and interesting.

Jack was cousin to the Duke of Marlborough. His father, Lord Randolph Churchill, the second surviving son of the 7th Duke of Marlborough, Conservative MP and one-time Chancellor of the Exchequer, had married Jennie Jerome, the beautiful daughter of a New York stockbroker. The family took a dim view of Leonard Jerome and opposed the marriage, but, taking into account the parlous finances of Blenheim Palace and the beauty of his future daughter-in-law, the Duke's view softened with Jerome's offer of a £50,000 dowry. Clarissa never knew her grandmother, who died of a haemorrhage eighteen months after she was born.

Goonie and Jack were regular visitors at Blenheim Palace. His cousin 'Sunny', the Duke of Marlborough, had married another exotic American beauty, Consuelo Vanderbilt, daughter of an American railroad millionaire, who had been forced into the marriage by her socially ambitious mother and is said to have wept behind her veil throughout the ceremony. After performing her duties as chatelaine of Blenheim Palace and producing two sons, an heir and a spare, Consuelo left. On her divorce in 1921 she married, for love, Jacques Balsan, a French textile heir and rather dashing pioneer balloonist and aviator. Goonie kept up her friendship with Consuelo after the split, and Clarissa and her mother were lent their *moulin* in Normandy and stayed at the main chateau where, Clarissa remembers, the sheets were so fine that they ruched up and became positively uncomfortable.

Clarissa, a longed-for daughter, was born on 28 June 1920. With her brothers, Johnnie and Peregrine, respectively eleven and seven years older, she was brought up as virtually an only child. Johnnie became an artist who conducted an erratic married life, Peregrine was an engineer who, according to Goonie, carried around with him an air of Chekhovian gloom.

Clarissa's schooling was patchy. At six she was judged an intelligent, enthusiastic and capable little girl, always delightful to deal with. At fourteen her headmistress reported she was clever, with a good brain: capable of doing one of the very best matriculation certificates, but her groundwork was poor. Certainly she was spirited and somewhat rebellious. She found her mother's concern and love overbearing: 'Why so hectic about me? I am quite well and happy, don't spend so much on the telephone,' she wrote perkily, aged ten, from her cousin's at Wroxham in Norfolk, where she was climbing trees and swatting stray bats in the night.

Within a year of leaving school Clarissa was restless. She discovered a hunger for knowledge and intellectual life and a delight in art and culture which her inadequate schooling had failed to satisfy. Having found what interested her, she set about educating herself. She failed to enter fully into the spirit of her 'coming out' in Society as a débutante – a year involving a busy social schedule – and spent much time attending daily art and philosophy lectures. Even so, her Aunt Clemmie reported to Goonie: 'On all sides I hear of Clarissa's charm and success and beauty. I am so glad, because I love Clarissa. I hope she will make a happy and brilliant marriage. She is made to shine.' Uncle Winston thought she had 'a most unusual personality'.

Clarissa was making her mark. At eighteen she was a beautiful, stylish and enigmatic figure, with clear blue eyes and golden hair likened to 'the colour of cornfields at sunrise'. An admirer – the writer James Pope-Hennessy – thought that she had éclat, combining 'the aristocratic traditions of the England that was worth living in' with a film star-like glamour. Hugh Fraser nicknamed her 'Garbo'.

She had a gift for deep friendship. Men loved her. Striking and unusual, she sometimes lacked confidence, though her natural poise and style belied this. She could give an impression of being aloof when, in fact, she simply remained silent if she felt she had nothing worthwhile to say.

She was, and is, impatient with convention and not afraid to be abrupt. Singular in her judgements, she has wit and an often mischievous sense of humour, with a keen sense of the absurd and strong antennae for pretentiousness and humbug. Nor was she concerned about what others thought – and some found her directness and intellectual honesty daunting. Many were, and still are, intrigued by her individuality. Of those who became friends in the discerning atmosphere of Oxford's academia, philosopher Isaiah Berlin thought her 'upright and downright', which amused her, and praised her 'noble and unbending pride and disdain for the minutest kind of cheating & compromise . . . hence your reproaches when I seemed to you to betray some clear standard of integrity or even manners'. Lord David Cecil delighted in her conversation.

In her twenties, she moved by choice almost entirely in literary and cultural circles, though she was also at ease in the social milieu of the most interesting British and European aristocracy. Her marriage launched her into the upper echelons of yet another world: politics, where she eventually found herself as chatelaine of No. 10 Downinng Street.

PART ONE

CHAPTER I

BACKGROUND

M y mother's family had lived at Wytham Abbey until, in the 1930s, my grandfather – having spent all his inheritance – sold the whole thing to a South African and moved to an incredible house called Oaken Holt, on the Botley Road out of Oxford, all 1920s beams painted high-gloss black.

The Abbey before the First World War had been a magnet for young men from Oxford and neighbouring houses to come over and see my mother. Among them Harold Nicolson, Winston Churchill from Blenheim and his much younger brother Jack. My mother married Jack.

Before the First World War my family had bought 41 Cromwell Road in South Kensington. My aunt, Clementine Churchill, and her three children moved temporarily into our house after my Uncle Winston ceased to be First Lord of the Admiralty in 1915 and was at the Front. The two families decided to pool their resources, money was tight, and my two brothers and their three cousins – Diana, Randolph and Sarah – all squashed into No. 41. Even so, Winston – rarely one to stint – urged Clemmie and Goonie to 'keep a good table ... Keep sufficient servants & your maid: entertain with discrimination, have a little amusement from time to time. I don't see any reason for undue skimping

... With £140 a month there should be sufficient.'

I was born and brought up in Cromwell Road, where my nursery window looked out on the multicoloured, multi-everything Natural History Museum. From an early age I was taken there and to the Victoria and Albert just along the road – it was considered educative. A near neighbour was John Lavery, portrait painter, looking like a little Irish jockey with sideburns. His wife, Hazel, was a majestic beauty with auburn hair and very pale skin. Lavery painted my mother three or four times and is credited with introducing my Uncle Winston to painting.

One of my early memories was hearing a terrible noise in the street outside. I was taken to the window and the narrow street beside our house was full of men and women, one woman with a red stocking on her head. The crowd were all screaming and shouting. I believe it was a protest against Uncle Winston putting Britain on the gold standard: they thought he was still living there.

Once Uncle Winston and Aunt Clemmie had bought Chartwell in Kent in 1922, I was often packed off there for holidays – my own family having no house in the country till I was about fourteen. My two brothers matched in age the elder Churchill children, but I was three years older than Mary, which, when one is a child, makes a big difference. However, we got along well enough during the holidays. I saw little of my older cousins, Diana and Sarah, who were already leading their own lives. Later, the only son Randolph and I became fond of each other, as we had friends and a sense of humour in common.

Mary lived in a wing of the house in the charge of Cousin Moppet – a cousin of my aunt's – so I only saw Uncle Winston at lunch, an event which took several hours and always contained dire prognostications about the coming disasters, coupled with loving conversations with, and feeding of, his dog or cat, the latter usually stalking about on the dining room table. As time went by the prognostications became more urgent. A year or so before the war he told us that the first thing that would happen would be a gas attack.

Each August we took a Norfolk house called Horsey Hall for the summer holidays. This was the time when I saw my father most. In London he would leave early in the morning for the City and come back late at night, go into the library, open his *Evening Standard* and I was allowed about a quarter of an hour with him. In Norfolk I could join him sailing on the Broads. Bathing in the ice-cold North Sea, spending ages each night with a pillow swatting mosquitoes flat on to the ceiling of my bedroom (before the days of DDT) and endless sunny days are my memories of these summers. My father liked having the daughter of his business partner to stay – Joan Vickers. I would see them sailing off together on Horsey Mere. She was very fond of my father; it was one of those friendships that crossed generations. He later backed her financially in her 1945 election campaign, but did not live long enough to see her elected to Parliament in 1955. She rose subsequently in the political ranks and ended in the House of Lords.

My mother would take me with her to the houses of her friends. At Mells Manor in Somerset, Lady Horner was the chatelaine (it was a Horner house).* She still bore traces of the features that had made her a muse of the Pre-Raphaelites – large, wide-set eyes, small nose, firm jawbone. She had a constant friend in attendance, Anglican Canon Hannay (aka George A. Birmingham, the novelist) who lived in polite juxtaposition to her daughter Katharine Asquith's Father

---

* 'Little Jack Horner / Sat in a corner / Eating his Christmas pie. / He put in his thumb / And pulled out a plum / And said, "what a good boy am I."' Mells had been in the Horner family since Henry VIII's dissolution of the monasteries. It is said that the Bishop of Glastonbury sent his steward (Richard Whiting-Horner) with the deeds of twelve manorial estates hidden in a pie, to bribe the King to save the monastery. He failed, the Bishop was hung, drawn and quartered at Glastonbury Tor, and Horner either stole, or was rewarded with, the deeds to Mells Manor.

d'Arcy, the renowned Jesuit priest. Katharine had been converted to Roman Catholicism in the 1920s when widowed after her husband, Prime Minister Asquith's son Raymond, was killed on active service on the Somme.

My childhood visits to Mells were dominated by insomnia. The church tower was a few yards from the manor house and every quarter was recorded. Mells and Breccles, Venetia Montagu's house in Norfolk, were two of the pioneers of private swimming pools in England – which meant a rectangle of greenish-grey cold water into which one happily plunged with shouts of pain and joy.

Katharine Asquith's son, Julian Oxford,* was called Trim as a baby by his father who, on returning from the war to see his son and heir for the first time, exclaimed 'Trimalchio' – the rosy child reminding him of the character in Petronius's *The Satyricon*: fat and bald. Trim had known me since I was in my cradle. Only four years older, he has always been a presence in my life, though never an intrusive one. I was often at Mells, listening to music with him and talking. He has stood by me in all my transformations, when he might have abandoned me in disapproval. He had a brilliant brain, but was renowned for his way of treating the simplest remarks with a long-considered pause before answering.

His friends have sometimes regretted that he never put his first-class brain to more active use. Drifting from the army in Palestine to various posts in the Middle East and to governorships around the world, he finally settled at Mells with his burgeoning family. After they had scattered and he was a widower, he resolutely remained in the old house, stoically alone and living eccentric hours. The only time he was tempted out of his isolation in later years – to France – he was as amusing, enthusiastic and discriminating as always.

---

* Julian Oxford: his grandfather, the Liberal Prime Minister Herbert Asquith, took the title Earl of Oxford and Asquith.

Breccles in Norfolk was the home of Venetia Montagu.* In the summer of 1930 she lent it to our family. She had a formidable, masculine mind. The excitement was the arrival of Venetia and her friend Rupert Belville in a tiny primitive aeroplane with their helmeted heads sticking out into the air in Biggles fashion – very dashing in those days. Venetia would read aloud to us at breakneck speed something quite complicated to follow, like Dickens. It put me off Dickens for life – exacerbated years later by my husband wanting me to read *The Pickwick Papers* to him when he was ill.

That summer my brother Johnnie filled Breccles with his own friends, including his then fiancée, Penelope Chetwode – who eventually married the poet John Betjeman. At the time, at ten years old, I was very keen on cricket and had been given my own bat. Alvilde Bridges, another of his friends, was particularly nice about throwing a ball to me. Later in life she was particularly nasty to me; and finally, nice again during the time she was married to my brother's old friend, Jim Lees-Milne. Jim had challenged me, aged eleven, to write a sonnet about insomnia. I didn't know what a sonnet was, but I did suffer from insomnia and the poem was much appreciated by my boarding school years later.

As my mother had remained a Liberal after my Uncle Winston had moved over to the Conservatives, I saw a lot of the interesting people in both Liberal and Conservative circles – the Asquiths' world and the Salisburys'. The Liberal Party leader from the 1930s was Sir Archibald Sinclair. My mother was a keen salmon fisher, so we stayed every year at the Sinclairs' hunting lodge, Altnabreac in Caithness – which they used instead of Thurso Castle on the coast – where his

---

* Venetia Stanley (1887–1948): daughter of Baron Sheffield, she became the famous recipient of Prime Minister Asquith's thoughts and feelings penned to her several times a day from the Cabinet table throughout the First World War. She was a close friend of Asquith's daughter Violet and married Edwin Montagu, Liberal MP and an Asquith protégé, in 1915. He died in 1924.

daughters, Catherine (with whom I later went to Paris) and Elizabeth, were constant childhood friends. Caithness gave me a permanent prejudice about Scottish scenery in favour of rounded mountains and golden deer grass as opposed to glens and heather.

At Plas Newydd on the Isle of Anglesey in Wales was another of my mother's friends, Marjorie Anglesey.* In London the Angleseys lived round the corner from us in Queen's Gate so I saw the five Paget daughters continually. Marjorie Anglesey was small and dark-haired with a little heart-shaped face – physically unlike her tall, fair-haired sister Diana Cooper. Her husband, Charlie Anglesey, played very little part in family life as far as I could see. Rose, being my contemporary, was the Paget girl I was paired off with most (when very young I apparently said 'I like being with Rose because I am cleverer than her'). Caroline, the eldest, had devastating charm and sex appeal, and used to come round to Cromwell Road to listen to my brother Johnnie playing the piano, which he did endlessly. She was very kind to me as a small girl, admiring my balcony garden. She had been due to marry an eldest son – apparently she was acqui-escent – when he was killed in a flying accident. From then on she did what she liked. When we were adults she was occasionally ruthlessly competitive. All the Paget girls crossed my path through-out my life.

Rushbrooke in Norfolk was a stunningly handsome house with a moat, lived in by my godmother, Anne Islington.† One evening everyone was choosing their very favourite book. When my turn came I piped up '*The Cloister and the Hearth*', by Charles Reade, being the last book I had read. The derision heaped on me by all the beastly grown-ups – and my mother's embarrassment – seared into

---

* Wife of the Marquess of Anglesey, whose family name was Paget.
† Married to the 1st Lord Islington, she was amusing and outspoken, and a friend of Liberals Cynthia Asquith and Edward Horner, and of Lord Ivor Churchill and Emerald Cunard.

me. They all thought him mediocre. Rushbrooke was subsequently bought by the scientist Victor Rothschild who never lived there and, like so many empty houses, it burnt down.

Pixton Park in Devon was owned by my other godmother, Mary Herbert.* I always rather dreaded going there as a child because even then I was conscious of the well-used sheets and towels, and the number of insects in the bathroom. Auberon, the only son, was a few years younger than me and I was flummoxed when, at the age of about seven, his first question to me was 'What do you think of the 5-year plan?' (Stalin's Five Year Plan to industrialise Russia after 1928).

My mother on one visit reported

the usual inconsequent chaos, Gabriel with a broken leg – her horse tumbled on top of her. Laura looking pretty, very painted and very at loose ends, two or three unknown scruffy young men and Mary with straggling hair welcoming harum scarum. Bed at 2-ish, dinner wasn't till 9-ish, then games. This morning they've all gone hunting either on horses or in motors. Papa off to Rothschilds to shoot and choose some orchids.

It was when I was staying at Pixton that I first saw Evelyn Waugh, in 1937. Evelyn was muted and on sufferance, as the family were hoping Laura, the youngest daughter, would not marry him – which, of course, she did. We played the board game Peggity a lot and he acquitted himself quite well at the agonising pastime of that moment, The Game. Worse than charades. In charades one acted out each syllable of a chosen word for the audience to guess the word. The Game was simpler and rowdier, with two competing sides acting out

---

* Daughter of the Protestant Irish peer Viscount de Vesci, married to the orientalist, wartime intelligence officer and Conservative MP Aubrey Herbert (1880–1923).

whole words. There was a tradition, begun, I imagine, by the clever-clogs in the nineteenth century, of playing paper games after dinner, variants of which involved somebody or something written down, paper folded over and passed to the next person, who did the same – the results being hilarious. They were good training, these paper games, needing quick responses, wit and enough knowledge.

In adulthood my friendship with Evelyn was all too brief. For a few years we would have lunch or dinner together whenever he came to London, and I found him gentle and charming. All the time I would be mentally contrasting this with his well-known wit and acerbity. Then one Christmas he sent me a card: my memory is of a concoction of lace with a simpering pastel picture in the middle. I probably threw it in the waste-paper basket along with others. Then I got an irate letter from Evelyn in January: I had not appreciated the beauty of the calligraphy or that the centrepiece was by a 'minor early-Victorian painter'. I enjoyed his riposte, saying we should swap it for something suitable – bath salts, artificial silk stockings, or *Life* magazine's *History of Western Culture*.

Lastly there were occasional visits to Blenheim. Consuelo was gone to a happier life in France and Sunny had married an American beauty called Gladys (pronounced Glaydis). By the time I saw her she had had one of the first facelifts and the wax had run down her cheeks so that she looked like one of Leonardo's anatomical draw-ings. In revenge for being married to Sunny she had transformed the enormous hall into kennels. Dozens of Blenheim spaniels in pens were breeding and barking all day long. The Duke would appear at dinner – a small table with my mother and me – in boiled shirt, white tie and the blue Garter sash.

Some years before the war we had moved from Cromwell Road to Regent's Park to a free-standing house with a garden. It was a bright escape. I loved the rickety Regency house overlooking the park, with its space and sky. After a while we also had a Buick car, and a house on the cliffs between Lulworth and Weymouth with a view of the vast bay and Guernsey on the horizon. Wandering on the cliff edge we would meet and pass the time of day with one or other of the Powys brothers, Theodore and Llewelyn, both writers – the only other human beings we ever met on cliff walks then. It was typical of my mother that they should have been her casual acquaintances. Lulworth Castle nearby was a burnt-out shell at this period, but was romantic with its four towers and the green ride thick with lenten lilies in the spring. My heart was always in Dorset from then on.

The only sensible schooling I got was a few years at the Kensington High School where I was up against the scholarship girls – I remember José, the tobacconist's daughter – and I really had to work.

Unfortunately it was thought at home that I was getting 'out of hand'. To this day I don't know why. So I was packed off to a fashionable boarding school, Downham, which was orientated to horses, with instructions that I should have extra drawing and music lessons. I did not settle at Downham and felt I wasn't learning much. My mother insisted I persevere. She placed little value on formal or academic achievement. When she reported that Lady Sinclair's daughter, Catherine, had matriculated she added:

> whatever that may mean … They are all very pleased but I do not really lay much store by examinations. What really matters in life is the individual's charm, looks, manners, capabilities and cleverness, sympathy, intuition and a certain amount of self-confidence and assertiveness, vitality and health – certificates or no certificates, matriculations or no matriculations, they don't matter if one is clever, charming, lovely and lovable – but I am awfully glad Catherine has done so well.'

If that was my mother's view, why wasn't I sent to Paris in the first place? – a normal routine for girls.

Finally I wrote to all my mother's friends telling them I was unhappy. As a result I left school without taking my school certificate, and at sixteen was sent to Paris – to be 'finished'.

CHAPTER 2

PARIS

Boarding school for girls makes them either silly or bossy. Paris was like the opening of a window on life. Everything seemed beautiful, exciting and free. Being sent there, albeit with two friends and a chaperone, was more than a window – it was a dazzling new world. One of my most vivid memories was the shock and thrill of going to the Braque exhibition – they were all the blue-green ones. I had never seen any modern paintings before, at home it had been portraits by Lavery and Sargent.*

My mother had asked the Ambassador, Sir George Clerk, to keep an eye on me – she thought that seemed enough. I had remembered Sir George as Ambassador in Istanbul when she had taken me to lunch at the embassy – then still on the Bosphorus – and he remembered me. So many wineglasses at each place setting had been puzzling. Also, there was no Ambassadress as hostess, but a pretty private secretary. I only understood about the Ambassadress later. In Paris she never appeared, until one day she invited me up to the top floor to see her little clay figures – sinister objects – which it was her passion to model.

---

* John Singer Sargent (1856–1925): successful portrait painter of his era and gifted landscape painter.

The embassy was full of intriguing first, second and third secretaries, who in different ways became lifelong friends. Valentine Lawford – with a charming melancholy face and curly hair – was my closest friend. Later he wrote the best account of being a secretary in my husband's Private Office. After being posted to Teheran he was sent to the UN, whereupon he threw over his career and left for Long Island to live happily with the great photographer Horst.

Quite different was the arrival, as Third Secretary, of a very young, tall, elegant boy – Fitzroy Maclean – complete with monocle. His speciality was already a fascination with anything Russian, and in Paris this meant lots of evenings in White Russian nightclubs, to which he occasionally took me. I was bemused by the Czarda and even more so by another club, the Boeuf sur le Toit, where the hostess was a black lady called Bricktop. At the Monseigneur a violinist would come up to the table and play violently under one's nose. Though it seemed exciting at the time I realised that it was from then on that I have never really enjoyed nightclubs, even though I seemed to be frequenting them until I married.

Sir Charles Mendl – a lookalike of Adolphe Menjou, the French film actor – went by the name of Press Secretary or Conseilleur Spécial, one of those permanent fixtures one found at embassies in those days. He had a handsome apartment on the avenue Montaigne, where he gave weekly lunches and served Cheval Blanc '21, which he refused to allow me to drink – more because he thought I would not appreciate it than because I was sixteen years old. Fitzroy let me taste the Cheval Blanc and I developed a palate which has given me immense pleasure all my life – though not a palate for the shepherd's pie he gave us with the claret.

Through Sir Charles I got invited to Lady Mendl's Sundays at her *pavillon* at Versailles. To get there they arranged that I would be picked up, so Hugo Baring, the banker, would arrive in his green Rolls-Royce at the house where I lodged in the boulevard Raspail.

He was polite though not very communicative and it must have been a huge bore for him.

Mendl had married Elsie de Wolfe, the interior decorator who preceded Syrie Maugham and the White Age of interior design. She specialised in Pompadour French, with the odd leopard-skin sofa and zebra rug. She received her guests in a gold-painted ante-room, standing very straight with her stick legs and simian face. It was much ritzier than other French salons to which I was sometimes invited and took place mainly in the garden. Much later, whenever my husband had not taken to one of my friends, he would say 'Café Society'. He should have seen what appeared at the Mendl Sundays – Indian potentates, remnants of the Austro-Hungarian Empire, playboys and playgirls, writers, painters, musicians, the more bohemian aristocrats and, looming above them all, the amiable figure of Grand Duke Dmitri of Russia.* A tall man with a melancholy face, he towered over every social engagement in Paris.

Being quite young, naturally I didn't take all this in my stride. I was excited by appearances and a feeling of danger, because I had no idea what was going on, and was treated as a sort of trophy adolescent. This perhaps was what made my 'coming out' the following year seem bland and superficial – no dangerous undercurrents there – and why I would fall for someone who could give me a taste of another side of life.

Meanwhile my mother was bombarding me with admonitions: 'You are moving around a rather loose crowd', 'Don't make up and powder too much', 'Rest in the middle of the day'. She finally wrote rather sadly, 'You have a trying mother and a not very congenial home.' Full of beans, I replied, 'I am blissfully happy – wish you

---

* Grand Duke Dmitri Pavlovich (1891–1941): first cousin of the doomed Tsar Nicholas II and one of the few Romanovs to escape assassination by the Bolsheviks during the Russian Revolution. Became a champagne salesman; known as a great womaniser – Coco Chanel among his conquests.

could realise how much & how different to what I have been used to in London. I feel balanced, content & satisfied.' Sometimes she parodied herself. This in 1938: 'Please don't ride – don't do any recreation that you don't really enjoy unless obliged to – ride if you have to cross the Alps on a horse, or go across a desert, or flee from the Turks – don't fly in an aeroplane unless you are in such a frantic hurry that you have to or you want to because someone you like is going – and it will be fun.'

A cultural muse was the writer Princesse Marthe Bibesco, who took an interest in me at this time. She had great presence and a breadth of outlook. Here was the salon world – badinage, politics, conversational fencing and good breeding – a feeling of enamelled civilisation. She had languorous eyes with lowered lids, possibly due to short sight, and wonderful jewellery – sapphires and emeralds or emeralds and rubies, instead of the boring English diamond mixture – and a lovely apartment on the Ile St Louis, standing like the prow of a ship against the Seine, with walls painted by Edouard Vuillard. When war came she fled to England and went to Cornwall – and grew anemones, I think. I was with her after the war in the foyer at the Ritz in London when Count Grandi appeared. He was Mussolini's former Ambassador to London and a leading Fascist; they greeted each other with open arms – 'Ma chère, mon cher' etc. Ah well . . .

All these activities were independent of my two friends, Catherine (Sinclair) and Anne (Powell), with whom I had been sent to Paris in the first place to study art. Most of the time we traipsed off to an atelier and painted. One day we decided we would like to go to the Folies Bergère, incredibly, and our poor old chaperone dutifully bought four tickets. There were very few women in the audience and certainly no sixteen-year-old girls. I had never before seen a naked female body. It was a very good example: Josephine Baker, the famous black dancer, wore nothing but a circlet of bananas. The only other time I saw her was thirty or forty years later when my husband

and I were driving down to the south of France and our embassy in Paris had quixotically booked us en route into Josephine Baker's hotel in the Dordogne. It appeared by then to be very run-down and we were shown into a scruffy yellow satin bedroom. Josephine was there to greet us, a sad old woman. When she died Paris ground to a standstill with people in the streets and the coffin drowned in flowers.

I returned from Paris to face my 'coming out'.

CHAPTER 3

'THE SEASON'

Paris had been for me a liberation and revelation from which I learned to cherish my freedom, painting and everything French. This made the English upper-class process for a girl to 'come out' – dances and meeting eligible young men – an anticlimax I failed to surmount. My escape was to go with Jeremy Hutchinson, one of the Liberal set, to the music hall in Stratford East and dinner at the Prospect of Whitby by the Isle of Dogs. I also discovered the left-wing weekly *New Statesman and Nation*, which I liked for its book reviews.

I was inclined to independent gestures. Marlene Dietrich had been appearing in all the newspapers dressed in a man's suit. I was very taken by this and went off to Simpson's in Piccadilly – then a men's tailor. They were rather taken aback, and probably checked with my mother. However, they duly made me a lounge suit in lovat cloth. Arriving that summer at the Angleseys' in North Wales my suit naturally astonished, and I like to think was admired by, all the Pagets. One of the young men staying there was particularly taken by it, to the extent that Marjorie Anglesey warned my mother against him.

In 1937, before I was going to any dances, there was a ball at Hatfield House.* My mother took me, togged up in a white dress

---

* A vast Jacobean edifice built by Robert Cecil, 1st Earl of Salisbury, in 1611, and occupied by the Cecils for four hundred years. The Old Palace, where Elizabeth I was confined for much of her childhood, is nearby.

girdled by a wreath of green leaves. I had always known the Cecil boys at their other house at Cranborne in Dorset – Michael, who had died, was my exact contemporary and friend – but this party was for his elder brother Robert's coming of age. Straight in at the deep end for me: the huge house all lit up, music blaring into the night and Robert, the birthday boy, seizing me round the waist to dance, and dance, and dance. After this particular event the social world unfolded rapidly, and Robert and I later gave a dance of our own for our friends in his grandparents' house in Arlington Street.

The so-called 'season' is a blur. One dance was very like another. Each year there was the Liberal Ball. One partner – stiff in his white tie and tails – was Donald Maclean.* He complained that I was not a proper Liberal girl like the Bonham-Carters and the Asquiths – I was too smart. It turned out that he wasn't a proper Liberal boy either.

My new friends in Paris had been older and more sophisticated, and I had also met 'Café Society', so the boys I was now confronted by – as dinner guests or dancing partners, let alone possible romance – seemed immature. I made a few friends – Richard Cavendish (of the Devonshire clan) was one. Just as Charles Mendl's wine excited me, so at Richard Cavendish's family house in Lancashire (Holker Hall) I tasted the best food in England. Robert Cecil remained a close friend for life and Charlie Lansdowne† seemed so sympathetic – a gentle, sensitive boy who, being unjudgemental and observant, could fit in with anyone – and was a particular friend. Charlie was killed in

---

* Donald Maclean (1913–83): a diplomat in the Foreign Office and son of Liberal Party leader Sir Donald Maclean, he was recruited by Soviet Intelligence at Cambridge in the 1930s to spy for the Russians during and after the Second World War. With fellow agents Guy Burgess and Kim Philby, a high-ranking member of British Intelligence, he defected to Russia after their exposure, provoking a major spy scandal in 1951.

† Charles Lansdowne had succeeded to the title, the Marquess of Lansdowne aged nineteen in 1936.

action in Italy in 1944. He had come to stay at the Moulin de Montreuil that summer – the mill belonging to Consuelo Balsan, a continuing friend of my mother's. Lunches at her chateau nearby were always elegant and simple and cool and beautiful, and her husband, Jacques, wrinkled and clean and full of *le sport*. He had a small pad permanently by his side to write notes to his chef: '*trop de sel*' etc.

Back from Paris, I had immediately enrolled at the Slade School of Art and at a strange institution called the Monkey Club, where an inspiring young woman called Monica fired me with the discovery of English poetry. During 'the season' I also started going to lectures at the Institute of Philosophy in Gordon Square and others on art at the Courtauld Institute. I was discovering the lacunae in my education hitherto and eager to make up for lost time.

That summer I was asked by Trim to go on a walking tour across the Apennines with his mother Katharine and his sister Helen. The tour started at Siena. I don't remember much walking – it was mainly wooden train journeys, third class. The mosaics at Ravenna were dazzling; the Piero della Francesca frescos at Arezzo were in their exquisite original colours, before being later ruined by restoration, and Piero's *Resurrection* in San Sepolcro was still hung in dramatic gloom.

Ben Nicolson (Trim's friend from Oxford and son of Harold Nicolson and Vita Sackville-West) had advised him on no account to miss Piero's pregnant *Virgin of Monterchi*. He told us it was known only to a few of the cognoscenti and to see it was something of a coup. Trim and I set off on the considerable detour alone. On arrival one had to search out the caretaker, who unlocked the chapel with a flourish. As we contemplated the painting – dramatic, as it was only a few feet away in this tiny space – the caretaker piped up, 'English lady here last week.' 'Oh really?' we said. 'Yes. A Lady Col ... Colefax.' Collapse on our part. (Lady Colefax was renowned only as a London society hostess with an interest in celebrity.) The next time

I saw the painting it had been whisked away to a building with white walls, spotlights, music playing – a nightmare.

Our tour ended in Venice. We had been living very simply for two weeks but thought nothing of taking up my mother's friend Juliet Duff's suggestion that we should call on Count Volpi* in his palazzo in Venice. His daughter was the chatelaine of a villa at Maser decorated by Veronese in collaboration with Palladio, which I visited years later in smart company. Then, Italian women in a town like Venice wore silk dresses, pearls and high-heeled shoes. We arrived for tea in old clothes and dusty shoes, worn for two weeks, and unwashed hair. They were polite but presumably appalled.

Some years later, when Iris Origo† came to see Isaiah and Aline Berlin in Paraggi when I was staying there, she appeared dressed like that after a steep climb in the blazing heat up a rough path to their house.

Another side trip from Venice was made to Asolo to see Freya Stark‡ – a friend of Trim's – who lived in a simple house with a big view. She gave an impression of pure integrity. I saw her once more, driving up from Venice to her home, and was again struck by her intelligence and honesty. Trim encountered her in Syria in 1942 'wearing crushed strawberry coloured shorts and garters, having just returned from picnicking on a donkey in the desert'.

At another time in another part of Italy I saw a bit of the writer

---

* Count Giuseppe Volpi, a diplomat and leading industrialist, was Chairman of the Biennale and was renowned for annual balls in his palazzos graced by the cultural aristocracy of Europe.

† Iris Origo (1902–88): Anglo-American heiress, married to the Marchesa of Val d'Orcia, she was a distinguished biographer and writer on life in the Italian countryside based on the estate, La Foce, which she developed with her husband.

‡ Dame Freya Stark (1892–1993): explorer and travel writer, and fluent in several languages, she was one of the first women to journey alone across the Arabian deserts, which she explored and mapped and wrote about. Later she worked for British Intelligence in the Middle East.

Muriel Spark. I loved her. She would arrive in an open-top sports car, full of enthusiasm and friendliness and determination to enjoy people. She was fun.

*   *   *

Back in London in September 1938, Clarissa continued her philosophy studies. It was a period of uncertainty and crisis as Europe gradually descended into war. Hitler had absorbed Austria in the Anschluss *of March 1938. In September he threatened Czechoslovakia. At the Munich Conference, the British Prime Minister Neville Chamberlain, with the French and Italian leaders Daladier and Mussolini, conceded Hitler's occupation of the Sudetenland region of Czechoslovakia. Chamberlain returned to Britain announcing he had averted war and achieved 'peace with honour'. Duff Cooper, First Lord of the Admiralty, resigned at this appeasement of Hitler. Warning bells sounded, not least from Winston Churchill, then out of office and languishing on the sidelines. Britain was suddenly preparing for war.*

Clarissa was at Holworth during the critical days at the end of September and was warned by friends not to return to this 'nerve-racking Armageddon atmosphere' in London. Friends were digging steel-propped trenches in their back gardens, trees were cut down on Primrose Hill to make way for anti-aircraft guns, the Victoria and Albert Museum was packing up paintings and families were removing their children and servants to the country.

James Pope-Hennessy* wrote of his 'terror of crouching under ground and the knowledge that St Paul's Cathedral and the Wallace Collection

---

* James Pope-Hennessy (1916–74): he corresponded regularly with Clarissa at this time, though his restless and sometimes erratic behaviour soured their friendship later. He was just embarking on his career as travel writer and biographer of, among others, Lord Houghton (Richard Monckton Milnes), Queen Mary, Robert Louis Stevenson and Anthony Trollope. He later kept dangerous company and died violently in 1974.

will be a heap of smoking ruins'. He was working on a book, London Fabric, *which describes his journey with a young companion – Clarissa, thinly disguised as 'Perdita' – round historic landmarks of London that were threatened with destruction. Perdita had sharp intelligence, directness and an original aesthetic sensibility. Pope-Hennessy warned Clarissa: 'Do not think of Perdita as a portrait of you, for that would be fatal; she is not', but it reflects his fascination with her: 'It is just that combination of youth and swift steely intelligence and dignity and looks that makes you what you are, unique', he wrote. Dedicated 'To Clarissa', the book was published on 27 September 1939 and won the Hawthornden Prize in 1940.*

*   *   *

James attached himself to me from the word go. He was small, with very black hair and heavy eyelids, quick as a lizard and always immensely appreciative and sympathetic – though after my marriage to Anthony Eden the friendship was over.

John was James's elder brother. Before the war he had seemed a pale, remote figure, engrossed in his work at the V&A and the British Museum. Later he went to the Metropolitan Museum in New York so whenever I went there I was welcomed warmly by an outgoing John, who gave me lovely dinners at his apartment – chiefly remembered for the constant attendance of Francis Steegmuller, whose books on Flaubert, Maupassant and La Grande Mademoiselle contrasted curiously with a huge one on Jean Cocteau. John had been transformed by America. Both the Pope-Hennessy boys had been moulded by their redoubtable mother, Dame Una. With her slightly oriental face and downright manner, she was the author of several books – when I knew her she was occupied in writing about the Victorian historian Agnes Strickland.

*

In the spring of 1939 I returned to Paris, mainly to pursue a rather hopeless friendship, but also to study medieval history and art. I stayed for almost four months, with only brief trips back to London. I wanted to immerse myself in French culture. I went to the Sorbonne dressed like a student in my mackintosh and with a leather case – to lectures by the poet Paul Valéry. And I managed to get a readership at the Bibliothèque Nationale, and was able to feed daily on the exquisite illuminated manuscripts and attend lectures on medieval philosophy. Paris in atmosphere was completely unmedieval. In the flush of discovery of the Middle Ages, I found I couldn't look at anything from the Renaissance onwards with any pleasure. An artist friend sent me to the Inspecteur des Beaux Arts at the Louvre, and from then on twice a week a *Moyen Age* expert guided me round Romanesque architecture and I was able to work with her at the Louvre.

Paris in that last spring before war broke out was entrancing. I lodged in the rue de Rennes in a room with yellow organdie curtains and posters of Rodin. On sunny mornings I would wake up and see my line of books caught by the sun in the most dazzling and wonderful colours. I bought two Java sparrows, pearl-grey with coral beaks. However, quite quickly the poor birds maddened me, waking me up in the morning by making an infernal noise – which even the Brussels sprouts on their 5 a.m. journey past my window in loosely constructed tin lorries, on their way to Les Halles, hadn't managed to do.

I was happy to be alone and went on long solitary walks. In Paris I was conscious of the sky, not as being a shell as in London but something infinite and freeing. However, I was feeling I was at a crossroads. I needed more direction to my life – I enjoyed studying, but I was weary of my useless dilettante academicism. What I really wanted was someone I could talk to three times a week who would inspire me and direct closely everything I read and did.

I was also anticipating with dread the possibility of war: I had such a sense of latent activity – I had so much to do before the world cracked that I thought it couldn't be just yet. Meanwhile the heat was getting me down – it was silent and expectant and unnerving.

*   *   *

Clarissa did not expect to return to Paris – gloomily predicting, 'In the autumn I shall be tossing hay with Vita Sackville-West in the Women's Army instead of living here, I should think.' It was a pessimism shared by her contemporaries – that Europe was drifting into a war that would change all their lives. Simon Asquith wrote of longing to go to Russia or Tibet or 'anywhere where one could escape these hellish crises which excite in one no feeling but despair tinged with a great zest for life. . . . But the issue is quite simple. Which is best: German domination over the world, or the End – probably for a long time – of Civilisation in Europe? It's idle to pretend a war wouldn't bring about the second.'

Trim visited Turin on his way to holiday in Florence and found it 'rather alarming' – it was chock-a-block with people in uniform, preparing for a visit by Mussolini: 'They were rehearsing – all ages down to little 6 year old boys with 7 year old boys looking after them and shouting out the step. Girls too – little Amazons in black capes who bore down on one if one tried to cross a street.'

*   *   *

On my return to London I began seeing old friends – Robert Cecil, Hugh Fraser, Julian Amery, Trim, Ben Nicolson – and one new, unique friend: the painter and writer David Jones. I expect I met him through Trim. He was a most unusual artist. Almost entirely a watercolourist: evanescent, dreamlike portraits or gardens or scenery. He had been seared by the First World War and wrote a masterpiece about it, *In Parenthesis*. Anyone who fought in the First World War seems to have a symbiotic affinity with others who had the same experience, whatever their background. Later, my husband Anthony liked *In Parenthesis*. David was more or less recovered from a breakdown – partly due to his apprehension about war – and at the time I used to visit him he was living by himself in a one-room flat in Harrow with a large window over-looking an urban panorama, which was all he had for immediate inspiration as he never went out. I don't remember any portraits at the time – he was doing his quite large scenes of flowers, birds, vegetation and people, in pale colours. He was very sensitive, reticent and sweet-natured. His book illustrations for *The Ancient Mariner* are exquisite. I had my copy on display at No. 10. Late in life he turned to calligraphy; the Tate had an exhibition of these some years ago. He would spend ages working on the quality of the chalky surface before inscribing the lettering, usually a personal inscription. Mine is in Greek, Latin and what I assume is Welsh, and hangs on my wall today.

*   *   *

After the Germans occupied Prague and the rest of Czechoslovakia in March 1939, anxiety about war intensified as Hitler's next territorial claim provoked Chamberlain's government to guarantee Poland against aggression.

Clarissa's mother reported to Clarissa from Chartwell in May:

When Papa and I arrived for luncheon we found Uncle W in overalls and Aunt Clemmie in her latest Molyneux tailleur.

War has been put off – I had hoped perhaps for good or for a very long time – but Uncle W is very war-like and talks as if it's put off for the present and that's about all – but anyway it's off – and then of course lots of abuse of old Chamberlain and all those footling Ministers and with reason – I don't know what the pro Chamberlains can say – unless they were only pro Chamberlain the man only, because he has completely volte-faced — has had to do every single thing he stood for not doing.

There is a feeling that Uncle W will be in the forefront if anything serious happens now again. He has risen in everybody's estimation as a Patriot — and all the fawners and grovellers and place hunters and toadies are hanging around — people writing him fulsome letters etc.!

* * *

My Uncle Winston, still out of office, was becoming increasingly gloomy about the developing situation and Britain's lack of readiness for what he saw as the inevitable war. Back from Paris, I took my friend Fitzroy Maclean down to see him at Chartwell. After Paris, Fitz had been posted to Moscow, had travelled extensively in Russia and was now back on the Russian desk at the Foreign Office. I thought my uncle would be interested in what he had to say about Russia. Winston wanted to know from him whether the Russians would come in on our side in a war. Armed with knowledge from a high-level German contact in Moscow about negotiations between Russia and the Germans, Fitz infuriated Winston by saying they would not.*

When I visited Chartwell again in July, Winston was still more pessimistic and warning that we would all be gassed. The news was that Hitler wouldn't march on Danzig, but concentrate on Poland instead. Someone had issued thousands of enamel badges with 'Churchill' written on them — and I heard that some Germans had come to Chartwell to assure Uncle Winston that Hitler meant everything, and more.†

---

* Germany and Russia were secretly negotiating the Nazi-Soviet Pact, 1939, whereby each agreed to remain neutral if either was involved in war, thus freeing Hitler from the threat of war with Russia if he invaded Poland. A further secret protocol divided Central Europe into German and Russian spheres of interest, with Poland divided between the two.

† Churchill was in contact with the few Germans who formed an ineffective opposition to Hitler at the time and who kept him informed of Hitler's plans.

In July I described the febrile atmosphere in London on the brink of war:

London has been rain rain rain. There is a panicky rush to finish the trenches & all the debutantes have passed or failed in their Red Cross exams. Catherine Sinclair has gone to Cornwall to learn to be a Land Girl. A huge cardboard stand appeared in Hyde Park & all the volunteers marched before the King.

Most of my friends were frayed – they all jumped a mile when a tyre burst in the street. So the parties got wilder and more oblivious:

I went to my last ball last week, & I watched them all swivelling round, powder, rouge, & tulle, & crepe – the black cloth, the red carnations, the pearl & onyx studs, the smell of expensive hair oil & Chanel numero cinq. Cold salmon mayonnaise, *framboises*. MENU. Hever Castle. July 18th 1939. Name please, MISS CHURCHILL – Number 8, numbers 13 & 14. Tzigane band in flame satin shirts – 'This Can't be Love'. 'You Leave Me Breathless'. 'My Heart Belongs to Daddy'. 'Hold Tight'. The pearl coloured dawn that rises over Hever Lake, & before that 20 Rockets soaring simultaneously up to the stars and falling on the soft smoke screen puffed out below. Three cheers for Gavin Astor, he's 21 today, & sent down from Oxford.

Three parties: one at Guildford Street, off Mecklenburgh Square, in two bare rooms with a bed and a sofa given by Ben Nicolson. Ben agitated and fussed for weeks before – and at the same time in two more bare rooms, Philip Toynbee's party:

dozens of artist's models and bohemians, covered in dirt and uncleanliness, on the floor, Craven A, white wine and beer – bonhomie, drunken affection and incoherence. Ben's party full of lions, Raymond Mortimer, Harold Nicolson, Spender, MacNeice, Virginia Woolf, Julian Huxley, Wyndham Lewis, Kenneth Clark. Then we had vodka, red wines, patties and pies – Du Mauriers. At midnight the celebrities were knocked off their feet by a violent inrush of Philip's bohemians, who settled down on the floor. Bare overhead lights shining on cheekbones and men's foreheads, dull and glistening hair, crooked and straight partings.

Then Ivan Moffat's* party in Fitzroy Square – a modernised flat with ancient objets d'art set in illuminated niches in the wall. Leopard-skin cigarette boxes, people setting out to get drunk instead of becoming so. Anne Powell and Philip Toynbee, the newest combination, were singing Communist songs on a divan – people were playing the Truth game in the boxroom. Austrians. Poles. Blacks brought by Caroline Paget. After an interminable time I seemed to be making soda-water with Ben (incoherent and sentimental and drooping) in the pantry. Later there was an accordionist playing penetratingly. Ivan, in enormous loose tweeds, his lock falling forward, his grin, his iron-sprung subtleties. In retrospect it was awful. For months Ivan had been working his way through his father Curtis Moffat's superlative cellar. I enjoyed that.

*

An invitation to Romania and the danger, and the strangeness, interested me. So August saw me bound for Romania via Venice. I was on my way to stay with my friends the Bibescos. My first trip on the Orient Express – an anticlimax. I lunched at the Lido with Douglas Fairbanks Sr and dined with the Volpis in a trellis-work courtyard,

---

* Ivan Moffat (1918–2002): grandson of actor Sir Herbert Beerbohm Tree, and son of actor Iris Tree and Modernist American photographer Curtis Moffat, Ivan Moffat became a successful Hollywood screenwriter, with *Shane*, *Giant*, *A Place in the Sun* and *Bhowani Junction* among his screen credits.

and afterwards hung about on the balcony in my hotel overlooking the Grand Canal. The heat was intense. I lay sprawled across the hotel bed listening to the jade-green water of the Grand Canal slapping the roots of the palazzos and the curious catcalls of the gondoliers gliding round corners – the mosquito nets were festooned above my head. We gondoled to the Veronese exhibition. I didn't like him but there were some profoundly perfect portraits.

On the way to Bucharest, each time we stopped at a station the whole train stuck their heads out laughing and shouting, buying and drinking bottles of *arangeata* – so eventually there was nothing for it but to do the same. From Bucharest we had two hours of hot training to Corcova, Antoine Bibesco's home. Elizabeth* and I went for drives in a phaeton – nose-to-nose epigrammatic monologues from her as we trundled through the delicious oak forests.

Back at the Hôtel de Grande Bretagne in Bucharest, Priscilla Bibesco (Elizabeth and Antoine's daughter) and I were asked what entertainment we wanted sent up to our rooms for the evening. We couldn't think. The next day M. Gafencu, the very good-looking Foreign Secretary, assured me over dinner that there certainly would not be a war. Heartened by this news, I ended up staying with Marthe Bibesco at her husband's ravishing red-brick castle, Mogosoëa.

I'd hardly got there before, sure enough, telephone calls started coming from my mother telling me to come home at once as Uncle Winston said there was going to be a war. 'M. Gafencu', I replied, 'says there isn't going to be a war.' In the end, Princess Marthe's husband, luckily an aviator with his own biplane, was able to fly me to Bucharest to catch one of the last planes out for London. This was via Munich where, as with all flights in those days having to make frequent stops, we landed among glum and stony-faced Germans.

---

* Elizabeth Bibesco: novelist, married to Antoine Bibesco and daughter of the former Prime Minister, H. H. Asquith, and Margot Asquith.

Meanwhile a Frenchman on board the plane claimed acquaintance and desired me to break my journey in Paris. I declined. A typical cross-section of three nationalities just before war was declared.

War was declared on 3 September at 11 a.m. The rest of September I spent mainly at Holworth, where my mother had retreated early to avoid the rush of the exodus. On occasional visits to London, a feature of the period was that we all had to carry a square cardboard box with an incredibly unwieldy gas mask inside it. Luckily, they were never needed and gradually disappeared.

Then, on 17 October I moved to Oxford – which changed my life.

CHAPTER 4

OXFORD

A t the time war was declared I had decided to live in Oxford. I lived in digs in St John Street. It was not in the ethos of my generation and class for girls to go to university, though it became common very soon afterwards. As a result, seriously clever girls did not have that opportunity. When Roy Harrod* asked me what I wanted to do, I answered 'Philosophy'. He fixed me up briefly with Freddie Ayer† as tutor, who wrote, 'Roy Harrod has told me that you want to read philosophy, and that you would be prepared to have me for a tutor. I should be very glad to take you. If you can manage it, will you come round to see me at 6.15 tomorrow evening so that we can arrange details? My rooms are in Peck Staircase 3.'

The lectures I had been to at the Institute of Philosophy in London had been about Kant and Schopenhauer. I had no knowledge of Logical Positivism and felt out of my depth as Freddie was pacing

---

* Roy Harrod (1900–78): economist, student and tutor at Christ Church, Oxford, friend of David Cecil.
† A. J. Ayer (1910–89): philosopher, then research student at Christ Church, Oxford. Had recently published his influential *Language, Truth and Logic* (1936), which introduced Logical Positivism to English readers. He worked on secret service missions during the war and was noted for his several marriages and his womanising, though not with Clarissa.

up and down expounding very fast. He was already in the uniform of a Welsh Guards officer and about to leave.

After this baffling experience I moved on to more orthodox tutors. Several dons took an interest in me, including Alick Smith, Warden of New College. However, when it came to my attending lectures, which would have involved wearing a gown, one Scottish don protested, 'No, she would be a walking lie.' This caused merriment among those who were trying to help me.

Oxford in the 'phoney war' was untouched by sandbags or people carrying gas masks: an enclosed beautiful world, where one saw friends walking down the street. In the autumn I wandered along the canal under the rusting chestnut trees, or explored my ancestral Wytham woods with Gay Charteris.* In winter, with Oxford under snow, gangs of toughies were going off to Port Meadow in mufflers and sweaters to skate. In summer, idyllic days 'punting down past the gasworks at sunset to eat lobsters, strawberries and cream, and hock in the twilight of a field of buttercups, all overlain by the setting sun'. I loved the day before everyone came back, because the citizens weren't visible and then ... suddenly the streets were rashed with blue shirts and corduroy trousers, and a general feeling of scarf and hair blowing in the wind.

My entrée to Oxford life was made easy by having known David Cecil† from a very early age, as he was a friend and admirer of my mother's, and I would find him in the drawing room at home perched

---

* Gay Margesson: daughter of politician David Margesson, she was one of Clarissa's contemporaries.
† Lord David Cecil: younger son of the 4th Marquess of Salisbury, he was an inspiring conversationalist, scholar, Fellow of New College (later Professor of English Literature and biographer of Lord Melbourne), noted for his idiosyncrasies and his sympathy. Isaiah Berlin described him running in and out 'with a voice like a crate of hens carried across a field'. He was the brother of 'Bobbety' Salisbury, friend and colleague of Anthony Eden.

on a chair while she reclined on the sofa, always with a rug over her knees. It was therefore natural that I should turn up at the Cecils', and I was immediately welcomed to their dinners and evenings, which were somehow contrived in spite of rationing, and usually ended with Ribena sorbet (obtained from the chemist – no coupons needed). It was there I met for the first time Maurice Bowra, Billa and Roy Harrod, and Isaiah Berlin, who formed the mainstay of my social life at Oxford.

David had a very steady set of values but, being so intelligent, he was able to weave academic distinction with good sense, wit and humour, which made his conversation a delight and encouraged his guests – even an abashed girl like myself – to join in. He used conversation more with an eighteenth-century sensibility, throwing in a subject to encourage others, darting to and fro to develop it. Although he enjoyed gossiping it was always rooted by a conventional foundation. He looked like a Beerbohm caricature – long thin legs, long face with the typical Cecil family high-domed forehead, limbs always in movement – elegant but not dandyish, sitting in his red sweater, drumming with his nicotine-stained fingers. Isaiah told me, to my astonishment, that when he first arrived at Oxford as a young don at New College, the person who had the most influence over him, and of whom he was most admiring, was David. I suppose the reason may be that David's intellect was combined with very English qualities of common sense and an ancestral moral grounding. Isaiah said he epitomised to him the clever Englishman. Added to which, of course, was David's delight in anecdotes and characters.

No evening at the Cecils' was complete without Rachel, his wife: birdlike, quietly clever in her gentle way, sometimes backed by her MacCarthy relations. Desmond, her father, was well known as a brilliant essayist and critic. He made a point of taking an interest in young people. It was he who recommended Joseph Conrad to me and I am grateful to him that I found Conrad quite early in life.

One person I greatly enjoyed meeting at David Cecil's was Joyce Cary. A small man with a brown face and white hair, faintly naval-looking, wiry and quite muscular. His novel *Mister Johnson*, about an African village, was a revelation. I found its style and approach completely different from any fiction I had read before – the most original novelist I know – and his *Memoir of the Bobotes* the best book about soldiers and war, although he was not, strictly speaking, a soldier and the war was a Balkan skirmish. In peacetime I have myself motored for hours from the Dalmatian coast up through wild uninhabited mountains to get to the capital of Montenegro, Cetinje. The surprise and the anticlimax when one finally arrives he describes perfectly: 'The government buildings are exactly like a convent, the Royal Palace like a Court House, the Embassies like a row of doctors' and lawyers', the Crown Prince's Palace like the local squire's.'

He was also a very good draftsman and had studied art in Paris. His ink brush pictures in the Bobotes book capture beautifully the Balkan soldiery. This also explains his interesting descriptions of the process of painting a picture in *The Horse's Mouth*. Joyce Cary's novels are highly flavoured. The intensely visual imagination, the painterly style of description and the almost pagan belief in the life force are characteristic. His novels are concerned with the right and the wrong way of living, and the right way is subtly made sympathetic to the reader.

Through David I met Isaiah Berlin,* a small dark man, a mass of quick movements and a torrent of words. I originally saw him with

---

* Isaiah Berlin (1909–97): leading liberal thinker, philosopher and historian of ideas, he was Fellow of New College and All Souls, and had recently completed his biography of Karl Marx. He was born in Riga of Jewish parents who moved to Petrograd in 1917. He arrived in England in 1921 and spent his adult life in academia, apart from war work in America with the Ministry of Information and the Foreign Office.

Trim at Mells before the war and he told me later it was his first taste of the English 'country-house weekend'. A relatively gentle introduction, I would say. He told me that he felt a failure with Lady Horner, but had a nice conversation with my mother about walks.

My first summons to his room was a postcard: 'Dear Miss Churchill, would you come to see me at 4 p.m. The door is first left.' So I proceeded to New College and found his rooms, in which there was a pale figure, obviously in the middle of a serious discussion and not wishing to be interrupted by a young girl. This was apparently George Katkov, historian and a disciple of Isaiah's. He was hustled out, and Isaiah and I settled down to what was to be one of many conversations mainly dissecting and gossiping about our mutual friends' idiosyncrasies, about whom he was immensely diverting. I could put forward an ill-constructed brick of a question and on it he would build an edifice that was always unexpected and interesting. I wondered if the Russian intellectuals of the pre-revolutionary period talked like this. I had long, long seances in those rooms, sitting amid a snowstorm of papers.

Isaiah had a complete disregard for time and place – talking to me on the telephone endlessly, or meeting me accidentally at 1 a.m. in Holywell, walking up and down discussing for an hour, me with my hair being ironed by the mist. I had never met anyone in the least like this – his exotic appearance, the deluge of words, the analyses laced with morality and spiced with frivolity. Until he went to America in 1940 we had all called him by his family nickname, Shaia.

Isaiah told me that when he was a little boy in Petrograd and the Revolution was starting, soldiers began ransacking bourgeois households. They appeared at the head of the Berlins' street, so Isaiah's mother told him to take her pearls and go and bury them in the snow on the balcony. What a memory. For his eightieth birthday

I got the embassy in Moscow to photograph the street and framed it for him.

Some time after our first meeting Isaiah said he would like to take me to tea with his parents. Off we went to Hollycroft Avenue in Hampstead. Mrs Berlin was there to greet us, a small woman with black hair and pink cheeks, smiling and shy. The sitting room was sombre and full of furniture. There was an effect of black and gold and red – very Russian. The tea was complicated and also very Russian. While we were munching away and not talking overmuch, Mr Berlin poked his head round the door and came in – he was small too but paler, and very neatly dressed. However, he remained standing and, after a few exchanges, made his excuses and left. I didn't see them for long enough to understand how this nice couple had produced this unique character.

Isaiah was a great correspondent. We all were – one would even write to friends one was seeing practically every day. The largest number of letters I used to get were after he had left for America to work for the Ministry of Information, and he was homesick. Letters would fly to and fro across the Atlantic. Thus Isaiah relayed to me two bits of American gossip: Christopher Isherwood saying he didn't feel the bombardment of London was *real*, somehow. And a description of California, where Aldous Huxley, Gerald Heard (writer on science and religion, educator, anthropologist, mystic and philosopher), Hunt Stromberg (American film producer with MGM), Isherwood and the Marx brothers all lived together. When Stromberg came into the room the Marx brothers all shouted, 'Give us a toone, Professor', and at dinner the Marx brothers jumped on bikes in the middle of dinner and rode round the dining room – which everyone thought immensely funny.

After Isaiah's marriage to Aline in 1956 there was a slight and subtle change to his life. Headington House was the largest private house in Oxford. He was surrounded by beautiful and valuable objects, pictures and furniture, which he hardly noticed, and his shirts were silk. While we would be enjoying a delicious meal and marvellous wine, Isaiah would be eating a single grapefruit with a glass of water – though there were odd chocolates and nuts all over the house, which he presumably snacked on.

The other mainstay of the group was Maurice Bowra, Warden of Wadham College. He had a bullish appearance and the voice of a sergeant major, which cloaked a formidable mind. A scholar and translator of the Classics, he was known for his wit and fluency. He had a mocking way of treating events, loved gossip and intrigue, and could be very waspish in his comments. I didn't, but his friends did, enjoy the witty scatological poems he wrote about them. Most were too racy to be published.* I did enjoy his shouting dinners, however, but I was dismayed when he asked me to stay at Wadham one weekend. I accepted out of bravado, then found him an unexpectedly shy and awkward host, though he was at pains to arrange a social round, including introducing me to Audrey Beecham, his friend and, briefly, to everyone's amazement, his fiancée. I was intrigued to meet her – she was square and ruddy and boyish-looking.

Of the undergraduates, the one I had known all my life was the eccentric Simon Asquith, with his pale face and scarlet hair. He specialised in amused skulking. His best friend, Raymond Carr, was a new experience for me. We used to listen to Mozart in his chaotically untidy rooms in Peck Quad and have long conversations over coffee

---

* Some were published in 2005 in *New Bats and Old Belfries* – a collection of satires on friends and enemies.

in the Cadena Café. Walking down the street with Raymond sloping along, hair flying, expounding his views in a loud voice, certainly drew attention from passers-by. This boy eventually became an excellent Warden of St Antony's College without ever changing his ways.

In my mind there were two groups at Oxford: the Cecil/Berlin/Bowra axis and the Longford axis.* I always thought another of my contemporaries, Nicko Henderson,† belonged to the latter. He subsequently became a lifelong friend and his humour was a godsend during the darkness and tension of wartime London, up to VE Day which we celebrated together.

Visitors from elsewhere were rare. Jeremy Hutchinson turned up as an ordinary seaman, having been sunk off Crete on the destroyer *Kelly*, commanded by Louis Mountbatten, and made the rounds of Berlin, Bowra and the Cecils. And a very young boy with curls appeared in my sitting room at St John Street: this was Tony Lambton,‡ come down to Oxford to collect the effects of his elder brother, a beautiful black-haired boy up at Christ Church, who had shot himself. Tony stood in the middle of my small sitting room and upbraided me for knowing someone as 'dreadful' as James Pope-Hennessy.

---

* Frank Pakenham (1905–2001): then a don, he had a more austere, more overtly Socialist political outlook. He was a recent convert to Roman Catholicism and later inherited the Longford peerage.

† Sir Nicholas ('Nicko') Henderson: career diplomat in the Foreign Office, he was Assistant Private Secretary to Foreign Secretary Anthony Eden 1944–5, and Private Secretary to five Foreign Secretaries thereafter. Later Ambassador to various capitals including Paris and Washington.

‡ Anthony Lambton (1922–2006): became a good friend of Clarissa's. Later MP for Berwick-on-Tweed, he was known for his directness, mischief and gossiping. Resigned as Parliamentary Under-Secretary at the Ministry of Defence in 1973 after being exposed in a call-girl scandal, then retired to Italy where he continued his mischief.

Once Harold Nicolson,* a friend of my mother, came down to speak at the Union. When one said something to Harold his little eyes just twinkled and he gave no hint of having seen the point – then suddenly he would begin in a charming and confidential way, 'Clarissa, tell me ...' but it always froze off: it was just a manner. I was admiring of his wife Vita Sackville-West's poem 'The Land', so when I stayed with the Nicolsons at their house, Long Barn, and Vita was remote and rather superior, I felt dunched, as I thought her an interesting romantic figure. But then, years later, after Anthony had become Prime Minister and I went to the Nicolsons' next house, Sissinghurst, to see the garden, I found a Vita transformed into an anxious, agitated host. I noticed at lunch that the napkins were very damp. I assume they had been dug out of a drawer and hurriedly washed for the occasion. I thought the less of her for worrying so much.

The cultural magazine *Horizon* had recently been launched and I often encountered its editors, Cyril Connolly and Stephen Spender, on their visits to Oxford, where Stephen invariably landed up at Isaiah's. Cyril became a friend, Spender I found huge, Germanic and ironic, telling endless accounts of his mastership at Blundells (where he was teaching for a term). I was once having breakfast with Isaiah and Stephen went lumbering into the bedroom where Mendl Berlin (Isaiah's father) was trying to sleep – minute in violet-spotted pyjamas. I concluded Stephen had charm of manner and he didn't seem half so *ingénu* as I had been given to understand, though Isaiah insisted he was.

---

* Harold Nicolson (1886–1968): then PPS to the Minister of Information, Duff Cooper, a prolific author and diplomat who had attended the Paris Peace Conference in 1919 and later became a Member of Parliament. Married to Vita Sackville-West, writer, lesbian, creator of the famous garden at their home, Sissinghurst Castle in Kent. Their eldest son, Ben Nicolson, was Clarissa's contemporary.

Horizon's enigmatic owner, Peter Watson, had inherited a fortune before the war, which he used to support the arts, particularly *Horizon*, and to collect paintings, which he had to abandon when he fled Paris. I thought he probably had a genuine feeling that a magazine like *Horizon* ought to exist so he was willing to back it. He had a pagan satyr quality which could be unnerving – to have anything to do with him would be asking for trouble – but in conversation I thought all his opinions were genuine. I remember saying to him that I thought the poetry in *Horizon* a great let-down compared to the rest, and he replied that personally he only liked stuff he could understand and that he left the whole business to Cyril. What I liked was his good manners. All the charm and politeness wasn't just ingratiation, nor did it signify that he really liked one exceptionally, but I could tell it was innate well-bred manners. David Cecil was the only other person of this sort who had them.

I quickly found philosophy and Oxford life a complete and absorbing escapism – having tutorials, reading, discussing and gossiping. One term I started to do logic, though I was surprised to find on a first reading how like a page of Gertrude Stein a page of philosopher Susan Stebbing could be. At this time I was very high-spirited – working six hours a day on my philosophy and attending classes given by Professor Price, about eight of us, where we had to read papers and debate philosophical questions. I couldn't believe that it was me doing something so difficult. On other days I would be working slowly and unseen, and in the evening go for a walk in the darkness and rain.

It seems curious that it was still possible to be discussing literature at such a time. Henri de Montherlant had just appeared in our lives (I found him fascinating but rather shockingly heartless – particularly about women), Sartre, Stendhal, Edith Sitwell, Lady Murasaki's *The*

Tale of Genji, which I had lately discovered, Proust (whom I read intermittently, finally finishing *Du Côté de chez Swann* decades later), Yeats – whom I then thought 'a good & noble poet bogged down by the faeries & table turning' – and modern poetry, which I didn't much like, apart from Dylan Thomas who 'employs modern imagery & metaphors with a certain poetic violence & nobility'.

The Cecils' was the house I frequented most often. In a corner of their drawing room there was often a small bald-headed man who rarely spoke and sat with bowed head. I eventually asked David who this character was and he said, 'He's called Lord Berners. He's having a nervous breakdown.'

Leaving David's one evening and embarking on my walk to my digs late at night (no danger in those days, in spite of the blackout), I was accompanied by the bald man who had sat in the corner, and we started to chat. After several of these night walks he said, 'I have a place not far from Oxford. We could take a taxi and visit it.' The place was Faringdon, a ravishing eighteenth-century house with a large lake and a well-proportioned symmetrical interior hung with Impressionists, Sisley, Derain and so on. I was surprised. Walking around outside, but never approaching us, was a figure in private's uniform. When I asked Gerald Berners who it was he said, 'Oh, that's my agent.'

One weekend I opened a drawer in the library and a deluge of photographs fell out: Diaghilev, Stravinsky, Gertrude Stein, the Sitwells, William Walton – the lot. There were also photographs of the 'agent', Robert Heber Percy, nicknamed 'The Mad Boy'. I was completely astonished; I had no idea about Gerald's past life.* His

---

* Lord Berners (1883–1950): Gerald Berners began a career as a diplomat but when he inherited the title in 1918 he concentrated on composing. He was a friend of Stravinsky and William Walton, of Italian and Russian Futurist artists and of Diaghilev, who commissioned him to write *The Triumph of Neptune*, choreographed by Balanchine (based on a story by Sacheverell Sitwell) for the Ballets Russes in 1926. (Diaghilev chose him over William Walton.) Later he collaborated with Frederick Ashton and Gertrude Stein on his choral ballet *The Wedding*

attitude towards life was that it should entertain him. He had a very subtle malice and humour without any pettiness. I found him amusing, scudding about whistling and blowing his nose with a blast like a pantomime trumpet. After an attack of flu, one academic's wife sent him a scarlet wool skullcap which he liked so much – it gave him an air of Ali Baba – that he wore it from then on. After a lifetime of fun and games, the idea of war had brought on a breakdown for Gerald. Under the benign yet stimulating atmosphere of Oxford he recovered for a while. He took digs in St Giles where, of course, he immediately made his landlady the focus of funny stories.

At heart he was a lonely and sensitive person – Oxford was exactly the right place for him to be. In the past his very real talent for painting and music – his pictures were of the Corot school and his music more jokey – had flourished. During the war he wrote two or three amusing books based on university characters, and revised and rehearsed the music for the ballet *The Wedding Bouquet* with choreographer and lead dancer Freddie Ashton and Constant Lambert.

*   *   *

Berners wrote two autobiographies and among his novels, The Girls of Radcliffe Hall, *a roman-à-clef intended for private circulation in which his friends are portrayed as girls in a boarding school of which he is the headmistress, and* Far from the Madding War, *in which the central character, Emmeline, was, according to Berners, based on Clarissa.*

The first impression of her was of gentleness and modesty . . . She was of rather diminutive stature, but her body was so well-proportioned that she appeared taller than she really was. Her hair, as a poetical

---

Bouquet, for which he wrote the music and designed the costumes. He was considered – by Stravinsky among others – as a dilettante, an amateur 'in the best, literal sense' of working for amusement rather than from necessity.

undergraduate once said, was reminiscent of a cornfield at daybreak
... Her type was more suggestive of the eighteenth century than of the
present day. She looked like a nymph in one of the less licentious
pictures of Fragonard. . . . Her manner was aloof and dignified. In fact
she was not the sort of girl with whom you might be tempted to take
liberties without encouragement. And encouragement in this respect
was one of the things that Emmeline never gave.

Prone to sharp comments, Emmeline wishes that one character, Pro-
fessor Trumble, a bore, would undergo a reverse psychoanalysis that
would give him some social inhibitions. When asked if she had ever tried
God Emmeline replies, 'I felt I wouldn't know what to do with him if I
found him.' As a child, she 'used to think that the Day of Judgement
meant that we were all going to judge God, and I still don't see why not'.

*   *   *

I never saw Gerald's well-known pranks and eccentricities. They
had been muted by the war and his breakdown. Though I would
come across haphazard signs of them. At the entrance to the wood:
'Beware of poisonous snakes', and in the library: 'This book belongs
to Lord Berners and is under a curse.' And he enjoyed dressing
me up wrapped in a curtain to be photographed in one of the
niches in a saint-like pose. He built a folly, a tower designed by
Lord Gerald Wellesley – a confusion of Classic and Gothic since
the designer had built a Classic tower before his patron returned
declaring he had wanted it Gothic, so he built a Gothic top. At the
entrance a notice: 'Members of the Public committing suicide from
this tower do so at their own risk.'

After a while Gerald started to see his friends and neighbours
again. On about my second visit to Faringdon I found his nearest
friends in the drawing room. 'Who's that girl?' asked Penelope
Betjeman truculently. She, who had once been engaged to my elder

brother when I was a child, was now married to John Betjeman.

A new arrival in the neighbourhood was Daisy Fellowes,* whom I had seen on and off, certainly not on equal terms, all my life. I only met her as an adult in 1940 when she took Compton Beauchamp, a beautiful house backing on to the downs not far from Faringdon. Like so many of the nicest houses of earlier centuries, it was facing north, away from the harmful sun. Gerald and I went over to lunch, taking Isaiah with us. I reported in a letter:

> We found Daisy in a turquoise jacket and Hugh S (her companion) very roving-eyed in velvet. Very sinister atmosphere, especially in the bedroom – she draws all the curtains of her bed like a box, & uses oil lamps. Isaiah and Daisy were rather taken aback by each other. However the fact that he had dined with Lord Beaverbrook broke the ice. There was a decanter that sang, & the Mad Boy got very drunk & drove us home zigzagging.

Daisy was a lifelong beauty and a lifelong siren who had the reputation of being ruthless towards other women. However, she considered the Churchills as 'cousins',† which included me, so my relations with her were always delightful.

---

* Daisy Fellowes (1890–1962): born Marguerite Decazes, she was an heiress of the Singer sewing machine empire – the niece of Winnaretta Singer (Princess Edmond de Polignac) who largely brought her up after her mother's suicide. A much photographed Society beauty with a sometimes caustic wit, she wrote poems and novels. Married first to Prince Jean de Broglie (which ended when she found him in bed with his chauffeur), then in 1919 to Reginald Fellowes. Generously hospitable on her Côte d'Azur yacht, though it was rumoured that people invented telegrams to greet them at the next port giving them an excuse to disembark.
† Reggie Fellowes's mother was Lady Rosamond Spencer-Churchill, sister of Lord Randolph Churchill – who was Clarissa's paternal grandfather. Clarissa was thus a first cousin once removed by marriage.

I admired the perfect quality of her surroundings – the silks, the velvets, the fineness of the sheets, the perfect food and wine. After I married, whenever I went to Paris she would give the most wonderful lunches for me – choosing all the guests I would want to see and would not be seeing officially. Years later, when we were house hunting, she lent us her final house near Newbury as a base. When the press asked her why, they got the 'cousins' reply. When Daisy came to a lunch party at No. 10 I was surprised to see that she had dressed herself very discreetly and plainly, with a dismal hat like a nursery maid's and no jewellery.

Nancy Mitford* was another visitor to Faringdon. Although her sister, Debo Mitford, was my exact contemporary, it was Nancy who became my friend – I met her when she had taken over the running of the bookshop, Heywood Hill, after Hill was called up and the shop became a casual social centre. After the war she moved to Paris for love of de Gaulle's aide, Gaston Palewski, who treated her heartlessly. She was another who gave a lovely and amusing lunch for Anthony and me – slightly more political and slightly more intellectual than at Daisy's – at her large ground-floor flat in the rue Monsieur. She was a good friend.

People were gradually being asked to spend the weekend at Faringdon. One of Gerald's guests was Princess Edmond (Winnie) de Polignac, one of the many refugees from France who chose to come to England rather than America. Princess Winnie was the most remarkable of the émigrés I met. Born Winnaretta Singer, of the sewing machine empire, she was therefore rich enough to be the greatest benefactor of French music and musicians before the war.

---

* Nancy Mitford (1904–73): one of the five daughters of Lord Redesdale, all of whom made their names. Nancy – renowned for her wit – was a biographer and author of several humorous novels about upper-class life, including *The Pursuit of Love* – based on her hopeless affair with Palewski, in which Lord Berners appears as Lord Merlin.

Stravinsky, Milhaud, Markevitch, Rubinstein and Cortot all featured at her famous musical evenings for her friends. When I was a child, even my mother had invited Prince Georges Chavchavadze to play the piano at a musicale at Cromwell Road, but Princess Winnie did it on a grander scale than anyone. By the time I met her she was an old lady, sitting on Gerald's porch making calm, rather resigned remarks, which nevertheless had a hidden bite. She was continually very good and attentive to me until she died.

Gerald and I visited Garsington one day, which could not have been a greater contrast to Lady Ottoline Morrell's* day, with her Bloomsbury salon of Aldous Huxley, D. H. Lawrence, Virginia and Leonard Woolf. Though the scarlet sitting room was intact, the walls were now lined with the tenant Mr Lewinsky's Gainsborough drawings. I remembered Lady Ottoline in childhood as a friend of my mother's – at her house in Gower Street. She had extraordinary looks and wore extraordinary clothes – a cross between a gypsy and a Gainsborough painting. One could see her coming down the street from a distance because of her hats. David Cecil called her a 'dream dresser'. The Duchess of Rutland was another – she wore a muslin wimple under the rest of her outfit. David called her daughter Diana Cooper a dream dresser too – for wearing naval caps.

After I had left for London, Faringdon housed American soldiers in the attic. They were a source of resigned amusement to Gerald. Though the house seemed every day more 'like a French chateau', he was mostly undisturbed beyond the sound of distant motorbikes. When he was snowed up, with food for only two days, he remarked,

---

* Lady Ottoline Morrell (1873–1938): eccentric hostess, socialite and literary patron, married to Liberal politician Philip Morrell. Between 1914 and 1928 they completely restored Garsington Manor, with Italian-style gardens and parterres outside, and vivid interiors. Her circle in Bloomsbury included the pre-eminent literary and political figures of the time.

'If it continues we shall have to kill and eat a soldier. It might be interesting to try the major, who is thoroughly impregnated with whisky and might make an excellent haggis.' There were drawbacks to the occupations:

I am told that it is regarded in America as *politeness* not to spare one a *single* detail. But it makes *me* feel like a motor car going up hill with the brake on. .... I had a visit from an American major. In desperation (for it appears to be another item of American etiquette that there should be no silences) I got him to explain – as he was an agricultural expert – the interior workings of a threshing machine. Robert came in, in the middle of it, and was very much surprised.

One day Gerald said we should go and visit an old friend of his. We went to the Athenaeum Hotel in Piccadilly, which was a nest of Free French – including Maurice Druon, the prolific author, later to become a Secrétaire Perpétuel de L'Académie Française – climbed to the top floor and entered a small room almost bare of furniture. We were greeted by a gaunt woman with a dead-white face and dyed hair, dressed in a very dusty black velvet gown. Like all Gerald's friends, I had no idea who she was, or what. In fact, she was the famous Marchesa Casati – who had lived in Paris before the war and gave fabulous parties surrounded by monkeys and snakes, and walked with a leopard on a lead followed by a little black boy. She was renowned for having covered two Nubian 'slaves' in gold paint – they barely survived the ordeal.

Before the war had ended I would be visiting Gerald in a home at Richmond. He had relapsed again into melancholia. His character, which was a conflicting mixture of frivolity and masochism, was too fragile and ill-suited to survive in the modern world. When I visited him for the last time at Faringdon in his ground-floor bedroom off

Aged three, with my mother.

Goonie Churchill
Lady R. Churchill – at the Hotel at
Torquay – where we stayed

My mother Goonie Churchill and my grandmother Jennie Churchill.

Winston and Jack.
Two brothers so unlike
in temperament and
appearance.

My hat, aged five.

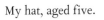

A good likeness of my mother by
McEvoy.

Above left: Picnic in Wales. With my brothers Peregrine, Johnnie, my father Jack, Perdita Asquith with Trim on her lap, Katharine Asquith, Helen Asquith.
Above right: Aged four at Tan y Graig.

Nannies and prams. With my Trafford cousins.

On Buster with my father in Rotten Row.

Mells June 1927.

The cold, green swimming pool at Mells Manor. C., Goonie, Lady Horner,
Trim (Julian Oxford) and his sister Helen Asquith.

'You are moving around a rather loose crowd.' Aged sixteen with leering
Austro-Hungarian in Lady Mendl's garden at Versailles.

Living it up at Lenzerheide with 'G' Wallace.

Weekend at Mells Manor. (From left) Katharine Asquith, the lurcher dog,
Conrad Russell, C., my mother, John Sparrow, Trim Asquith.

Isaiah explains it all to Trim.

A weekend at Cranborne, the Salisburys' home in Dorset. Charlie Lansdowne and his young brother, Ned. In the background, Robert Cecil shows me how to work the camera.

John Sparrow, Desmond Shaw Taylor, C., Trim and Eddie Marsh.

The Hatfield Ball, 1937. Robert Cecil's twenty-first birthday. In the white dress with the laurel leaf belt.

In Normandy, the Moulin de Montreuil, lent to us by Consuelo Balsan. Fitzroy Maclean, Kitty Mersey, Priscilla Bibesco, Trim, James Pope-Hennessy.

the front hall, he was lying in bed with the scarlet knitted skullcap on his bald head – and only a sad moroseness remained. He died soon afterwards.

Though I was largely insulated in my charmed Oxford existence, the war was impinging more and more on all our lives.

CHAPTER 5

INVASION

At the outbreak of war, Churchill had been called back to the government as First Lord of the Admiralty. Absorbed in her Oxford life, Clarissa visited only occasionally – and mainly for family events. She went in October 1939 to her cousin Randolph's much publicised marriage to Pamela Digby. Like many young men, Randolph was determined to get married and beget an heir before he left for war. He achieved both, though the marriage did not last.

Clarissa's long-standing male friends were being called up on military service and dispersed around the country into very unfamiliar surroundings. James Pope-Hennessy wrote to her from Chatham barracks of his sheer exhaustion and dead fatigue, working in an office with 'trestle tables, gas-fire, bells ringing, a constant fuss about ration cards, black-out materials – typing letters to the Regiment for the Sergeant-Major'.

Trim Oxford observed his changed circumstances with bemusement as he was moved from one place to another, with only occasional leave:

Got up at 6. Cold wet winds blow all day off the sea and in the evening we creep home to slate bungalows – bare dusty boards inside – where 15 of us sleep elbow to elbow on iron racks. My elbow mates are particularly uncongenial. How I wish I was an officer. . . . Hair mostly *cut off. . . . I have been issued with 7 different brushes for cleaning things with – also a little white hat band to say I am a gentleman – which, rightly or wrongly, seems to make very little difference, though I believe it gives me the entrée to the Majestic Hotel in Folkestone.*

Being under army discipline was tricky – 'I've not yet got out of the habit of treating people with reasonable courtesy – & hear myself beginning all my orders with the words, "Could you . . ."' The discomfort of army life was considerable. At Northampton he spent two nights in the clock golf pavilion of Kettering municipal park before being billeted with the rector of a neighbouring village – an improvement on 'three weeks of very strenuous work with pick and shovel and barbed wire including one entire night shovelling and wiring with two hours' sleep on the windward side of a gorse bush'. After one leave it was 'back to my wooden hut. No food, sheets, light, lavatories or hot water and the work more strenuous than anything so far. We carry enormous loads down to the river nearby – boats, beams and girders – build bridges out of them and then pull them down and carry them up again. It's much more endurable than you might think – or than you might think I think.'

Clarissa saw these friends occasionally on leaves, but as the phoney war continued it became increasingly difficult. Meanwhile the German armies advanced steadily across Europe.

In May 1940 Prime Minister Neville Chamberlain resigned.

*   *   *

My uncle was appointed Prime Minister and I went up to see him on a brief visit. It was the day Holland and Belgium were invaded, and we dined at the Admiralty. He was terribly pessimistic – not at all virile and courage-giving as he was usually. Lloyd George (who had been Prime Minister during the First World War) wanted to sue for peace but Winston thought there was just a chance we would pull through.

As the Germans advanced rapidly through northern France, I was shaken at the prospect of defeat. I wrote to James Pope-Hennessy, 'I have imagined so completely what it will mean ... one knows that life as we have lived it & Europe as we have known it (known it so little too – that's the bitter part) will never be again.' What I cared about was the disappearance of France from my life and the threatened presence of Germans.

We were in such a haven at Oxford with its atmosphere of scholarship and civilisation, so when Arras and Amiens were taken it was the double pain – first, the devastation of northern France; second, the potential havoc here. 'They *can't* get Paris, can they?' I wailed. 'They're as near as Oxford is to London now. Think of *Germans* in Paris.'

Others were getting even more jittery. Cyril Connolly came down to Oxford in May. He was thinking as a matter of course about going to America when the Germans came – he knew it was wrong but was nevertheless hatching plans if it became too intolerable. When he said he had plans for trimming *Horizon*'s sails towards Fascism so that when the Germans invaded it would be spared, I don't know if he was really serious, because he also said he'd got addresses of IRA writers whom he would get to write things and then keep them by as future contents of the *Horizon* Nazi number.

*　　*　　*

By the end of May, British troops had retreated before the German onslaught and were fighting a rearguard action on the coast around Dunkirk.

*　　*　　*

I went to London on 31 May and had lunch at my uncle's – which was a nightmare, with news of people's deaths coming in, and Winston's exhaustion, and the barbed-wire entanglements everywhere – and then Johnnie my brother coming home, his clothes drenched by sea water having just escaped, after the War Office had given him up, from Dunkirk – having been bombed at the HQ twice a day for twelve days.

The German advance towards Paris had begun. My Uncle Winston's speech* was intensely moving and seemed to me the most brilliant piece of oratory I'd ever heard.

*   *   *

The British were trapped at Dunkirk, the massive evacuation of troops began and Britain prepared for invasion. Paris fell on 14 June. Three days later the French government sued for peace. In Britain, the fear of invasion was pervasive and unnerving.

*   *   *

That summer Oxford was deserted and very hot. In St John Street there was a sad tricolour hanging from one of the windows – against the flat stone façade and the green gush of Wellington Square at the end of the street. Even in New College gardens at night, where the moon was absolutely full and honey-coloured in the twilight sky and there were masses of bluish trees, there was no peace – the aeroplanes droned overhead night and day without stopping. Soon Canadians and Australians arrived, who roared about all day long in cars with camouflage fishnets in which branches and bright green paper fuzzy stuff were stitched. I felt they were a comfort, a rather desperate comfort.

---

* 4 June 1940: '... We shall not flag or fail. We shall go on to the end, we shall fight in France, we shall fight on the seas and oceans, we shall fight with growing confidence and growing strength in the air, we shall defend our island, whatever the cost may be, we shall fight on the beaches, we shall fight on the landing grounds, we shall fight in the fields and in the streets, we shall fight in the hills; we shall never surrender.'

Meanwhile the intelligentsia were not exactly bearing up. I wrote:

Raymond M[ortimer] was saying he *thought* he would probably shoot a parachutist if he met one. Cyril Connolly was saying he wouldn't and they were exchanging the names of sleeping draughts, of which they intended to take an overdose should the Germans win. Raymond has had, as he himself says, a very happy life and is now getting old. So why not? But it was unpleasant and squalid. Stephen Spender and Leonard Woolf have a suicide pact. All this was pretty bad . . . Gerald keeps on asking what is the best form of committing suicide just as if he was asking for a cold-cure. If one is planning suicide one ought to keep it to oneself, & not implicate all one's friends!

From James in the forces at Chatham came news that the country was preparing for an invasion any day and destruction was imminent: 'The sirens wailing for hours, eerie and exciting, springing up all over the dock yard, first in the distance then nearer and nearer till they reached one's bedroom window – an almost sprouting growth of noise'. They were 'anticipating a big landing on the aerodrome nearby. Up almost all night and every morning at 3.30, with the searchlights glittering in the night sky. They are issuing rifles.' Trim was as usual laconic: 'The new invasions should slightly alter things . . . Owing to the general panic here of the Germans landing at any moment in Folkestone, we are all confined to barracks and made to spend our time putting up flimsy barbed wire fences to keep them off.'

The whole fabric of Oxford was dissolving and the spell irretrievably broken. It became impossible for me to go on doing philosophy. Even if it were still possible, my tutor was being called up and Isaiah was trying to be sent to the embassy in Moscow. Finally, discussing with David Cecil one day how we would behave if the Germans came, I realised how unrealistic and irrelevant my life had become. I felt that I ought to be doing something, so I joined Chatham House, then evacuated to Balliol College. I sat on the lawn proof-reading their surveys of the foreign press destined for the Foreign Office, but also quietly sub-editing. I thought the occupation futile, but it kept me calm and resolute in the face of the deteriorating situation.

I learned to type, went on a Red Cross course and even thought of doing civil defence exercises. I wrote: 'The parachuters [sic] here are having a field-day tomorrow. It really is farcical – Simon and all dressed up as nuns etc. . . . & trying to creep into Oxford while other parachuters try & stop them. I shdn't be surprised if assiduous farmers kill some of them, or at least half a dozen spies creep in too!' I had also been filling beer bottles with pitch and petrol, and learning how to throw them, what's more, 'but I know I should never do it unless I was going to be shot anyway'.

Forty years later I was invited to a party at the Imperial War Museum for all those in the German Black Book (a list of those to be immediately rounded up by the Germans after the invasion). They were an incongruous collection of Left and Right wingers, who were mostly taken aback by being in the same room with each other. We would all presumably have come to an abrupt end anyway. One day I was looking for something in a chest of drawers in my husband's dressing room when I came upon a large capsule dis-coloured with age. I couldn't figure it out. I showed it to Anthony who said in a surprised voice that it must be his cyanide pill. Both he and Winston had been given them in the war in case they were captured.

Dr Brown from the village was asked to come and remove it. The deadly object had been rattling around in his sock drawer for thirty years and through four house moves.

*   *   *

The Battle of Britain began in July 1940 with Luftwaffe *attacks on convoys at sea. By August RAF fighter pilots were repelling waves of attacks on the South-East, which reached the London suburbs in mid August.*

On 7 September German bombers broke through the defences. The docks were set ablaze. The Blitz began – in nightly mass raids the Germans bombed London and industrial centres.

Throughout the second half of September there were daylight raids on London, then on major cities in the provinces, which continued until May 1941.

*　*　*

Once the danger of invasion had faded the atmosphere changed from the feeling of hopeless apprehension to a solid, stoical one – we could 'take it', and take it we managed to do for the rest of the war.

Although the worst damage was in the East End, the West End was also hit. A friend wrote, 'Everything when it collapses is the colour of dust, even curtains & furniture and all the biggest buildings seem to be made of twigs and sticks and plaster and an ash-like substance.'

Regent's Park had had it badly. Nearby Cambridge Terrace was a row of gaping houses and all the windows of our Chester Terrace house were blown in. I visited there, chiefly to salvage my books, on a windy gusty day, with the gale tugging at the cardboard protecting the empty window frames. The top floor was waterlogged. My Maggy Rouff and Lelong ball dresses were, symbolically enough, lying under a layer of rain and dust in a heap on the floor. I didn't know what principle to use in taking my books away, as I wanted none of them at that moment and in theory they were all replaceable. I dropped one of the purple glasses I had bought in Baker Street but it all seemed so futile, the floor was littered with broken glass and there seemed no point in picking it up again.

There was destruction everywhere. Back in Oxford when I bicycled a mile or so beyond Cowley, there was an enormous plague pit of twisted aeroplane bodies – great mounds of wreckage glistening in the sun. A curious inversion of the autumn landscape – the sky was a dark, sultry sea-green and all the trees misty ochre-coloured.

At the height of the Blitz in November I saw Chequers for the first time. I wrote:

It was less awful than I had anticipated. Rather the Stockbroker-with-taste's place all the same. Very much Tudor, and set in the folds of the Chilterns, very much Bucks. But the luxury was heavenly, quantities of rare foods, fires, lights, drinks, etc. Winston was in terrific form, if not exactly spirits, and oozing charm. The house was heavily guarded, and the password 'Athens'.

My mother was there, looking like an Ingres portrait. Astonishingly, I wrote that I 'was going up to London for the day, to Worth [the smart dressmaker] to try and get some nice clothes – I hadn't had a stitch since the war began'. The irony of this seems to have escaped me.

On brief visits to London I met my friends in the Foreign Office – Nicko Henderson, Valentine Lawford back from France, Fitz trying to get into active service – and left in Oxford were only a few of the usual crowd, many of them already in uniform so we met only on brief leaves. Isaiah had returned from America for a term before taking up a Ministry of Information post in Washington. I went more frequently for weekends with Gerald and his motley guests at Faringdon, and visited Trim at Mells before he was posted to Egypt and then Palestine, where he remained for the rest of the war.

In April 1941, after a final term at Oxford, I got a proper job at the Foreign Office and moved to London.

CHAPTER 6

WARTIME LONDON

I returned to London for good in 1941. After some enquiries I began work in the basement – what Gerald called 'your catacombs' – of the Foreign Office, decoding. Although Valentine Lawford was up above in the Private Office, I was oblivious of what life might be going on in the handsome, spacious room of Anthony Eden, the Secretary of State for Foreign Affairs. The basement was a dismal place. Sometimes I would be paired with Anthony Nutting, whom I already knew and liked, then at the start of his career.* 'A for apple, B for brother,' we droned as we replied to another complaint from Sir Reader Bullard in the Middle East.

Social life outside the office went on quite gaily. Pamela Churchill – as she now was – and I had rooms on the top floor of the Dorchester Hotel: not as glamorous or as expensive as that might sound, since it was not a popular floor to be on during the constant air raids. This was the time of the heavy bombing raids, which were, of course, concentrated on the wretched East End, with only an odd near miss on the hotel and the occasional fatality among one's acquaintances.

---

* Anthony Nutting: later picked out personally by Eden as a promising politician, he became Minister at the Foreign Office in his government and resigned over Suez in 1956.

At one time or another there were friends and acquaintances on every floor, hostesses Lady Colefax and Lady Cunard, and several American bigwigs including Averell Harriman, President Roosevelt's Special Envoy to Britain, who had a suite on the first floor. Pamela and I refused to go to the air-aid shelter under the hotel, but remained in the foyer during the raids. When the bombing got close one night a noted gossip columnist and peer (several gossip columnists were peers then) threw himself flat on the floor. We all looked at him with embarrassment.

I had known Pamela at boarding school where she was a plump redhead who was mad about horses. We went to dances in 1938 and she did not seem to have changed. I was surprised when a charming and dashing friend of mine, Hugh Fraser, told me that they had secretly planned to run away together. At the last moment she had had second thoughts. I felt that was the moment that the real and future Pamela showed herself.

She combined a canny eye for chances with a genuinely warm heart. At any rate she was consistently kind and thoughtful to me, but she had no sense of humour. We would often have tea or lunch and after I was widowed she asked me to Birchgrove, then the house she and Averell used at Yorktown Heights. It had belonged to Leland Hayward, her second husband. This was the only time I met Kissinger – rather too weighty in conversation and surprisingly lacking any trace of European humour.

The Harrimans next had a house in Middleburg, Virginia, with an open-air swimming pool heated to 90 degrees giving off clouds of steam in the freezing Virginian winter. One day the local Master of Fox Hounds was ill and Pamela took his place. She had a wonderful seat – something to do with the shape of her thighs. As the field moved off I noticed tagging along some fifty paces behind, two black riders, exquisitely accoutred and marvellously mounted. I remarked on them to a fellow guest called Luther, who said, 'Those are Paul

Mellon's hunt servants, following to be sure that his hedges are not damaged.' Virginia was still Virginia.

The last time I saw Pamela was as Ambassador at the American embassy in Paris when she was still determinedly learning the ropes. Our own Ambassador later told me she had been excellent at her job – mastered her brief and argued her case. I found she still retained a certain competitiveness. At dinner at our embassy, where I was staying, I was chatting with Maurice Druon who was a guest of honour and had made a flattering speech about Anthony. Pamela evidently thought I was monopolising him long enough, crossed the room and broke it up.

*

I first met Cecil Beaton in 1940 when he was photographing the Blitz with James Pope-Hennessy. We became friends immediately. I realised soon that not only was he a stalwart friend – appreciative, but not uncritical – he also had a steely base underneath his perceived persona. I always found him sympathetic, amusing and sharp about everybody. At that time he was working for the Ministry of Information, having moved from glossy magazines. He was an atmospheric photographer, never making a statement like Cartier-Bresson, simply trying to catch the spirit of his subject. Technically he was apparently a nightmare to work for: couldn't work his cameras, couldn't fix the lighting – but he achieved the result he wanted. He was constantly the best photographer of women. He knew the most flattering angle of the sitter's face like no other. He wished to make the camera do the work of a painter or designer. However, when he took some photographs of me in Wiltshire, which I thought ravishing (because I am not usually photogenic) they were sent to me with a scribbled note saying 'horrible pictures – none at all like you'!

I have a better memory of Cecil Beaton than most of my friends because he wrote me so many letters in the war – from the Middle East, and from India and China where he was working on photographic assignments for the Ministry of Information and was also official photographer for the RAF.

When Beaton went to the battlefields abroad – or to gun-sites, RAF stations and Navy shipyards here – the glossy magazine image disappeared entirely. With stoicism he traversed the Hump in China in a bucketing aircraft or accompanied a forward patrol in the Burmese jungle. By being uncompromisingly himself, industrious and professional, he earned the respect of the three Services, even where the initial response might have been wary.

His letters to me from all over the world during the war were a wonderful diversion from bombed and blacked-out London, though I didn't agree with his taste when he said Bombay was the city he liked best. It was also fun for me to answer him with all the news from my end. After he died my own letters were returned to me by his literary executor. David Cecil once said to me 'the only way to get our letters back is to write immediately to the family of the deceased and as they are in a state of shock they will do what you ask.' A typical piece of unsentimental Davidism. I hadn't written, but luckily for me they were returned to me anyway.

When Cecil was in England, most weekends in the war he took the train to Salisbury and spent a few days at his house, Ashcombe. He would return with boxes and boxes of flowers, branches of apple trees or lilac, and would send round to me at Rossmore Court a bunch of striped tulips or old-fashioned roses and jasmine. These bouquets seemed so fantastical in my flat in wartime that they engendered in me a determination to have a garden if ever we got out of the city privations.

I spent only one weekend at Ashcombe. A perfect rose-brick farmhouse, elegant, with Georgian windows and porticoes, set in a combe of the Downs and surrounded by ilex trees and ruined grottoes in the garden. But on going inside one entered a circus tent. Everything seemed made of papier mâché and every colour clashed. Cecil's bed was adorned with seahorses and barley-sugar columns. I think there were even joke balloons, or so it seemed. I was completely shocked.

When wartime drabness was at its worst he had a wonderful suit made for me in grape-coloured velvet – from a theatrical dressmaker's: a jacket like a side-saddle jacket, a skirt long and flared, then unheard-of, and a lace jabot. I turned up at Cyril Connolly's dressed in this new suit – 'Well, we can't compete with *that*,' said his assistant, Sonia Brownell, to his mistress, Lys Lubbock. I had nothing else like it until Daisy Fellowes gave me a smoky-orange Dior chiffon dress when the 'New Look' came in after the war. It was beyond belief.

Towards the end of the war Cecil turned to theatre design and production. His over-the-top theatre designs and costumes were just what we needed. The costumes in *Lady Windermere's Fan*, which we all went to see at the Oxford Playhouse, were the first unstagy authentic-looking period clothes I had ever seen on the stage and at the same time effective. Isabel Jeans in flamenco pink from top to toe in the last act was breathtaking. Cecil made this production especially stunning as he longed to give everyone a real visual treat after the war. He repeated this in the film *An Ideal Husband*. I wrote to him that I thought his designs for *The Return of the Prodigal*, directed by and starring John Gielgud, had been the perfect backdrop for 'Dame Sybil Thorndike twitching and mouthing for laughs in the most endearing fashion'.

In June 1941 my mother, who had for a long time been in frail health, became terminally ill. She had been living with her half-sister – my Aunt May, married to Lord Fitzalan – in a grace-and-favour house,

Cumberland Lodge in Windsor Park, where I used to visit her. She was only fifty-five when she died. The funeral mass was in Windsor. We then went on to Chequers. My aunt and uncle had loved her very much, and I think all who knew her appreciated the rarity of her charm and the inconsequential beauty of her mind. I had lost someone of such uniqueness of quality, whom I had had the immeasurable good fortune of having had so close to me.

One day in 1941 when I set out for the Foreign Office it was pouring, but I carried on across Green Park and down Whitehall and worked all day in my soaking clothes. Coming out again into Downing Street in the evening (the FO entrance was then on that side of the building), my Aunt Clemmie was emerging from No. 10 to get into her car and she gave me a lift, evidently noting the state of my clothes. I am not clear what happened next, except that Sir Charles Wilson (afterwards Lord Moran), my uncle's doctor, appeared in my bedroom at the Dorchester next morning and shot me off to St Mary's Hospital where I remained for some time with inflammation of the kidneys.

When I recovered I was still feeling very ill and stayed for a few weeks with the David Cecils at Rockbourne, their house near Salisbury. It was like the Austen-ish house that one finds in every village, usually painted yellow or cream, with one side near the road, separated from it by a wall, and the other overshadowed by tall dank trees and a sombre lawn. The exotic jungle effect was accentuated in every room by thick swinging creepers hanging before the windows shutting out light and air (but letting in damp). From my bedroom I could see just beyond the thick trees, when they bent and formed a gap, that there were downs and sky – 'but somehow my life has so shrunk now, like a hide water carrier unused, that it is really impossible to imagine one can get it stretched out again,' I wrote. The Cecils were delightful in these surroundings – they looked like a couple by Zoffany – and Jonathan, the little boy, was dressed like an early nineteenth-century print with pleated linen skirts and blouses cut wide at the neck – later he was to become a successful actor.

I then went on to Chequers, where I was lodged in the Tower Room, which I described to Gerald Berners:

It is rather nice being here. I am alone all the week (except the Scotch housekeeper, ex-governess of Kenneth Clark!) & live in one of the towers where Lady Jane Grey's sister Mary (a plain girl who looked like a red-haired parlourmaid) was kept prisoner for years by Queen E. The walls are covered with what I suppose to be the Elizabethan equivalents of graffiti executed to while away the time [but, according to the guidebook, copies of letters she wrote to Robert Cecil pleading for her reprieve]. The prison effect is enhanced by the guards who clump round the outside of the house all night, & detachments of Coldstreamers who march up and down all day.

O dear, O dear, I wish I could find someone to stop me feeling ill. The quack has got me into the brandy habit & I consume Winston's rarest & best all day long. I don't know what will happen next week when he appears!

One weekend when my aunt and uncle came down, the Duke of Kent came to lunch. I liked his looks and I was taken by his eagerness to talk to me throughout the meal. It was only a year later that he embarked on his final and fatal mission when his aeroplane crashed in thick fog. Whenever the PM was at Chequers we saw a film every night – a Nazi horror film and Walt Disney one night, Marlene Dietrich and *Underground*, *Cottage to Let* and newsreels.

One day Oliver Lyttelton, a Minister of State, came to lunch. He was a man of immense charm and wit, as many women of his generation discovered. He was accompanying some important envoy from Roosevelt, and the good-looking but rather reclusive 'Gil' Winant, the US Ambassador, was also there. I asked Winant what American authors I should read and he sent me several volumes by the American novelist Winston Churchill. This writer had been the reason why my uncle always called himself Winston S. Churchill – Spencer-Churchill being our full name – to avoid confusion.

I ended my convalescence at Faringdon. Staying there, I made friends with Alice Astor,* who kept me up all night with her troubles. She was quite exceptionally nice, earnest, battered, foolish and beautiful. She always gave me the impression of not knowing even then why her life had been such a muddle, and it was simply the agonising dissatisfaction that drove her on.

Up till then I had still been living at the Dorchester Hotel and had briefly resumed my job at the Foreign Office, unfortunately having to give up the original plan of being sent to Lisbon. After voluntary work with the Women's Voluntary Service, I joined the Ministry of Information through Brendan Bracken, then the Minister.

It was at this time that Alice offered me one of a pair of the little cottages of her large Regency villa called Hanover Lodge in Park Road (now dwarfed by the Mosque) and allowed me to do it up with her decorator. While waiting for this, I stayed at the Etoile Restaurant in Charlotte Street, a place I knew well from pre-war meals, owned by a charming Italian family who by then had been interned on the Isle of Man. It was acutely uncomfortable, with two bedrooms, one

---

* Alice Astor, daughter of American millionaire John Jacob Astor who went down on the *Titanic*. She was notable for her generosity and charm – but was always troubled and restless. She surrounded herself with artists and writers, and was patron of the Sadler's Wells Ballet and later the New York Ballet. She married four times.

occupied by the actor Miles Malleson, who had a distinctive face, no chin and wobbling lips, and consequently always got the comic parts in Restoration plays; I believe at that time he was a Communist. Mine was, I wrote to Gerald,

> a rickety but quite nice room, with pink-washed walls and flowered linoleum. I have stablelized [sic] my day very pleasantly, reading all day in the London Library, and evenings in the Fitzroy [a popular drinking hole] & scrumptious meals here or at the White Tower – the noise is simply terrific – street noises of shuffling & shouting till 2 a.m. & restarting again at 6 a.m. – & I have to sleep in earplugs.

When the Hanover Lodge cottage was finally ready I was at Faringdon, and Gerald hired a car and drove me up to see me in. The cottage was rather damp. After five months I left and it was used by Freddie Ashton, who also found it damp. I had first met Freddie when I was about sixteen when Rose Paget took me to the tiny theatre in Notting Hill where the nascent Ballet Rambert danced: lithe Robert Helpmann, youthful Freddie Ashton and a ravishing ballerina, Pearl Argyle, who died very early.

Freddie became a great friend, always with an original 'take' on people, so ideal to do things with, and perfect taste – 'Don't come to stay this weekend,' I once said, 'because the rhododendrons are still out.' His ballets are my ideal of what dance should be: witty, ingenious, but also romantic. His *Symphonic Variations* (1946) is abstract ballet at its highest level, the purest distillation of an art, bringing tears to the eyes – and no gymnastics.

In December I moved down the road to a block of flats at Rossmore Court, where I remained until I married ten years later. I was again

on the top floor – through endless bombing raids, then the doodlebugs and the V2 rockets.

In February 1944 I wrote to Cecil Beaton:

Some beastly raids. We all mind very much now somehow though
you have no idea how beautiful they look from the 7th floor. Snow
on the rooves, red flares rising, white flares falling, searchlights
hitting the bank of cloud, & dozens of fires raging on the hills all
about me. It is icy cold – snow, gales, no spring yet & all the croci
flattened on the grass – at least that's how it is in London.

Places hit so far:

London Library (biography section)
Partridge's in King St also Spinks etc.
Wardour St
Also the Treasury.
The World's End Pub in King's Road (Lord Crewe evacuated
by ambulance, prostrated not injured – & Lady Crewe's
dinner-party showered with glass!).

From my flat – my eyrie, as all my friends called it – I could see
Regent's Park, Hampstead and Highgate stretched out before me,
with the white cliffs of Albany Street on the right, and a castellated
stucco pub, the Windsor Castle, in the foreground. I was taught how
to make goulash, or a version of it – because one got more stewing
beef on one's coupons than any other meat – and brewed glühwein
to mask the taste of the Algerian wines we drank. I entertained in my
dining room, which an acquaintance decorated for me in what I
imagined was an Etruscan style. In the sitting room I had a grotesquely grand gesso chaise longue which had been given to my
mother by Ivor Churchill (my favourite Churchill, younger son of
Sunny and Consuelo Marlborough), several Empire chairs and a

Derain, given to me by Gerald Berners, above the mantelpiece. One of the first things that happened to me was a burglary by the painters working in the kitchen. They said that, as they had found my jewellery in an old rubbish bin, they assumed it was rubbish. I had assumed it was a clever place to hide it. I got the jewellery back.

I saw more of Cyril Connolly after I had moved to Rossmore Court. He now invited me to his regular dinners at Bedford Square. He suffered from accidie – the death of civilisation and so on – but in our personal friendship he was always playful. A civilised, indolent epicurean who realised that he had never fulfilled his potential, he saw his entertaining as a means of getting writers and artists to meet – to keep culture alive amid the chaos of war. He took his entertaining very seriously, as far as was possible in wartime, with the food and wine, the silver and china, once generously buying me a pretty tea-set he had spotted in the Marylebone High Street.

Later he became my near neighbour when he bought a house in Sussex Place – one of the grander Regency terraces with cupolas and Corinthian columns. The soirées at Sussex Place were full of old and new friends. George Weidenfeld remembers I took him there for the first time and he thought he was unsuitably dressed, being in a brown suit, which he discovered was never worn in London, though I remember Jeremy Hutchinson had a brown suit before the war, so I think it was rather nonsense.

Cyril's 'Comment' in each issue of *Horizon* beautifully reflected the condition of literature at that time. On the other hand, he never forgot his creature comforts. It was typical of him that at a later date he kept up his constant moans about the privations of post-war Britain. There is a notice appearing in the September 1947 number appealing to American *Horizon* readers: 'If you have liked anything in it this year, send the author a food parcel: orange juice, tomato juice, butter, bacon, rice, tea, honey and tinned meats are all particularly acceptable to brain workers. They take two months to arrive, so begin now ... c/o *Horizon* etc.' One forgets for how many years after the war's ending rationing continued – food, drinks, clothes, fuel.

Though Cyril had a reputation for inefficiency and sloth, later on when staying at my cottage I took him to Fonthill to see the rhododendron valley – a spectacular sight – whereupon my little car stuck in the mud. We were miles from any other human being. To my astonishment Cyril jumped out and began gathering sticks together to put under the wheels, thus releasing the car. I would have had no idea what to do.

At about this time I also made friends with Elizabeth Bowen. I got to know her through proximity. She lived in nearby Clarence Terrace and my flat overlooked her. I admired her books, naturally. But the fact that she liked Jane Austen and didn't like George Eliot meant that I didn't feel more than admiration for them.

Elizabeth used to have a small collection of half a dozen people for drinks – or what passed for drinks at that time – or teas and dinners, with some new faces for me. She presided in a calm yet stimulating way, drawing people out and commenting cleverly, with her sweet husband, Alan Cameron – who had no interest in her friends – ministering with the teacups or the wineglasses. They seemed relaxed and happy with each other.

Elizabeth was always smartly, carefully dressed in a non-chic way, and her large frame was diminished by her charm and intelligence; she never forgot one was there and took care that the most minor member of the party had a small part. The house never felt like a permanent home and it seemed that she and Alan were camping there, with sparse furniture and a lot of bare boards – the warmth came from her. Her heart must have been in her beloved Irish home, Bowens Court. Clarence Terrace was bombed in the war and, as I was staying in Oxford at the time, she and Alan moved into my flat in Rossmore Court until her house was repaired.

*   *   *

Halfway through the war Emerald Cunard* had returned to London from America and took up residence in a suite at the Dorchester Hotel. My relations with her were at first slightly rocky as she fell in love with Valentine Lawford and imagined he loved me. She was very wrong, though we were indeed friends.

She was the best hostess I have ever known. Not only did she value eminence in all walks of life, the eminent all came. She then orchestrated the table, bringing in a violin, French horn or a bassoon, to perfection. She would introduce one section in turn with a flattering epithet – 'so and so is the most Eminent Philosopher/is our most Famous War Hero/is a cross between Voltaire and Garbo/is the greatest Expert on the Middle East, etc.' The men rose splendidly to these compliments and grabbed the table – except the War Hero, who was too drunk.

Once, when I took Isaiah for the first time to one of Emerald's dinners, it was the night of the Foreign Office Middle Eastern pundit's turn. As he talked on I began to wonder about Isaiah. Sure enough, when some slighting reference was made to Weizmann,† Isaiah felt impelled to intervene, saying that it so happened he had just come from visiting Weizmann, who also lived at the Dorchester, and the expert was wrong – and he enumerated the reasons why for

---

* Emerald Cunard (1872–1948): an American who made her mark as a London Society hostess. Divorced from the foxhunting Sir Bache Cunard of the shipping line, she was cultured and witty, and counted among her friends writers, social and political figures, musicians and artists. She financed Sir Thomas Beecham with whom she had fallen in love.

† Chaim Weizmann (1874–1952): Berlin worked with Weizmann during the war, gathering support for the foundation of the State of Israel. Weizmann, also an eminent scientist/chemist, had assumed leadership of the World Zionist Organisation in 1920 and represented the Zionist cause from then until he became Israel's first President in 1949.

a while. I hope Emerald, as a good hostess, was pleased with the evening. Ann Fleming certainly would have been; she enjoyed a little bit of contretemps at her table.

We gravitated to anyone who was still able to provide social sustenance, however depleted. Moura Budberg* gave regular drinks parties that were really basic – gin and Kia-Ora. There were the usual friends. One night I went and the room was full of strangers. I had come on the wrong day. Her life was evidently compartmentalised. She was one of those Russian women who were very pretty when young and in middle age became completely rounded.

Ava Wigram† was a widow at the time I knew her. She had a mini-salon in her mini-house in Lord North Street (the only large house there belonged to Brendan Bracken) into which she inserted and promoted me. She was naturally very satisfied when I married. Her food was superb, in spite of rationing, and she was foreseeing enough to have kept a cow in Sussex. One day after the war I was lunching there and was next to her new husband, the Scot John Waverley, who, as John Anderson, had been a wartime Home Secretary. I asked him why he hadn't built deep shelters as the Germans had in Berlin – the Anderson air-raid shelters being corrugated-iron huts. Taking another dollop of the cream, he said, 'It would have been bad for mor-rale.'

---

* Baroness Moura Budberg (c. 1891–1974): descended from Ukrainian aristocracy, she had married first a high-ranking diplomat, Count Johann Benckendorff, and later, briefly, Count Budberg, the Tsar's Court Chamberlain, but is better known for her romantic adventures – as the mistress of British agent Robert Bruce Lockhart, whose life she saved, then of Russian writer Maxim Gorky, who protected her in revolutionary Russia, and later English writer H. G. Wells. An enigmatic presence, she travelled freely between Russia and the West. After the war Alexander Korda brought her to London Films as a script reader – perhaps another of his wartime intelligence contacts.

† Wife of Ralph Wigram, a Foreign Office official who provided Churchill with intelligence on pre-war German rearmament plans. After his sudden death in 1936 she married John Anderson who became 1st Viscount Waverley in 1952.

Earlier in the war I started to see Ann Fleming – then O'Neill – yet another denizen of the Dorchester, who became a great friend. In 1944 she married Esmond Rothermere, owner of the *Daily Mail* and Associated Newspapers, and moved to Warwick House. This gave her scope for holding her large parties. If Esmond was present I was always seated next to him because Ann said he could not stand any of her other friends. Apart from Emerald she was the most entertaining hostess. The difference in the generations showed. Ann's table was more racy, more daring, wits could make jokes and polemicists argue freely. When the Labour government came in, most of the political guests were Labour – but the other guests were all my old friends from the artistic world and it was mainly to the latter dinners I was asked. Ann was able to stimulate them in a way that one saw nowhere else.

She was not a loyal friend in the sense that a quip was never missed if it amused others, but she was a loyal friend in an unpriggish and genuinely concerned way. She was relentlessly inquisitive and one found oneself helplessly revealing personal details. Mockery of her friends was affectionate and not spiteful. Only if her personal emotions or pride were involved was she unforgiving.

During the V1 attacks, Ann took Bailiffscourt, Lord Moyne's house near Littlehampton. Bailiffscourt had been created by Lady Moyne, who was apparently only able to exist in a medieval ambience. Thus the furniture including the beds, the pottery, glasses and cutlery were all fourteenth-century. This made eating quite tricky, as the forks only had two prongs. Floral decorations were likewise limited to weeds such as cow-parsley.

While we were at the banqueting table one day Ian Fleming, who was in Naval Intelligence, arrived from London and announced as he entered the room, 'The Germans have a new deadly weapon.' It seemed ironic – here we all were, having a weekend with clever, amusing people in a millionaire's fantasy house, to be told there was a new deadly threat to test our nerves. This presumably was the V2 rocket.

In 1952 Ann divorced Esmond and finally married Ian Fleming, with whom she had had a long affair. They bought a smaller, well-proportioned house in Victoria Square. Ava Waverley's cook came to Ann. She had been superb, but Ann's lack of interest led to a gradual deterioration in the cuisine. Dinners continued as before – though the table was perforce much smaller and more people had to look in afterwards. Ian would put in an appearance, having dined elsewhere, take one look at us all and thump upstairs.

Ian was writing spy thrillers while working for the *Sunday Times*. Soon after, to our astonishment and Ann's rueful embarrassment, the James Bond books took off and Ann and Ian were able to buy a country house in Wiltshire. Sevenhampton was at the end of a very long drive with a sloping garden down to the lake and a swimming pool built by Ian. Ann loved Sevenhampton. It was one of those English country houses with a beautiful main room downstairs, one good bedroom upstairs, and the guests in a wing with bedrooms not unlike a boarding school in size and comfort. On the whole the guests came locally for lunch: Stuart Hampshire from Oxford, Roy and Jennifer Jenkins from East Hendred and, of course, the Berlins. At weekends she loved to hear Paddy Leigh-Fermor reading aloud from Robert Burton's *Anatomy of Melancholy*, but as the years went on and her health weakened, bridge took up more of her time and new friends fitted that pastime. I was never able to learn the game, though Duff Cooper advised me to, as he said it was often the best way to get through a country-house weekend.

Another of her close friends was Evelyn Waugh. When I married he disapproved so strongly that the curtain fell on our friendship. It was tweaked rather mischievously by Ann years later when I arrived at Sevenhampton, to find Evelyn standing in the drawing room. We both seemed equally embarrassed – he handed over an inscribed copy of *Gilbert Pinfold* and left. Ann gleefully said afterwards that he had said, 'She looks like Doris Castlerosse' – the wife of a once celebrated gossip columnist and renowned *poule de luxe*. When he once asked wistfully whether I ever enquired after him, Ann replied, 'Naturally not.'

Later a deadly blow occurred, from which Ann never recovered. She and Ian had one child, a boy called Caspar, my godson. He committed suicide in 1975. He was twenty-three and at Oxford – clever and charming, but with a dark side. His circumstances and the general ambience of the time were too much for him to cope with.

*

Lucian Freud remembers we first met in the Café Royal during the war, when I was with Cyril Connolly and he was with his father-in-law, the sculptor Jacob Epstein, and the bombs were falling in the blackout. After the war I used to see him often at Warwick House dinners and I remember him hurtling about in a large Bentley – I think perhaps the same one that he still uses. Although we met for lunch or a drink from time to time, we never began talking until much later during sittings when he was painting me.

Next to Isaiah, I enjoyed Lucian's conversations most of all. He too has the capacity for building up a subject and then elaborating it, which I find stimulating and which enlarges my own views; he can cause me to change my mind and see things differently. I respect his choice of the painters he admires from other centuries and at least see the point of his prejudices. His determination to stand most of the day and night at his easel has taken its toll on his health but the results are large, powerful bodies with every face completely catching the character of the sitter. He is exotic and sharp – but good at friendship, and expects it in return.

At one point in the war I made friends with an intriguing man-about-town, who had the added attraction of shameless access to the black market. Lord Queensberry* won me over with sheer charm and Shakespeare's sonnets, and also the most magnificent chickens. As I wrote to Cecil Beaton:

I am becoming anti-high-brow, anti-scholar, & I liked finding someone who buys up the Brontë letters knowing nothing about them except that they move him. We had a nice dinner after the Queensberry Club a night or two ago – with Venetia [Montagu] (tremendously alert – in on the conversation all round the table), Quintin Hogg pontifical – swept aside by Venetia, Raimund,† Emerald [Cunard] (she & I were given, as non-drinkers, a bottle of 'sparkling burgundy' between us, which we both found dis-astrously potent) in a new hat, white with nodding black feathers – tremendously seductive. And oh the food!

Another evening I was dining with Francis Queensberry – a dinner for Glenn Miller. I think I was the only woman, oddly. There was much bawdy talk in which Glenn Miller took no part and he looked embarrassed. He was a great figure in wartime London, with his band and their famous tune 'In the Mood' playing at every club and party. Some time after this dinner his plane disappeared in the

---

* Francis Queensberry (1896–1954): grandson of the Marquess of Queensberry who gave his name to the rules of boxing and became notorious for his litigious pursuit of Oscar Wilde because of Wilde's relationship with his son, Lord Alfred Douglas ('Bosie').

† Raimund von Hofmannsthal: son of the Austrian poet Hugo von Hofmannsthal, he was taken up by Henry Luce of Time Inc., worked for 'March of Time' docu-mentaries, and became his roving ambassador in Europe and editorial consultant for *Time*'s London office.

Channel and the mystery has never certainly been solved – possibly friendly fire. Planes going down in the Channel seem to have been happening for various reasons to friends and acquaintances over the decades.

*

My father had been installed in the annexe at No. 10 Downing Street in Storey's Gate. In early 1944 I stayed at Chequers again as a convalescent after having my appendix out:

> the strain of which was naturally a knockout, though I rather enjoyed the operation itself, I mean being gassed. Winston however was as loving, humorous, great, and utterly seductive as ever, in a series of quilted Chinese dressing gowns, & champagne for every meal. Clemmie was also in a quilted dressing gown (I don't wonder, the house was icy, & I slept in my fur coat). Pam [Churchill] was there too, with green sequins in her hair, doing a mother-act over her child who had bronchitis.

That year I also spent Christmas at Chequers. Winston had set up in the Great Hall a huge mock-up of Berlin as it looked after the Allied blitz bombing – in other words, in ruins. I was shocked by the sight. In the cinema there on Christmas Day, we saw Olivier's *Henry V*, which had caused a great patriotic stir at the time.

*   *   *

In June the Germans had unleashed a new menace, the V1 rocket, pilotless aircraft known as 'doodlebugs', which were launched night and day on London and the South-East from mobile landing sites in France. The attacks continued until January 1945. But with the successful Allied landings in France on D-Day, June 1944, and intensified bombing of enemy territories, the long struggle to defeat the Germans was under way.

*　　*　　*

By this time one was getting rather frayed. The doodlebugs were particularly unnerving. You would hear the approaching drone, then when the drone suddenly cut out you had no idea how close to you the bomb would fall.

Life at Rossmore Court continued. My friends and I dined off a table covered with a blue and red taffeta cloth, which I imagined looked eighteenth century. I had discovered George Eliot and thought *Middlemarch* one of the most wonderful books. It became my favourite book for years. I thought there was a feeling of air and visual sensitivity, which I always missed in Austen.

I discovered Diderot's letters to Sophie Volland and thought them the best letters ever written:

> It must have been so nice to live in an age when the knowledge of the universe was of a size & kind *comprehensible* to the human understanding – the mind was seen as a combination of faculties, the body as a combination of humours, the world as physically, three-dimensionally and morally reasonable – which are the terms our minds naturally think in – nowadays we are weighed down by knowledge of complexes, of biology, of relativity, and of unreason – no wonder we are all exhausted.

Meanwhile, Alice Astor and I began going each day to an improvised factory off the Euston Road where we sat holding red-hot irons soldering parts for submarines beside a good-looking older woman, who was Lillie Langtry's daughter – she was rather severe but had a marvellous profile.

There was privation and exhaustion as the war neared its end. The American P X rations helped – which one got from U S soldier friends – though I can only remember Spam, peanut butter and

Hershey bars, and of course Camel cigarettes, with their sweet taste. England had only produced Passing Clouds in a pink carton, and Woodbines. In May a friend in Hampshire reported that there were quantities of rooks for sale and not much else. Eating out at restaurants was still possible, though. At the Hungarian Czarda it was chicken paprika, at Rules the excitement of jugged hare or venison: 5s. was the limit on food.

After the liberation of Paris in August 1944, we were all longing to get back to France. Duff Cooper* returned as Ambassador, but only a gradual trickle of people succeeded in getting through the red tape. Cyril Connolly was among the first – he went over in January 1945, to my envy – reporting for *Horizon* on French culture. He suffered, rightly, from the post-war depression – that the quality of life and literature would never be the same again.

Meanwhile Duff Cooper in Paris was playfully thinking about my future:

14 July 1945

I was reminded of you only two nights ago when I was talking to your distinguished uncle, his wife and his little daughter.... I had been telling them of the last legitimate Bonaparte who is in search of a bride, and whose emissary asked me not long ago what there might be suitable in the English marriage market. He started by Princess Elizabeth, but when I indicated that he was aiming a bit

---

* Alfred Duff Cooper, 1st Viscount Norwich (1890–1954): diplomat, politician and friend of Clarissa. Also a biographer (of Talleyrand and Douglas Haig) and poet. Charming and urbane, he married Society beauty and eccentric Lady Diana Manners in 1919, a union which survived his infidelities. Entered Parliament in 1924, became First Lord of the Admiralty in 1937 and resigned in 1938 over Chamberlain's Munich agreement with Hitler. A friend of Winston Churchill, he re-entered the wartime Cabinet as Minister of Information in 1941, then was responsible for Britain's liaison with the Free French led by General Charles de Gaulle in North Africa. Became British Ambassador to France 1944–8.

high he gradually descended to Miss Mary [Churchill], saying that he was sure the idea would appeal to me as an historian – the idea that the last of the Bonapartes should marry a descendant of the great Duke of Marlborough. Mary, I think, was rather tickled by the suggestion but Clemmie said, somewhat acidly, that she thought he had much better marry you – who were equally descended from the great Duke, and who were much more the kind of glamorous type that would appeal to a Frenchman.

The young man in question is six foot six, extremely handsome, has fought bravely in the War and in the Resistance, has been decorated, is a student of history, has edited memoirs, is altogether admirable and quite desperately dull. How would you consider him as husband with a hundred to one chance of becoming Empress of the French? I think he would be very easy to deceive which is always a good point in a husband.

The war ended. On VE Day I lunched with Elizabeth Bowen and ended the evening with Nicko Henderson watching the fireworks.

With peace in Europe, we began to pick up the threads of our lives. Though the stringent conditions did not ease at once and rationing continued long after the war, there was relief that it was over. I summed up London:

I am very gay & happy, & obliged to rest only a very small amount now. Isaiah says I am quite unrecognisable from last year – & as for my figure I can only say that Cecil now tries to force food down my throat because he thinks I am too thin! . . .

We have occasional dulcet summer days when one can picnic in the Park or walk in Hanover Lodge garden after dinner. People are beginning to have cars, one or two people – there is a little champagne from Paris, & Bébé Bérard from Paris – & the

Comédie Française – & some Frenchmen in my life – & a Polish prince (tremendously gentlemanly, lived all his childhood in the Royal Palace in Vienna) – & Eric Duncannon home on leave, very good looking & more intelligent – & Duff, for whom my affection is unbounded – & still dinners at Emerald's with the curtains drawn tight on the hottest summer evening on the longest day of the year – & the same voracious femmes de 30 ans – & more airy more raffish dinners on the floor above at Daisy's, with Gerald, & drunken Hugh S. & Daisy with a French dress & a rose tree on her corsage, & lots of iced hock.

Then there are balls in the 'Galerie des Glaces' downstairs in the Dorchester –with everyone in their mummified balldresses, & the really rich ones in new dresses, at a price – rather empty floors & lots of waltzing (at which I am becoming adept – oh what we have missed – & oh the boredom of those sexy modern dances – once one has really waltzed nothing is like it – becoming giddy makes it into something so unique, that, plus the rhythm is something more satisfying than any drug could ever be).

I paid visits to Mells – a lovely life and admirable – they ran the village, every decision depended on them, with the cows, hoe, scythe etc. A welcome change to my Faringdon existence of the last few years. Mells was real life.

I also made a full-blooded excursion into the Dudley world: rich, loud, coarse, comfortable, worldly – great fun – swimming pools, gin rummy, stimulating crude admiration of one's looks.

I had been thinking for some time what I should do after the war, what direction to take. Journalism seemed the only answer.

Portrait, aged about seventeen.

A youthful David and Rachel Cecil.

At Oxford, Isaiah Berlin developing an argument to David Cecil.

At Faringdon: one of Gerald's japes.

… and another.

Faringdon House.
Gerald Berners in foreground.

MISS CLARISSA CHURCHILL, *niece of the Premier* ; LADY JULIET DUFF,
LORD BERNERS *and* GREGORIO PRIETO *were snapped at Mr. Prieto's
Private View of paintings and drawings at the Lefèvre Galleries. They
were gazing intently at a portrait of Lord Berners holding triumphantly
a large fish. Prieto studied at the San Fernando in Madrid ; at the
Museums of France and England, and was later awarded the Spanish
Grand Prix de Rome.*

At Long Barn, 1940.

At Long Barn: Nigel Nicolson in Guards officer's uniform, Vita Sackville-West, James Pope-Hennessy in private's uniform.

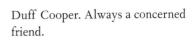

Duff Cooper. Always a concerned friend.

Cyril Connolly at the window of the *Horizon* office in Bedford Square.

Creating the ballet, 'Les Sirènes'. Cecil Beaton and Freddie Ashton with Gerald on the piano.

London Films publicity department. Sorting out the stills.

The fascinating cigar-smoking Orson Welles with Alex Korda.

Brilliant, clever and very French, director Julian Duvivier on the set of Korda's production of *Anna Karenina*.

« blanc » de qualité : Jean Hugo, aux tempes argentées,
un fidèle parmi les fidèles habitués de la maison.

Smoking with Jean Hugo in Paris.

Drawing by Jean Hugo.
My husband's favourite.

Summer in Wiltshire. Stas Radziwill, a great friend, and a young
Lucian Freud in tartan trews.

In Cecil Beaton's judgement, 'a horrible picture – not at all like you'. I liked it.

Peter Ustinov
on some issues of the theatre today
(page 94)

Elizabeth Bowen, Graham Greene and V. S. Pritchett
on the writer and society *(page 55)*

Clarissa Churchill
on Julien Duvivier, French film director
(page 98)

Contact (1947) with fellow contributors Peter Ustinov, Elizabeth Bowen, Graham Greene, V. S. Pritchett.

CHAPTER 7

POST WAR

W hen war ended I needed a job and Cecil Beaton got me one on *Vogue*: not fashion, thank goodness, but a column called 'Spotlight', which covered all things cultural, at £8 a week. I managed to live on this because one could clock up 'expenses' and because in those days all social life was paid for by one's men friends. Thanks to Cecil, and also to 'Spotlight', because most writers and artists are not averse to publicity, I met and often made friends with many artists and writers.

By the end of the war, those who had spent it in England were weary and emotionally stale. I was longing for escape and my thoughts naturally turned to France.

I had been introduced to Nicolas Nabokov* by a mutual friend. To me he was Nicolas, from his French past; to Americans he was Nicholas, or even Nicky. A composer, he wrote music in the

---

* Nicolas Nabokov (1903–78): cousin of the Russian writer Vladimir Nabokov, he was born into a family of Russian gentry who fled to the Crimea in 1918. Nicolas moved briefly to Germany, then settled in Paris in 1923, studied at the Sorbonne and embarked on his musical career, before moving to America in 1933. He became a US citizen in 1939 and worked for the US Strategic Bombing Survey and as cultural adviser to the Allied Control Commission during the latter stages of the war.

Stravinsky mode and worked with Diaghilev in Paris long before the war. At the time I met him he was in uniform and working in various US cultural outfits. I was entranced by his Russian-bear appearance: very tall, with a Slav face and a forelock. He had the usual Russian bass voice and delighted in the same kind of jokes and interests that I and most of my friends enjoyed. I think he had a curiously soft centre, though; there was something not sturdy about his character. Perhaps that was why he married four times.

Nicolas was by then on the US Control Commission in Germany and suggested I should visit Berlin. I managed to get a permit in December 1945 by being engaged to write two articles about what remained of cultural life there – for *Vogue* and Cyril's *Horizon*. By this means I was able to make my first post-war trip to Paris. After a few halcyon days staying at the embassy, Nicolas and I flew to Brussels where we lunched *à quatre* with Hansi Lambert, head of the Banque Lambert, and M. van Zeeland, the Belgian Prime Minister. Hansi was quick-witted and not suffering fools. The luncheon seemed awkward; I suspect she had intended to have a tête-à-tête with the Prime Minister when Nicolas invited himself with me in tow.

I then had to fly separately on an RAF flight, while Nicolas flew straight to Berlin. I wrote:

Flew from Brussels this morning strapped on to the bucket seat of an unheated Dakota (the apparatus let out a gust of oily-smelling hot air and then stopped) . . . a naval officer beside me obligingly wiped the frost off the inside of the window . . . flying over the Ruhr I noticed nearly all the factories appeared to be working . . . smoke from their chimneys hung in round white puffs like thousands of parachutes over a vast area.

I was deposited at the HQ of the British Army of the Rhine at Bad Oeynhausen, where I was surrounded by astonished airmen. I gave as my reason for being there that I was en route to Berlin to write articles for *Horizon* and *Vogue*. They had never heard of *Horizon*, but '*VOGUE!*' they screamed, doubling up with laughter. A car of the British Control Commission then drove me to the capital.

What I saw in Berlin far outweighed anything I had seen in London.

... All along the road the bridges were down, each river and ravine was full of twisted iron girders. The outskirts of the towns were hollow and pitted by shellfire. As I neared the centre of the city it seemed as if I were reaching a different climatic zone, a mountain top where no living thing could survive and the vegetation gradually thins out and ceases. The gutted crowded streets gave way to a vast area as formless and without plan as a jumble of rocks on barren soil. The interior bricks of the houses have been torn out by high explosives and scorched by incendiaries so that even on a rainy day the ruins are an intestinal pink.

The upper echelons of the US and British forces were sanitised in the Grünewald in handsome intact villas. I stayed in the American Zone, facing Admiral Doenitz's house, in a well-heated small villa smelling of beeswax and still full of the former owner's books and furniture. German bourgeois bad taste was the most flamboyant in the world. In the British officers' mess (a Nazi's ex-home) the walls consisted of grey and puce marble banded by horizontal lines of turquoise-blue enamel.

The Berlin Philharmonic played on Sunday afternoons in our zone in the Theater des Westens. It had been de-nazified and was conducted by a young Romanian called Celibidache, who tended to rhapsodise. The British troops applauded indiscriminately with true British politeness. I wrote:

Drove home tonight through this warped devastated town behind a lorry full of Russian soldiers huddled one on top of the other and wrapped in blankets. It gave a lurch rounding a bend so that one of the soldiers rolled out, still rolled in his blanket, like a sack of potatoes ... he started to yell to his comrades ... but the lorry roared away out of sight ... Could we stop, I asked, and pick the man up? No, that was not allowed, only the Russians could do that ... and so we left him, shouting 'Tovarich' to himself among the ruins. ...

I was unable to get to the opera – then run by the Russians – but Nicolas reported that the opening night was a fantastic event among all the desolation: generals and military of four nations arriving through the dead streets, filled with that sweetish nauseating smell of death and ruin, to a brilliantly lit opera surrounded by de luxe German policemen dressed up for the occasion in white gloves and impeccable green uniform. A crowd of motley Germans swamped in a sea of uniforms and loud American majors. A magnificent performance of Gluck's *Orpheus and Eurydice*, the incredibly pure music, so remote, so heavenly beautiful – all this in the dark of a hungry desert.

All the same, Berlin didn't know how to animate the arts in 1945, so they imitated Weimar of the 1920s. When I returned to Berlin in the 1990s it was to see all the new buildings – the Jewish Museum designed by Libeskind, the Reichstag just rebuilt to a Norman Foster design, the National picture gallery and the Berggruen Collection, and to go to *Tristan and Isolde* at the opera, while staying in a hotel in luxury with the best pillows in the world – unobtainable in England.

The last time I saw Nicolas his forelock was grey and he was with his last wife at a lunch of the Isaiah Berlins' in Oxford. I was wearing velvet breeches, then in fashion, and he remarked on this in Russian to Isaiah. Nothing complimentary, no doubt.

*

One advantage of the Berlin assignment was that en route I got back to Paris at last. Though our embassy had reopened in October 1944, after the German retreat but before the war ended, few had been able to get there. Those who succeeded and who had the good fortune to know the Coopers lodged at the embassy.

I had known the Ambassador, Duff Cooper, all my life but we only became friends during the war. He was a consummate writer – he gave me his *Talleyrand* in 1944 (by then it had already gone into seventeen editions and nine translations), an example for all biographers unable to wean the essentials from the details. Apart from being wonderful company he was also a faithful friend, affectionate, concerned and discreet.* In London he often used to take me to the theatre. One day he asked which play I would like to see. I said *Peer Gynt*, being at that moment in my Ibsen phase. Of course the play was impossible, but Duff, foreseeing this, instead of refusing my suggestion, took a box, went to the back of it and fell asleep. Evenings usually ended with cold partridge at the dear old cream-and-gold Savoy Grill, now twice destroyed.

After the drabness of London, the drabness of Paris seemed subtly different. It looked splendid – no bomb damage, but the mood was resentful. The people in the streets seemed deadened and hollowed out. London was shattered but had triumphed. Paris was intact yet violated. Sartre wrote that there was not a single person without a friend or a relation who had been arrested or deported or shot. Outside the diplomatic privileges there was nothing but acorn coffee and privation. Embassies, as in England throughout the war, are

---

* He died suddenly at sea on New Year's Day 1954. Not long before, he wrote to Clarissa, 'Darling – you are the only woman I have ever loved without asking much or indeed anything except a peck on the cheek in return.'

exempt from shortages. This made our embassy a magnet not only for friends but also for the French *gratin* and those literary figures who could endear themselves to the Coopers.

Jean Cocteau* was one of those who had ingratiated himself and I suppose because my name was Churchill and his war record had not been very sound, he latched on to me vigorously. I visited the set of *La Belle et la Bête*, the film he was working on with Jean Marais who wore a fantastic mask as the beast which took him hours to put on. Cocteau immediately ordered me to be made up and photographed as a souvenir. The result was that I looked like a film star, or rather a starlet, and not myself.

I met but did not talk to Camus, to my sorrow, for I admired him the most. I reported for *Vogue* on Camus and the intellectual atmosphere in Paris in 1946:

> How to bear life at all, rather than how best to live, is the pre-occupation of the Existentialist school of writers in France. Camus' characters seek to combat the chaos and absurdity of life with unflinching logic.
>
> Camus is wise. Both in *The Outsider* and in his play *Caligula* he is concerned to show that existentialism when put into practice is too antisocial to be tolerable. In formulating this conflict Camus has created a fertile and genuine subject for art. In the eighteenth century, after faith in religion had waned, the idea of progress took its place.
>
> In France, faith in progress, or indeed faith in anything, became, to some, absurd. 'Life is absurd,' says Camus, and the existentialists stoically accept this contingency, and accept also

---

* Jean Cocteau (1889–1963): leading French intellectual for over four decades from the 1920s. Though he thought of himself as a poet, he was also a Surrealist film maker, designer, and wrote novels and plays and a ballet for Diaghilev with the Ballets Russes. Friend of Proust, Gide, Picasso, Satie and others.

the simple facts of existence and non-existence as the sole reality. Existentialism has swept over the intellectual youth in France, one girl even walked barefoot from Finland (it is said) to see the maestro Sartre.

Existentialism – as fashion and philosophy – was pervasive. Jean Hugo wrote to me after visiting a monastery that 'talk among the monks was all of existentialism and the Café Flore'.* I cannot remember where I met Jean Hugo. Great grandson of Victor Hugo, he was a burly man with cropped hair and great charm, looking rather like a French *ouvrier*. A highly rated painter, inevitably he had done sets for the Russian Ballet and was part of the lively raffish group. I have a number of his tiny landscape watercolours and a charcoal drawing he did of me, which I kept in a drawer until long after, when my husband found it and liked it enough to get it framed and hung.

I went to stay with Jean at his house, Mas des Fourques, in the Hérault, where one heard the faint chug and whistle of a train a long way away. He took me to a bullfight in Nîmes, which I did not enjoy, and to Montpellier, where we were peaceably drinking in a café when his mistress appeared and a noisy row ensued on the pavement – a terrific scene with Jean explaining plaintively *'Mais non, mais non'*. We met many times over the years in Paris before I married.

Nicolas organised my social life in Paris. I always stayed with the Coopers and when he used to come to fetch me from the embassy for a night out he remained stubbornly in the hall and refused to come up to the Salon Vert, the room at the end of the first-floor *enfilade*, which was the private sitting room. Nicolas had a mania about the Coopers – of whom, ironically enough, he disapproved – and said he did not want to meet them. After this had happened a few times Diana asked me who it was who insisted

---

* Where Jean Paul Sartre and Simone de Beauvoir held court.

on waiting downstairs, and I said 'A Russian composer'. I heard that later on, when he finally met Diana, they naturally got on like a house on fire. After a few years, it was Louise de Vilmorin always with Diana in the Salon Vert, as by then Louise had moved into the embassy permanently.

After the Labour government won the 1945 election, Ernest Bevin took over from Anthony Eden as Foreign Secretary. The Coopers were apprehensive about whether they would stay on under the new regime. Luckily Diana got on with Bevin. I was present at one dinner when the evening ended with the two of them alternating in singing songs. However, after three years, the Harveys* in 1948 replaced the Coopers, who retired to the beautiful house they had bought at Chantilly with this in mind.

Through Nicolas I sampled the very many parties given by rich cultured people, such as used to exist in England but had been quenched by the war. They all seemed very energetic – I thought it was to do with their recent liberation, but perhaps they had other aids. Nicolas always purported to me to have a certain discrimination about them. Some had got to America or England during the Occupation, some retired to their properties and some equivocally stayed in Paris.

Marie-Blanche de Polignac, married to Comte Jean de Polignac, was the daughter of Lanvin the dressmaker. Nicolas first took me to lunch with her, then to her parties. She was sweet and vital, and a talented pianist. Her evenings were musicales and her guests were not only the usual writers, artists and men-about-town. Marie-Blanche and her aunt, Winnie de Polignac, were seriously musical, patrons and performers whose evenings were to promote composers.

---

* Sir Oliver Harvey: former Deputy Under-Secretary at the Foreign Office, British Ambassador to France 1948–54, succeeded by Sir Gladwyn and Lady (Cynthia) Jebb.

In Princess Winnie's case, Stravinsky, the pianist Cortot and so on, while in Marie-Blanche's day it was Francis Poulenc with his long melancholy face, solid-looking Georges Auric, the pianist Jacques Février, Satie, Milhaud and Rubinstein, Menuhin and Horowitz.

Marie Laure de Noailles was another great patroness. By the time I knew her she was ravaged, with a heavy body and very black hair. I could not quite take it. I knew everyone around her was talented, ground-breaking, charming, but it all seemed the end of the line. However, in her day she had been immensely knowledgeable in Italian and German art, and had gradually developed into a major patron of the Surrealism and Dadaism of the 1920s. Salvador Dalí was a frequent presence. During the Spanish Civil War she had been on the extreme Left – hated Léon Blum and so on. Her husband Charles entered into all her artistic forays in spite of seeming to be a throwback to the nineteenth century – straight-backed, polite, clever, cultivated – consequently he became a friend of ours after I married, particularly as he was an internationally renowned gardener. Knowing him as I did with my husband, I find it hard to realise that he had been a partner to his wife's taste in promoting all the extreme modern painters and writers.

The Noailles' huge house in the place des Etats Unis had two full-length Goyas confronting one in the hall and splashed around were Davids and Rembrandts. Then, in Marie Laure's part of the house, Dalí, Magritte etc. Years later, when Charles took Anthony there – curiously enough to see Marie Laure's modern paintings – it was a failure as Anthony wasn't into that sort of modern. I believe her grandson, who inherited the house, built an underground swimming pool, but never lived there.

The third Marie was Marie-Louise Bousquet. She had a famous but more formal salon in her new flat, place du Palais Bourbon – a lot of the same people, but somehow behaving in a more decorous manner, partly because there was practically nothing to drink. She seemed smaller and plainer than when I knew her before the war. At her salon I was introduced to the Abbé Mugnier, the great converter, who was already very faint and frail.

All these women had emblems which they used on writing paper, brooches, cushions. Marie Laure had a leaf, Lulu de Waldener had a ladybird, Louise de Vilmorin a four-leaf clover.

At the British embassy, John de Bendern was one of Duff Cooper's succession of private secretaries. These were exactly that – not diplomats, but acquaintances of the Ambassador. De Bendern was bouncing with *joie de vivre* and charm. After a few years, in some *quartiers* of Paris there would always be a funfair and we would love to zip on the switchback, or hang upside down on the great wheel. He was a champion golfer of France, and had survived the eccentricities of his father by being debonair and vital.

*

Covering Shakespeare at Stratford was part of my remit for 'Spotlight'. Once it was *Love's Labour's Lost*, directed in an intelligent and unusual way with the costumes in the period of Watteau. I was enchanted by it visually, gave it a rave review and met the director – a very young boy called Peter Brook. We made friends and I remember going to the Arts Theatre in London with him to see Alec Clunes in *Hamlet*, and at dinner afterwards deciding it came nearer to the spirit of Shakespeare's day than some of the more modern versions of our time. Peter Brook once said to me that he liked directing Paul Scofield more than any other actor, as he was completely free of 'interpretation', he lived his part. Another eminent actor thought too much – he was sure that Lady Macbeth was pregnant and that must influence the interpretation of his role as Macbeth.

John Gielgud in *Hamlet* was probably the first time I saw any Shakespeare. I must have been pretty young. It defined for me the only way the verse, with respect for the metre, should be spoken, to give the words their resonant meaning and emphasise the poetry – never mind trendy costumes or scenery. Peter Brook understood this. Dining at publisher Graham C. Greene's years later in the country, John Gielgud, who lived in an exquisite pavilion a few yards away, sat next to me, resolutely silent while Arnold Goodman held the table. By the pudding he suddenly saw an opening and for the rest of the meal it was one amusing theatrical anecdote after another.

I liked Peter Brook for being such a visual director. When he was ballet critic for the *Observer*, we saw *Accolade* and *The Olympians* at Covent Garden, and I think his experience of ballet as well as opera reinforced this visual sense, though it was at odds with modern popular theatre production in London. I saw Peter's *Mahabharata* in Glasgow – I am not sure the hangar-like space it took place in was ideal. I say 'took place' because it is unlike any conventional drama. He immersed himself in Indian religious and dramatic themes and, indeed, I believe took the whole cast round India beforehand so that each member, presumably, could extract his own special reactions.

Peter did *Titus Andronicus* at Stratford and I went with Anthony, who was President of the Stratford Memorial Company, later the Royal Shakespeare Company. It had Olivier and Vivien Leigh in the main roles. When we went round afterwards, Vivien said, 'When I am doing Lavinia I always think of you.' Well, Lavinia has both hands cut off and her tongue cut out and is raped, so what Vivien meant I dread to think.

London crassly lost Peter Brook. If we had grasped the chance and given him what he wanted – independence and a large auditorium to do what he liked with – I believe he might have stayed in England and not left for good, going to Paris instead. In England artistic experiment was frowned on, whereas in France it was natural. Much later, when I was at Downing Street, I suggested his name for an honour, but the Honours Committee rejected it, saying he was 'too young'. In spite of abortive attempts in later years to join up with him in Vienna and Paris when we were both there, I never saw him again until he was given an honorary degree at Oxford University and we met once more.

*

During the war, theatres had been filled by plays which ran for one, two, even four or five years. It seemed that the West End managers simply couldn't run a flop. War has always driven people to theatres. Companies like John Gielgud's, or the Old Vic, and plays like Peter Ustinov's *The Banbury Nose* were scarce, and the important London theatres were mainly filled with American farces and genteel English middle-class comedies.

At the New Theatre in 1946, Rodney Ackland's adaptation of Dostoevsky's *Crime and Punishment* had John Gielgud as Raskolnikov conveying a terrible cumulative tension, Peter Ustinov as the detective and Edith Evans as the consumptive neighbour. I went to Somerset Maugham's *Our Betters* and was surprised by the 'slowness, almost boredom of the first one and a half acts. One could see the platitudes and jokes coming a mile away – but then of course all Maugham's stuff *is* platitudinous in texture, it is only when the cynicism really starts backfiring that things shine – (or in his books the excellent narrative power and plot)'. The play was set in the 1920s:

I would like to have grown up in the 1920s [I wrote]. For all their crudity, cynicism and perversity, they had an atmosphere of electrifying excitement which would surely have galvanised even my own wan and bewildered generation. I feel the strongest possible nostalgia for Dada, Futurism and everything which they symbolised. And the women's fashions! How much I love that sleek curl pasted onto the cheek, those deep mysterious cloches, that collarbone neckline, the hip-waist, the skirt made of hanging beads like the entrance to an Italian Trattoria. The women of those days had something we have lost – It.

After seeing *Our Betters* I went to a party where the Duchess of Kent was. I found that either one was being (apparently) too fresh and she was royally offended, or one wasn't paying her enough attention and she was really offended. She rather inexplicably picked me out to go to the Milroy with her and John Profumo – so I dragged Aly Forbes along and we sat up till 5 a.m. I was interested because I had never really seen her much before.

Glyndebourne reopened with Benjamin Britten's *The Rape of Lucretia* and I went with Isaiah Berlin. The cabbages planted in the gardens during the war were being grubbed up and replaced with those electric-blue delphiniums, which used to radiate in the twilight as one crunched along the gravel paths between acts.

A Russian season also brought the première of Eisenstein's film *Ivan the Terrible*. I wrote, 'Whatever motives of propaganda may have inspired it, Eisenstein's method of building up every dramatic moment on the screen by means of large synthesised stills is always memorable, and an added interest will be the music of Serge Prokofiev, who has incorporated ritual songs and old Russian hymns into his score.' In France, Georges Lampin had just completed filming *The Idiot*, with France's new young actor Gérard Philipe in the name part. I was very taken by the looks of Gérard Philipe. He was unforgettable as the emperor in the Camus play *Caligula*.

I met Rudolf Bing in about 1946. He was forty-five, tall and thin, with a high domed forehead, delicately boned. He conversed softly and eloquently in a wistful, bantering manner, pacing up and down the room or seated, resting his long hands on the arms of his chair.

Rudi came to England in 1934 from Austria – under the patronage of John Christie who had recently built Glyndebourne opera house beside his house in Sussex, and who reunited Rudi with his colleagues from the Berlin Städtische Oper, Fritz Busch and Carl Ebert, as conductor and producer. I wrote at the time, 'When a man who has been successful and experienced on the continent comes to this country, rehabilitation is extremely difficult – for both sides. But the newcomer also must be open-minded – though the quality he stands most in need of is a superabundant tact.' Rudi did not necessarily have tact. He insisted on his own way and his own views. His El Greco features masked his acumen and drive. He combined an exceptional business flair with a love and wide knowledge of music, and he had the Austrian's genius for mixing music with gaiety and with life. I had been to Glyndebourne before the war when Audrey Mildmay, John Christie's wife, was singing in a Mozart opera on a tiny stage. Bing was the manager and had got it all going. He went on to run the Metropolitan Opera in New York.

Towards the end of 1946 Rudi asked me if I would like to go to Edinburgh with him as he wanted to see if it would be suitable for a Festival. We stayed in a freezing-cold hotel near the railway line. He had chosen Edinburgh, I think, because the castle hanging on the crag reminded him of Salzburg. I could never forgive the Scots for having driven that railway bang through the ravine in the centre, covering everything with layers of soot. I was dazzled by the National Gallery, though – such a Vermeer, and a Goya – and the Bridgewater House collection there, with five Raphaels, seven Poussins and three Titians in one room. Pre-Fringe, the Festival was a remarkable cultural event. The first year had the Vienna Philharmonic and Louis Jouvet's company for starters.

Rudi and I also went to see *Antony and Cleopatra* with Edith Evans and Godfrey Tearle. I reported to Cecil that

It was less upsetting and painful than I had expected. I have always

94

thought her such an exquisite actress, but this part brings out her limitations, the emotional rather than the physical ones oddly enough. Her appearance is a masterpiece of make-up – except for a scraggy neck & hunched shoulders one isn't appalled. She wears a black wig, rather wiggy, of hair the shape of mine – but the trouble is 1) a bad voice for this part, too querulous in tragedy, & not rich enough in pleasure 2) no sexual passion, 3) inability to convey pride or majesty. She is like an outraged dowager, not an empress (do you remember how good Gérard Philipe was at being an emperor in *Caligula*? It is a strange knack evidently).

Old Tearle gave a good performance as Mark Antony in a dull sort of way – stupid, soft, corrupted. But the production I thought poor – silly touches in it – & the Motley décor & costumes! a ghastly mess – the scene throughout (38 scenes – 3 hrs perf: with only one interval, much too tough going) was a factory chimney descending from the roof with incredibly complicated intersecting platforms all the way up it, & a sliding door at the bottom like a department store lift, which rumbled open each time to reveal Cleopatra dressed as a Spanish Infanta surrounded by waiting women dressed as Creoles – Cleo finished up dressed in brown-black rep as for *Desire Under the Elms*. The men wore traditional Roman costumes, except Mark Antony who occasionally wore an Apache tam-o'-shanter. In the final scene, dying Mark Antony was levered up to waiting Cleo on one of the platforms by means of a rope-pulley – like a horse being embarked onto a ship.

This account so amused Alfred Lunt and Lynn Fontanne, the most famous acting couple in America, when it was read aloud to them in New York that they asked for a reprise a few days later, which is why, if it pleased them, I quote it here at length.

On the other hand I said of Edith Evans in *Crime and Punishment*:

'Dame Edith Evans as the consumptive wife of the drunken neighbour is beyond all praise – the woman's latent hysteria and visible
despair, the raw, wounded snobbery, have been pared down to a
shape that is wholly credible and incredibly moving.'

Also at this time I met George Weidenfeld. I was introduced to
him by a fellow Austrian. We soon began to have lunch and dinner
and I was flooded by George's fertile plans and ideas. He was only
starting on his meteoric rise but after a few years – behold there was
Weidenfeld & Nicolson, and horizons were broadening. His personal
warmth and friendship were a pleasure, and many evenings were
spent at a nightclub called Les Ambassadeurs, a house in Park Lane
with huge tall rooms run by some dubious Poles – not to dance, but
to talk. Later I drove him to Salzburg where I ended up staying at an
ex-bishop's palace. Through George I also made great friends with
Marcus Sieff, later the Chairman of Marks & Spencer – still at that
time in uniform. We dined, too, with the legendary Lord Marks and,
from his forceful manner, I was not surprised to learn that it was his
father who had started the original penny bazaars in Leeds.

The winter of 1946–7 was one of power cuts and fuel shortages –
the coldest of the century so far. I had no heat at all in my flat, the
bedroom was freezing. People forget how long the rationing and
privations went on for. Snoek (a form of barracuda packed in tins)
and whale meat were available, but everything else was in short
supply. Everywhere seemed in gloom. I remember on a visit to
Switzerland looking out of the window and being exhilarated to see
the whole town lit up. The further excitement was visiting the Beyeler
Collection in Basel, with room after room of Impressionists. Most of
our nation's paintings were still stored in the salt mines of Wales.

By the end of 1946 I had decided to leave *Vogue*, largely because they
didn't pay enough. I was far from being a successful career woman.

Audrey Withers, *Vogue*'s editor, was moderately regretful, but I felt more and more that there I was tied to *Vogue* and London on £500 a year and being made to do more and more office work, whereas I considered my job was to do an efficient 'Spotlight'. It appeared that they had been wanting to make me into a features editor and that I was no use to them simply as a writer, as the increase in the paper allowance wasn't going to materialise for some years. I escaped when Alexander Korda offered me a job in the publicity department of London Film Productions.

CHAPTER 8

FILMS

Korda's offices were one of the large stone houses in Piccadilly, near Hyde Park Corner, number 146. The head of my department was a kind and cosy man, Ralphe Thompson, husband of C. A. Lejeune, then the leading film critic. On various floors were gentlemen seated behind large desks – one a businessman, one an airman and one predominantly a gardener. I only realised long afterwards that they had all been in Intelligence, together with Korda,* during the war. His PA was a handsome sailor. After a while it turned out that I should have joined the NUJ as a requirement for the job, which I duly did. Sadly the post-war period of Korda films was not as good as the pre-war, with the exception of *The Third Man* and *The Fallen Idol*. I soon learned that the publicity department was regarded by everyone working on the films with veiled hostility. You would have thought the opposite.

Korda was starting again; having been such a successful film

---

* Alexander Korda (1893–1956): born in Hungary, Korda moved to Britain in 1930 and was the founder of London Films and Denham Studios, and the guiding force behind the success of the British film industry in the 1930s. With his brothers, Zoltán (director) and Vincent (art director), his films were lavish and often visually stunning, though not always successful. He continued to be a major producer until his death.

maker before the war with films such as *The Private Life of Henry VIII* with Charles Laughton, *Rembrandt* and *The Four Feathers*, I felt that he was rather weary and not happy this time round. He had married and divorced Merle Oberon, and now had a minor star, Christine Norden, in tow, and was only bolstered by the companionship of two of his three brothers, Vincent and Zolly. He was immensely charming and very Austro-Hungarian.

During the production of *An Ideal Husband* and before I qualified for my own car – a Standard 8 – Cecil would pick me up in the morning in a grey Rolls-Royce provided for him as designer. Duff (Cooper), who, as always, was keeping an eye on me, wrote, 'Sounds mysterious. What do you actually do at the studio after having got up at 7 a.m. to get there?' Later, when I suspect Alex was losing interest in film-making, and the publicity department was moved to another office, Duff wrote: 'Distressed to hear you have been moved to a room without a sofa. What next indeed. How do they expect you to do your work?' He had a point.

An Ideal Husband premièred in November 1947, with Paulette Goddard immensely miscast as Mrs Cheveley. Glynis Johns as Mabel Chiltern gave by far the best performance and the audience reacted to her immediately. At the première all the contact girls climbed into landaus and processed slowly down Piccadilly to the Carlton Cinema, where the crowd milled around and gaped at them. Alex stood in the floodlights to receive the Mountbattens. The press was not over-enthusiastic, and it was not a commercial success.

I was delegated to go with Paulette Goddard to Brussels to publicise the film. One night she announced she wanted to go to a porn show – the Korda representatives in Brussels were taken aback but managed to make some arrangement. The next night I had a message from Paulette: 'Sugar: Will not be back at 4. I have an idea that we will be seeing each other from 5.30 to 3 a.m. So then – P.G.' I recall only that we climbed a flight of shabby stairs and entered a room to be greeted by two men in black suits. There was a baffled pause and Paulette evidently decided this was no go and we left.

*

Julien Duvivier was a small dynamic man. The director of such French film classics as *Pépé le Moto* and *Un Carnet de Bal*, he was brought over by Alex to direct *Anna Karenina*, with Vivien Leigh as Anna, and an unsuitable discovery of Korda's – a young Irish actor called Kieron Moore – as Vronsky. Julien had been more responsible than any other Frenchman for creating what is known as the 'realistic' French film. This was his proper province. But, being a professional, he had undertaken the making of various types of films, not all of which he had excelled in. *Anna Karenina* was one of these. It managed to avoid any hint of Tolstoy. Of all Tolstoy's works, this is the one with a plot that can easily be reduced to a trite modern tale. David Cecil used to laugh and say how curious it was that in Tolstoy's book Anna was presented as a seductress with a swaying walk, like a sailor.

As the production ground on, Alex thought Julien Duvivier was not doing a good job so he was immersing himself in Tolstoy in order, as he thought, to get it right. This was a mistake. Duvivier was sometimes accused of being dictatorial. His intransigence came from his conviction that he was recreating a work of art, and that to do this the director must plan and execute his film without interference, without the opinions or considerations of others. For this reason, and the gross miscasting of Anna and Vronsky, even Ralph Richardson as Karenin could not save it. It was a failure.

Julien was the first sympathetic character I had met in the film world so far – apart from Alex – and we would dine regularly, with great gaiety, in his suite at the Savoy. After what must have been a frustrating day in the studios, he would be singing 'People will say we're in love' – a popular tune – as he bounced into the room. This had no personal connotation – we understood each other perfectly. I imagine he was making the best of a bad job as regards the film, and was doing Alex a favour. Alas, we did not have serious discussions, just a lot of fun. I never saw him again after the film was finished and he left for France – his parting letter: 'I am leaving you those nice records [memories] which have enlightened my evenings in this god-damned land of liberty and tea. It seems that I shall have to work in Hollywood.' He sent me a delighted message when I married.

The next event was being sent to Paris to help with the publicity for *Bonnie Prince Charlie*. I was put in the Hôtel Normandie, but the noise of the couple next door was too much and I forced the film people to move me to the Hôtel Raphael by the Arc de Triomphe, an ancient hotel of unspeakable luxury where I had a soundproof suite. *Bonnie Prince Charlie* was not a success. The Prince was David Niven, who was dissatisfied, as he said he was not being paid enough.

Meanwhile in London Carol Reed was going to direct a film version of Graham Greene's *The Third Man*. The lead was Orson Welles, whom I found delightful. Less conceited, more intelligent than I had anticipated – and fantastically funny – an appearance like a very handsome bullfrog, green eyes and black curls. I saw him as a modern version of an extravagant, creative, vital Renaissance figure – cruder, of course, and slightly debased – he could only have come out of America. Also I found him pleasantly patient, polite and humane.

Both Joseph Cotten and Orson were always arriving late for their shoots in London and Vienna. They were enjoying themselves in Paris or Rome. There was only a four-week shooting schedule in Vienna and Orson was particularly tardy. He had to be chased all over Europe, which he thought was amusing. He was more used to directing than acting, and therefore didn't care. The first crisis came when he refused to go into the sewers in Vienna because there was water running down the walls. Carol Reed took this resignedly, simply saying, 'We shall have to build the sewers in Shepperton.'

Orson also enjoyed inventing his own dialogue as he went along, the most famous being 'What did the Swiss ever produce? The cuckoo clock.' Which was probably cribbed from James McNeill Whistler anyway. The next crisis was when he refused to stay more than a few weeks in England, which meant that all the sets had to be built like lightning, including the sewers. Carol Reed again took it all in his stride. By this time the participants were said to be on Benzedrine.

The unexpected plus was that Anton Karas's zither theme tune proved to be one of the most famous pieces of film music ever. It made the film known worldwide. The French press were ecstatic about it and said Carol Reed was the best director in the world. However, there was a difficult relationship between David Selznick and Korda all through. It was a Korda film, produced by London Films, but Selznick provided money and Americanised the film when it was shown in the States. Korda to Selznick: 'You know, David, I hope I don't die before you. I hate the thought of you sneaking out at night and scratching my name off my tombstone.'

In March 1948 Korda sent me to New York to publicise *An Ideal Husband*. I sailed on the *Queen Elizabeth* and stayed at the Plaza Hotel where Valentine Lawford kindly lent me his room. I saw Nicolas Nabokov, had dinner with Alice Astor and the painter Tchelitchew, and dined at Cole Porter's – then to Washington where I stayed with Alice at Rhinebeck, her house on the Hudson, before returning to London.

Landing at Heathrow, then a small airport in a field, I was met by friends. As I stood on the edge of the airfield, they didn't recognise me. I had bought a long 'New Look' coat and Marietta Tree had sent me to the most fashionable hairdresser in New York, who had cut my shoulder-length hair quite short. Thus transformed, I resumed my usual routine in London.

*

Life now took on an added dimension.

After Cecil Beaton had been forced out of Ashcombe by the farmer from whom he had leased it, he moved to Broad Chalke, a village in the Ebble valley, and an equally exquisite house called Reddish. This time he did not create a circus tent but a mini-Houghton with damson flock wallpaper and lots of gilt furniture. I had been yearning for a foot in the country. A few years later, thanks to an advertisement in the *Salisbury Times*, he alerted me to a cottage for sale at Little London, outside Broad Chalke, which I bought immediately. The cottage was at the end of a long lane which, when I bought the house, was unmade-up mud. I blithely wrote to the council to say I would not pay my rates unless it was surfaced. They were so amused, the chairman told me later, that they tarmacked it. Today one would probably be arrested instead. I kept the cottage's name – Rose Bower – because it was funny.

I was, I wrote to Cecil, 'so excited that I cannot sleep. I have never owned a bit of earth before, or anything in the country – I have longed for it so much that it is overwhelming now that it has really happened.' At twilight the rooks came to the trees in the field and a black cloud of starlings gathered and flew regularly over the cottage and into the downs each evening. I was bewildered, too, by the sweetness of all the village people. When my car refused to work one morning I made the acquaintance of Mr Bundy and family, who towed me behind their tractor. It showed me how radically different it was from urban life.

Little London was a hamlet of three cottages. Mine had a Gainsborough view down the valley with a wych-elm in the foreground. On one side was the River Ebble, a winterbourne and so far upstream was a mere trickle – too small for trout, let alone the crayfish which Antony Head* conserved on his part of the river lower down in the valley.

On the other side was Mount Sorrel, a chalky ploughland down with plovers nesting. The Ebble flowed into a valley with villages. One of them was Alvediston, where we eventually spent the last years of Anthony's life. Unless you are a big landowner and don't want to be crawling round the edges of farmers' fields, it is essential to be near the downs where dogs, and you, can be free for ever – with views to north and south.

And now – a new life and a new set of friends in the country, as well as Cecil, whom I saw there whenever he was at home. Lady Juliet Duff, a friend of my mother's, lived at Bulbridge, Wilton. She had been a statuesque beauty and unexpected muse of Maurice Baring and Hilaire Belloc, though a touch foolish herself. I had visited Belloc long ago at his house in Sussex where he sang songs and recited his verse. He looked like a rugged peasant and had a guttural French accent. Baring's letters to Juliet are devoted but also, while not exactly mocking, treat her flippantly. Baring was a friend of my mother's too and a figure of my childhood. His brother was the Hugo of the green Rolls-Royce in Paris. Someone interesting was always staying at Bulbridge. One time Willie Maugham remarked, with his stammer, 'The c-c-cows are lying down – that means it is going to r-r-rain.' 'Oh, not in *Wiltshire*,' replied Juliet vaguely.

In the valley to the south was Cranborne, so I was able to see Robert† and Mollie Cranborne. Where Tony‡ and Violet Powell lived, at the Chantry in Somerset, there was a different feeling from

---

* A colleague of Anthony Eden's, later Secretary for War, then Minister of Defence in Eden's Cabinet.

† Formerly Robert Cecil, one of Clarissa's friends from childhood.

‡ Antony Powell (1905–2000): British novelist, acclaimed as among the greatest of the twentieth century, and likened to Proust. Most famous for *A Dance to the Music of Time*.

the other houses – ancestral portraits on the walls and a gentleman's library, the wines produced with ceremony and Tony disappearing to make his speciality curry. He was always enthusiastically welcoming and interested in what one had to say, and Violet provided a perfect match. Anthony got on with Tony.

In a modern bungalow in the grounds of Stephen Tennant's Wilsford Manor later on I met the unlikely figure of Vidia Naipaul. I was immediately hooked. His face in those days was clean-shaven, with black, black hair and large black eyes. I like his recent rather beatific persona – with a Buddhist smile and short beard – which comes, I believe, from a final contentment. When I first met him I held him in awe and was so proud to know him that, when an Italian girl came to lunch with me at the same time as he did and argued and contradicted him, I was mortified. Everything he said seemed unusual, sharp or wise. He is a master of words and feelings, neither Eastern nor Western.

Cecil Beaton, was at the time having a complicated relationship with the great Greta Garbo. After a huge palaver and shilly-shallying she finally came to Wiltshire. As we all know, a wonderful face. I was also impressed by the smoothness of her skin. With a low and melodious voice, nothing she said was of the slightest interest – and very often made no sense – but one was enchanted all the same. I believe one would react in the same way if one had not known it was Garbo, the legend. I was very conscious that it was – particularly on a drive to see a Noël Coward play in Bournemouth, when I was wedged in the back seat between her and Cecil. Cecil observed, 'Who can resist the fascination of Greta when the allure is turned on, & it was certainly turned on for Clarissa's benefit.'

One afternoon at Rose Bower, when Bridget Parsons* was

---

* Bridget Parsons (1907–72): daughter of the Earl of Rosse, a great beauty, much photographed, who had discriminating taste and intelligence and was a close friend of Clarissa.

staying with me for the weekend, I got a warning call from Reddish to say that Greta was walking on the downs and heading my way, and the press were around. Looking out of the front door I saw this legendary figure striding down the slope of Mount Sorrel towards me. Each time she came, she always examined everything over and over again – the wallpaper, the books, the kitchen – with many exclamations of delight. What was she really seeing and feeling? I was at my cottage most weekends that autumn, and got quite used to going with her to the Saturday market in Salisbury (she was a great window- and market-stall-shopper) and to the Great Yews, a private forest of yew trees belonging to the Radnors on the downs, and toing and froing between Rose Bower and Reddish.

I decided to leave London Films and the kindness of Alex Korda – dearth of money again – and went to work for George Weidenfeld, who was a patient employer. The offices were in Cork Street and my immediate boss was a rough diamond from Glasgow called Jack Winocour. I remember seeing him again years later when I was with my husband at some function, and he was much smoother towards me. The magazine we worked on was called *Contact** and I rather enjoyed trying to cajole people to write for it. Some of them wouldn't. One who did was Elizabeth David. She was so eager and charming that one would not have thought she was already an eminent cookery writer. More than that, pre-eminent. I still prefer her recipes.

At this time, probably because of *Contact*, I met and made friends with Alan Ross. Not good-looking, but he had a way with him, and was gay – in the original sense of the word – and ignited one. He had

---

* *Contact* was set up by George Weidenfeld as a monthly publication of essays and articles on British and European literary, political and social topics. With paper restrictions still in force for magazines, it had a hardcover book format, appeared irregularly and lasted until 1951.

been in the Navy in the war and once narrowly escaped drowning when he was trapped in the ship's hold as it was flooding. We used to meet at Cyril Connolly's and I continued to see him through two girlfriends – one of them a great beauty and a writer herself – and they both came to stay with us at Alvediston in the 1980s. Finally he married Jennifer Fry, ex-wife of (the 'Mad Boy') Robert Heber Percy, and they went to live in Sussex, near, I think, Plumtree racecourse – Alan could own a racehorse by then – and also near Sussex County Cricket ground. He was a great cricketer and reviewed matches for the *Observer* and was a poet, writer and, above all for me, editor of the *London Magazine*. I had a last lunch with Alan at Daphne's, the hip restaurant in Kensington, where I used to go with Freddie Ashton, to find him the same humorous, teasing, easygoing friend.

After George had moved into his grand apartment on Chelsea Embankment, with its Popes by Francis Bacon, I loved going to his book launch parties, full of old friends, or new ones made. His warmth showed itself again a quarter of a century later when I was once more alone. Not having seen most of my friends during my marriage he immediately asked me to the book parties again. On one occasion, when he had invited me, he added his reason in a puzzled tone: 'You are on Antonia's* list.' As so long a time had passed George used to tell so-and-so to come over and talk to me. One of the so-and-sos was Harold Pinter, who was gently sympathetic and very good-looking. Over the years, whenever we meet, I admire his passions for and against nations, people, events. His plays are surely the only radically new approach to drama in over a century, and his poetry is constructed with great purity and emotion.

---

* Lady Antonia Fraser: author and historian, published by Weidenfeld. Antonia had first encountered Clarissa at Oxford in the 1940s, when her father, Frank Pakenham (Lord Longford), was a don there and Antonia was a schoolgirl. They became friends later.

*

In August a group would gravitate to Venice every year – the nucleus being the Coopers and the base being the Hotel Gritti, which had recently opened. One year Robert and Mollie Cranborne (formerly Cecil) were also staying at the Gritti. We had a plan that I should drive my car behind the Cranbornes all the way to England, so that I would not be alone. They were in his grandfather's Rolls-Royce. The Rolls had a gold grille, a rubber horn that honked on two notes, and had been made especially high to accommodate this grandfather's top-hat. When they had gone to pick up the car at Maestre – where one left cars when staying in Venice – they found several mechanics had crawled underneath it, unable to believe their eyes.

I had visited the Villa Maser with its wonderful Veronese frescos and was transfixed by the quality of the lawn – the most incredible lawn of fine bluish grass – and got the name of the nursery where we could buy turves en route for England. This we did – the boot of the Cranbornes' Rolls taking lots for the lawns at Cranborne and I a few for my pocket-sized lawn at Rose Bower. Both lots died soon after being laid.

I was in my Morris Minor, Robert, a dashing driver at the best of times, at the wheel of his Rolls. This was the signal for Robert to drive as fast and dangerously as possible. I managed to keep up, cheered on by Italian drivers who realised what was going on, until we got to Robert's favourite route over the Alps. Oh no, not the Brenner Pass, but something called the Little Brenner Pass – this was like a rough riverbed with hairpin bends. Half the time I seemed to be going backwards and, at the summit, to find Robert and Mollie laughing was the last straw. Robert had always been inclined to mad extremes of humour.

Another year the Cranbornes decided to stay at a *pensione*. When they called at the Gritti to see friends, the management were so appalled – they looked like tramps – that they were put up at the hotel in the best suite gratis – 'Ah, Signor Milord . . .'

I went in August 1951 to Sicily. Fulco Verdura was a dynamic, clever, amusing, impoverished Sicilian duke, who had made a great success designing uniquely beautiful jewellery in New York. He combined gems with an imagination and flair unlike any other – and the New York millionaires loved them. That year he had taken a house at Taormina where Bridget Parsons and I were among the half-dozen guests. I was enchanted by the Sicilian atmosphere – darker, rougher than the mainland, with different things to see: the Greek temples, then unspoilt, Roman mosaics and strange Moorish towns.

In Palermo, apart from the dazzling gold cathedral, we visited a Sicilian prince living in solitude in a vast Arab house – or rather an Italian palazzo subsumed into the North African atmosphere. Fulco's own family home was more or less ruined. One evening was spent at a nightspot, where Bridget and I experienced dancing the tango with Fulco. He was a renowned master of the tango, but he had to tone it down, I fear, to accommodate two English girls.

In Venice that summer, Princess Aspasia* of Greece gave a party in the Eden Garden, which she had leased. Built by a Miss Eden in the nineteenth century, this was a very large narrow garden built along the Giudecca, which also had a villa. Fulco and I were invited. It was a sinister event – so dimly lit that one was stumbling about, with only occasional flares lighting up people's faces. The Princess was said to have the evil eye and Auberon Herbert had warned us that we were to take care when shaking hands to put one thumb inwards.

Venice was in a ferment that year about the Beistegui Ball. Charles

---

* Aspasia Manos, widow of King Alexander of Greece – who had been killed by a chimpanzee bite.

Beistegui was a Mexican millionaire with a passion for England. He had a house near Paris, Groussay, done up like a stage set for an English stately home – smoking rooms, stags' heads, chintzes – the French were thrilled by it. The ball at the beautiful Palazzo Labia in Venice seemed as fraught as some royal event at Versailles – people became frantic at not getting invitations. Some Americans arrived in their yachts and anchored at the Lido, waiting and hoping they would get to the party. As far as I was concerned they needn't have worried. The Palazzo Labia was so subtly lit that all the exquisite costumes the guests had slavishly created seemed colourless. Only Diana Cooper shone, as Cleopatra, in a sort of pageant held in the great vestibule and backed by the Tiepolo frescos of Antony and Cleopatra. A friend and I ended up hanging out of a balcony and looking at the crowd down below looking up at us.

But by then I was again wondering what direction my life should take. George had given me the opportunity of a career in publishing. But I never really wanted a career. My life at *Contact* was soon to end. In January 1952 I became engaged, secretly and to the surprise of all my friends, to Anthony Eden.

PART TWO

The cottage in Wiltshire, Rose Bower.

At Rose Bower with a burgeoning pear tree.

The sitting room. The wallpaper is 'climbing fuschias' bringing the garden indoors.

Greta Garbo is delighted. The cat less so.

A rare impromptu scene. Garbo talking to me on the terrace at Reddish House.
An illicit photo taken by Cecil Beaton from his bedroom.

1935: AE as the youngest Foreign Secretary for 150 years. The latest models of government cars in the background.

A wedding portrait.

Left: My cousin Randolph rallying to my side. Confronting the press outside No. 10 Downing Street after the announcement of my engagement, 12 August 1952.

Right: Greeted at Caxton Hall for the marriage ceremony at which the Prime Minister was witness.

The reception at No. 10. We pose in the garden with Uncle Winston and Aunt Clemmie.

A period portrait.

In at the deep end, my first
launching in Belfast.

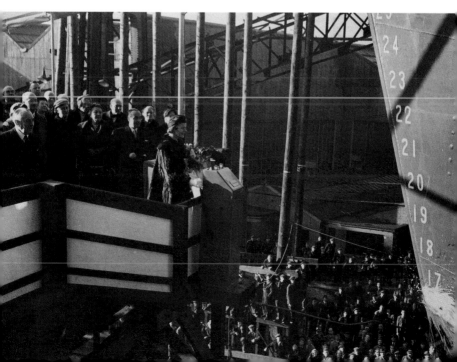

Tiara time.

Embarking on HMS *Surprise* as AE convalesced after his operations. AE is wearing his Trinity House cap and blazer.

On HMS *Surprise* before weighing anchor in the South of France. (From left) Unknown, Nicholas, my stepson, Bridget Parson dissociating herself, me, AE gazing at Babe Paley.

Tomorrow is Already Here. For all politicians, a good title.

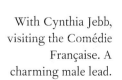

With Cynthia Jebb, visiting the Comédie Française. A charming male lead.

A day off from the Geneva Conference. Before lunch at Evian.

An official trip to Paris, 1954. I escape to Chantilly. (From left) Liz Hofmannstahl, Diana Cooper, Juliet Duff, me, Aly Forbes.

INTRODUCTION

Cate Haste

Clarissa met Anthony Eden in 1946 and they began going to dinner and the theatre, though not on a particularly regular basis – as friends. Each was absorbed in their separate private and social lives. Still handsome and dashing in his early fifties, Eden had been leading a virtually bachelor existence for some time before he met Clarissa. His first wife, Beatrice, had never been at ease with life as a politician's wife and had pursued her own outside interests for much of their marriage. They had two sons, Simon and Nicholas. The death in action of the elder son, Simon, aged twenty, at the very end of the war seems to have tipped the marriage. Beatrice departed for New York with another man in 1945 and they divorced in 1950.

Eden was at the peak of a distinguished career. Elected to Parliament in 1923 as Conservative MP for Warwick and Leamington, he rose rapidly to become Foreign Secretary at the age of only thirty-eight (the youngest in that office for 150 years), after serving as Britain's representative at the League of Nations. At a time when dictators were tightening their malign grip on Europe, he established his reputation as a skilful diplomatist, internationalist and statesman. But after only two years at the Foreign Office, he resigned in 1938 over Neville Chamberlain's policy of appeasement towards Mussolini following the Italian dictator's invasion of Abyssinia, earning the admiration of some, *including Churchill, and the hostility of the appeasers. He returned to government in Churchill's wartime Cabinet as, briefly, Secretary of State for War, then Foreign Secretary for the war's duration, and was influential in shaping the United Nations Organisation as the framework for post-war diplomacy. Though out of office following the Conservative defeat in the 1945 election, he returned to Churchill's Cabinet as Foreign Secretary on their re-election in 1951.*

The announcement of Clarissa's engagement in August 1952 astonished her friends as much as his. Most knew Anthony merely as a remote public figure and politics was not her milieu, despite her Churchill pedigree.

Clarissa had confided to only a few. Cecil Beaton had heard rumours that Eden was in love with Clarissa and encouraged her to think what an interesting life she could create for herself, but Clarissa took her time. He approved when, 'shy & embarrassed, [she] told me that she was thrilled at having made up her mind to marry Eden'. Isaiah Berlin wished her 'gaiety and glories and splendours of every kind, 'like the Tintoretto Paradise', but 'now, I am afraid, you will inevitably (do what we may) sail out of my life in a very princessy & swan-like way'. Duff Cooper warned, 'You will find, I expect, that you have many more friends than you used to have. Even in London I heard echoes of things to come: "I used not to like her, but she has become much nicer lately. I was saying so to Mrs Slander and Lady Sneerwell and they both agreed."'

Only one friend disapproved violently. Catholic convert Evelyn Waugh penned an intemperate outburst from White's Club – where, he later conceded, 'the mind was not at its brightest' – accusing her of apostasy for marrying a divorcee. Clarissa had been brought up a Catholic. His fury at her lapse from the Faith – 'Did you never think that you were contributing to the loneliness of Calvary by your desertion?' he thundered – was complicated by his personal feelings for her:

As you must know, I fell in love with you and so kept away. You simply became a rare treat which now & then came my way. But I . . . hoped that if you were seriously tempted to apostasy, you would trust me by asking advice. . . . I don't think it presumptuous to believe that I might have influenced you, if I had not fallen in love with you. . . . I think you were left in childhood with a conception of the Church as being a sort of club, from which one can resign at any moment if the cooking deteriorates. I don't think you saw it as a complete way of life. As a friend I might have shown you.

Clarissa sent a dignified reply, but their relationship never recovered.

The marriage was for Clarissa a switch, at the age of thirty-two, from the world of culture and the intellect and sensibility, which suited her personality, to that of political intrigue, ambition and manoeuvring for place. She arrived with no experience of political life to take on the duties of Foreign Secretary's wife. Inevitably she found that she had far less time for friends from her old milieu – as they had anticipated. Few were to Anthony's taste and formal engagements took up much of her time.

She absorbed herself in the new life. Beaton noted that she was 'still the same strong uncompromising character – great distinction – but surprising revelation that she is in love'. She 'looked quite changed, a smile always on her face'. When he commented on her conventional appearance, she countered, 'But you do see that just at the moment I should be looking conventional, don't you? In a few years' time I'll be going around without a hat again – but not now.' Beaton was relieved that 'after a while she relaxes into being the marvellously sympathetic person I love'.

There was a further twist. Since 1942, when Churchill formally advised King George VI to appoint Eden as Prime Minister if anything happened *to him, Eden had been seen as the unchallenged successor to Churchill as Conservative leader – the Crown Prince in waiting. Clarissa's Uncle Winston was seventy-eight when she married. In due course it was expected she would take over as chatelaine at No. 10 Downing Street when he finally decided to retire. Churchill still commanded respect and popular support, but his colleagues in the inner circles of government became steadily convinced that his retirement was due. Though outwardly calm, Anthony vented to Clarissa his growing frustration at her uncle's erratic interference in foreign affairs and his lack of focus in government. 'I cannot go on like this with this old man. I must escape somehow,' he exploded. With no personal ambition to reach No. 10, Clarissa supported Anthony and her loyalty to her husband was absolute.*

She took a keen interest in day-to-day events. She began keeping a diary – of her own experiences and a record of what Anthony told her of the political to-ing and fro-ing in Cabinet and on the wider political stage. These diaries form the backbone to Part Two.

*   *   *

DRAMATIS PERSONAE OF
PRINCIPAL CAST IN DIARIES

NIGEL BIRCH – Minister of Works 1954–5; Secretary of State for Air December 1955–7.

PATRICK BUCHAN-HEPBURN – Chief Whip 1951–December 1955; Minister of Works December 1955–7.

'RAB' (R. A.) BUTLER – Chancellor of the Exchequer 1951–December 1955, when he was moved in Anthony Eden's Cabinet reconstruction to Lord Privy Seal and Leader of the House of Commons.

MARK CHAPMAN-WALKER – Head of Communications, Conservative Central Office.

WINSTON CHURCHILL – Prime Minister October 1951–April 1955.

HARRY CROOKSHANK – Minister of Health 1951–2; Lord Privy Seal and Leader of the House of Commons 1952–5; raised to the peerage in 1956 as Viscount Crookshank.

ANTONY HEAD – Secretary of State for War 1951–6; succeeded Sir Walter Monckton as Minister of Defence October 1956–7. Later the Edens' neighbour in Dorset.

DERICK HEATHCOAT AMORY – Minister of Pensions 1951–3; Minister of Agriculture and Fisheries 1954–7.

VISCOUNT KILMUIR (formerly DAVID MAXWELL FYFE) – Home Secretary 1951–4; Lord Chancellor 1954–7.

ALAN LENNOX BOYD – Secretary of State for the Colonies 1954–7.

SELWYN LLOYD – Minister of Supply 1954–5; Minister of Defence April–December 1955; Secretary of State for Foreign Affairs December 1955–January 1957.

GWILYM LLOYD GEORGE – son of David Lloyd George and Minister of Food 1951–4; Home Secretary 1954–6.

OLIVER LYTTELTON – personal friend and contemporary of Eden; Secretary of State for the Colonies 1951–4; elevated to the peerage as 1st Viscount Chandos and returned to his business activities.

HAROLD MACMILLAN – in Churchill's wartime Cabinet with Eden during the Second World War. Minister of Housing and Local Government 1951–4; Minister of Defence October 1954–April 1955; Eden's Secretary of State for Foreign Affairs April–December 1955; Chancellor of the Exchequer December 1955–January 1957; Prime Minister 1957–63.

SIR WALTER MONCKTON – Minister of Labour and National Service 1951–5; Minister of Defence December 1955; Paymaster General October 1956.

'DICKIE' MOUNTBATTEN (EARL MOUNTBATTEN) – former Viceroy of India during Partition, 1947; Commander of the Mediterranean Fleet 1952–5; First Sea Lord 1955–9.

ANTHONY NUTTING – Under-Secretary of State for Foreign Affairs 1951–4; Minister of State for Foreign Affairs 1954–November 1956.

ANTHONY RUMBOLD – contemporary and friend of Clarissa. Took over from Evelyn Shuckburgh as head of Eden's Private Office (Principal Private Secretary) 1954.

'BOBBETY' SALISBURY (MARQUESS OF SALISBURY) – long-term personal friend and contemporary of Eden; Lord Privy Seal 1951–2; Secretary of State for Commonwealth Relations March–November 1952; Lord President of the Council November 1952 until his resignation in 1957.

EVELYN SHUCKBURGH – Principal Private Secretary at the Foreign Office 1951–4; Assistant Under-Secretary in charge of Middle East Affairs at the Foreign Office 1954–6.

JAMES STUART – Secretary of State for Scotland 1951–7.

'JIM' (JAMES) THOMAS – Eden's Parliamentary Private Secretary in the 1930s, resigned with Eden in 1937 and subsequently in the Eden 'group'; First Lord of the Admiralty 1951–6; raised to the peerage as Viscount Cilcennin 1955.

CHAPTER 9

MARRIAGE

The second phase of my life began with my marriage to Anthony Eden. He was the only minister to have been continually in office, together with my Uncle Winston and John Simon, for the full span of the war. For the latter years of the war he had had the virtually physically impossible burden of not only the Foreign Office but the post of Leader of the House.

I first saw Anthony Eden when I was about sixteen at his great friend and colleague Bobbety Cranborne's house in Dorset. I remember his eruption into the room, partly because he was as famous as a film star, but particularly because he had on Sunday country clothes. These consisted of a bottle-green tweed jacket and bottle-green pinstriped tweed trousers – a take on the black jacket and pinstriped trousers worn by politicians in London at the time – and this struck me as imaginative. I think this suit went to the Victoria and Albert Museum eventually.

The second time we met, nearly ten years later, we hardly spoke. I sat next to him at a dinner party where he was monopolised by a foreign lady anxious to marry some Englishman of prominence. Towards the end of the meal Anthony turned to me and muttered, 'Perhaps we could have dinner sometime?' Intrigued and amused, I accepted.

When we got to know each other better it became apparent that we were, on the face of it, a surprising couple, as people hastened to point out. Most of my friends were writers or critics or painters. Most of his were politicians, but we shared a love of art and books.

At this time Anthony was out of office. He seemed untouched by fatigue – working at the Westminster Bank, going to the theatre, playing three sets of tennis on end – he exuded energy. A few years on and it was back to the Foreign Office – the midnight boxes, the 8 a.m. arrival of his private secretaries in his bedroom, the endless trips across the Channel. This was the world I was entering.

I started to stay at his house in Sussex at weekends. At Christmas 1948 I reported: 'It was excruciatingly cold – no central heating & electric fires switched on a second before you came into the room.' On the South Downs near Binderton there was a hunting lodge designed by Sir Edwin Lutyens where Anthony had permission to take his guests. It had been redesigned by its owner, Edward James, and his friend Salvador Dalí, painted purple and green outside, and had lime-green sheets hanging out of all the windows. It contained several Dalí icons: the Mae West lips sofa – very uncomfortable to sit on – and the telephone with the lobster receiver invented by James himself. He was the major serious patron of Surrealism in England. When I said to Anthony one weekend, 'I am going over to see Edward James' (thanks to Gerald Berners), it was the only time I ever saw his face darken over anything I ever said or did. I went over, nevertheless, to the huge house James lived in at West Dean. By then he was no longer the willowy figure, but stocky, with a bristling beard. Tilly Losch, the lovely dancer he had married, was long departed. He seemed pleased to be able to talk of mutual friends.

Anthony would have made a good eldest son. He would have managed the family estate in County Durham with shrewd competence. He wrote an excellent book about his early life, though I had to urge him not to be so discreet about his childhood. To have grown up with a beautiful, not very clever, selfish mother has happened to many. To grow up with a father such as Sir William Eden was exceptional. The awesomeness and the eccentricity of Sir William were compensated for in the young Anthony by a natural responsiveness to his father's artistic sensibility and talent.*

But Sir William's exceptional character had to be coped with. Children with overwhelming parents often erect a protective shell. In Anthony's case it resulted in a debonair social manner, a preference for unexpanded relationships and a conventional reaction to human behaviour in general. He was not a complex man. To his legendary though brief tempers, the reactions of the budding diplomats and politicians under him can only be compared to huffy housemaids, however overworked they may have been.

As for the First World War, although he said they were the best years of his life for the comradeship, he absolutely refused to explain or describe the horror.† What I think came out of the ordeal was a lifelong sympathy for ordinary soldiers which he then transferred to the people of England. He always seemed happy chatting to the man in the street and, above all, to soldiery. He never felt at ease with the True Blues. Early on he once said to me, 'I'm not really a Conservative. I'm an old-fashioned Liberal.' After all, his greatest

---

* Sir William Eden (1849–1915): a gifted painter, he had an explosive temper expressed in outbursts of extremely colourful invective, but also a sense of humour, though bitterness and disaffection with life dominated his later years. He was known as 'The Bloody Baronet'. In aesthetic taste he was exacting and ahead of his age; for instance, he was among the first to champion the painter Degas, much to the horror of his neighbours in County Durham, where he lived at Windlestone, Anthony Eden's birthplace.

† Eden described the comradeship and bravery of the soldiers in *Another World*, a moving account of his First World War experience, published in 1976, a year before his death.

influence had been Noel Skelton's *Constructive Conservatism* (1924), which outlined a 'property-owning democracy', and there were those who maintained strongly that the ideas developed in Conservative Central Office in the 1940s had already been formulated by Anthony.

But he was not an intellectual, nor was he an inspiring writer or orator. This was at odds with his aesthetic sensibility, which was strong both in literature and in paintings. Going up to Oxford at twenty-three years old, having been through the First World War, he founded the Uffizi Society to invite artists to come and talk to undergraduates. Other members included young men such as Edward Sackville-West, Eardley Knollys and David Cecil, and figures such as George Moore and Roger Fry came to give the talks. Certainly at this time he was already buying those paintings he could afford, though his taste seemed orientated to France rather than England. Consequently the French loved him for it. Years later his great friend, the painter Dunoyer de Segonzac, wrote under one of his etchings, '*Pour Sir Anthony Eden, ami de la France et des arts. En hommage.*'

He carried his culture lightly. It was part of normal life and he would have thought it pretentious to flaunt it. When the time came for a portrait to be done for his old college, Christ Church, Roy Harrod asked Anthony who he would like to paint him. Kokoschka, said Anthony. Roy Harrod gamely went ahead. Kokoschka always refused commissions abroad, but to Anthony's surprise and delight he said he would like to accept the commission. It would have cost £6,000 in the 1960s. Christ Church, one of the richest of Oxford colleges, said it was too expensive – or were they scared? Elizabeth Frink was keen to do his bust in the House of Commons, then she became ill and died.

He had had knocks at every phase of his personal life and, like many Englishmen, hadn't known intimacy. He was happy when it came to him later. Although he was older than me we had both led single lives. The announcement of our engagement in the papers was met with consternation and astonishment by friends on both sides.

His colleagues, while happy that he would no longer be alone, were wary of his choice. My Aunt Clemmie thought me too independent and totally unsuitable, and my own friends were dismayed, or, at best, doubtful. My aunt being away on holiday, we went down to Chartwell to break the news to my Uncle Winston. He congratulated us with his usual magnanimity.

I did not anticipate the publicity furore – and nor, I think, did Anthony. He had wanted the announcement to be made in August – as he said that was the 'silly season' when it would slip in relatively quietly. Of course, the opposite happened. I arrived at No. 10 from Rossmore Court to an empty house – my unfortunate aunt had not yet arrived back from Capri where her holiday had been ruined. The banks of press photographers outside, the hollow house, my only visitor being the jeweller bearing several wedding rings for me to choose from, put me in a state of shock which lasted through the wedding and the wedding reception at No. 10. The wedding week had been like entering a typhoon – as one saw it approaching one did not realise or imagine what it would be like – then suddenly the whirling blast of cameras and telegrams and flowers until one felt quite bruised.

Of the wedding reception, a family affair, I can only remember my godmother, Lady Islington, being offended when she was not included in the wedding photograph, and my dear friend and cousin Randolph lurching up to me and saying 'I give you two years to knock him into shape' – meaning that, as he had consistently attacked Anthony in the press, he would lay off for two years.* He kept his word to the exact day.

---

* Randolph Churchill (1911–68): journalist. Irascible and erratic (though not without charm), Randolph disliked Eden and attacked him in print, especially the *Evening Standard*, in a vitriolic book and around London's gentlemen's clubs. Briefly MP for Preston between 1940 and 1945, he failed on numerous occasions to get re-elected. Jealousy may have informed his hostility to Eden, his father's Crown Prince. This episode severely strained Clarissa's relations with Randolph, who in due course resumed his increasingly venomous attacks on Eden.

We honeymooned in the north of Portugal, a country we both loved, half pastoral, half eighteenth century and the Gothic made exotic and unserious by African influences. On our way back we called on Salazar – then Portugal's President – in a fortress on the sea with great doors unfolding until we got to a very simple house where he lived in a tiny room with chrome furniture. Everything he said was detailed, shrewd and terrifically knowledgeable. This was my first encounter with a leading European figure.

Back from honeymoon, I was thrown into a world of which I had had no inkling. Politics had never played a part in my life, though at lunches at my uncle's before the war I had heard a lot of it, including the prediction that war was inevitable.

My desire was to make everything as easy and pleasant as possible for my husband. I had had no conception of what his life would be like – the hours he worked, the triumphs and setbacks, the constant crises.

The Foreign Secretary's official flat was in Carlton Gardens. It was rather dark and had not at that time been enlarged to face the Mall. We did not dream of altering the décor in those days, though Anthony had his own furniture and some pictures, and the corps diplomatique gave us a wedding present of several French eighteenth-century Aubusson carpets, which I chose. These came streaming into the house just as Anthony arrived home from Moscow. He was taken aback and felt that he should have been consulted – what about his own beautiful Persian carpets? We escaped the confusion to walk up Bond Street to look at the Géricault exhibition.

Official entertaining in the big rooms on the first floor at Carlton Gardens was easy as the menu and the flowers were in the hands of Government Hospitality and I did not yet have the confidence to interfere in the catering, as I did at No. 10. The government cellars were full of first-class wines. All that was required of me was to cope at dinner with the guest of honour – be it the Shah of Persia, young King Hussein of Jordan or old General Marshall, architect of the Marshall Aid plan. More problematic was learning the day-to-day ropes. Anthony was preoccupied and all his officials were used to a bachelor; helping a wife did not occur to them. Anthony had grown accustomed to being surrounded by staff and private secretaries who were there to do his bidding. I tried to adapt to this new life in a flat surrounded by someone else's possessions and two resentful old retainers. I was not used to someone coming home every day for lunch and expecting a fish or meat four-course meal each time.

My first visitor at Carlton Gardens was the wife of the then head of the Foreign Office, Lady Strang, who came to tea. Though I did wonder what I had got myself into when her opening remark was 'I hope you are not going to denationalise steel – it is doing so well.' I had previously had no views about steel.

Next, the ambassadresses came to tea in batches; one of them I knew already, Odette Massigli, the French Ambassador's wife, and I made great friends with another – Anna Hägglöf, the Italian wife of the Swedish Ambassador, Gunnar Hägglöf, an old friend of Anthony's from pre-war League of Nations days. She was a great ally, and able to joke about the quirks of our official lives.

On one of many embassy evenings, this time with the Austrians in Belgrave Square and without Anthony, I found myself on a sofa with a member of our government, Selwyn Lloyd, then Minister of State at the Foreign Office. He immediately began to tell me that Anthony never delegated any of his work and that he ought to have the man immediately under him elevated to Cabinet rank in order to relieve him of some of the burden. 'Don't think that I say this because that means me,' he added, wanting me to have a word on his behalf. In my innocence, as a baptism of political fire I was shocked by this blatancy. In addition, he wished me not to go to the airport to meet

Anthony from Paris, which was also done so tactlessly that I resolved to go, even if it meant waiting four hours in fog.

I met Anthony's other colleagues and their wives. One of my favourite wives was Biddy Monckton. I never got to grips with Walter Monckton [Minister of Labour, later Defence], but she was fun and took the right attitude to all the shenanigans. She had had an eventful past, which probably helped her sense of proportion.

The wife with great charm was Sylvia – first married to Buck de la Warr (Paymaster General), then to David Maxwell Fyfe (later Lord Kilmuir – a key Cabinet figure). She never seemed like a political wife. Perhaps being Rex Harrison's sister was a mitigation.

It may seem odd not to mention Dorothy Macmillan, but I really never knew her. At the Geneva Summit Conference in 1955, which she attended as Foreign Secretary's wife, we bathed one morning in the Lake against the advice of all the locals, who warned that it was unhygienic. Harold Macmillan played no personal role in my life, either before or during the Suez Crisis, though inevitably I formed an assessment of his character from the wings. I only observed him close to after he had resigned as Prime Minister, on his constant visits to Anthony in the 1960s down in Wiltshire. I would have to meet him at Salisbury Station, where the stationmaster was waiting for the train in full rig, as Harold was a Gold Card Holder (having been on the board of the old GWR), and drove him home in as much silence as possible. He only ever came for some specific reason: once it was to ask Anthony to back his return to politics as Prime Minister. Nothing came of that.

All Anthony's Private Office boys were, in very different ways, talented and clever. Guy Millard had anyway been a friend of mine for years; Evelyn Shuckburgh was charming but too highly strung – he couldn't stand the heat during the Geneva conference; on the other hand Tony Rumbold, another old friend, was wonderfully laid back.

To me, one of the most bizarre events was the State Opening of

Parliament in the House of Lords that November. It was a Venetian scene. The peers appeared to be huddled in heaps on the floor of the House, dressed in very creased red robes with Peter Pan collars of white rabbit tied under the chin with tape, indistinguishable one from the other. The Heralds were charming gnarled old men in cloth of gold – Field Marshal Alexander, carrying the Sword of State, was impressive with a face like St George; Bobbety Salisbury carrying the Imperial Crown, rather scowling and shifting his strap. The Crown was suspended from his shoulders like a tray of matches.*

Visiting the constituency was much more daunting, as I had had no experience of political life whatsoever. Anthony's constituency consisted of Warwick and Leamington. Originally it had also had Stratford-upon-Avon and part of Coventry. When the division came in 1948 Anthony gave up all the easy rural areas. I soon realised that he had been adored by the workers in the constituency for many decades. Even the annual visit to the Lockheed factory's Christmas party was a love-fest (not exactly a Tory milieu). Anthony's nephew Fulke Warwick lived at Warwick Castle, but we always stayed at the house of the Party Chairman, Mrs Mills, although when I went up there by myself I would stay with Fulke.

As the wife of the Foreign Secretary I had no official car, so I used Anthony's old Hillman Minx. This continued at No. 10. One evening I was going alone to the Jordanian embassy for a dinner in honour of King Hussein's mother, Queen Zein. So I set off in the Minx in my long dress, long gloves and tiara, and parked in front of the embassy. When I came out at the end of the evening there was a

---

* The reason Lord Salisbury carried the Crown was that the Queen had not yet been crowned. It was the only time during the reign when this happened. Later the Queen would have worn it.

flock of limousines and chauffeurs ranged in front, and my car had been pushed by them right down the street. I told this story to John Waverley* as a humorous tale, but he was outraged and reproached Anthony's Private Office for not getting me transport. It then turned out that there had been a perfectly good car and driver used exclusively by my aunt for official occasions. A slight hitch occurred at the start of this when it was run into by Miss Coral Browne, the actress, in Queen's Gate.

Immediately after our return from honeymoon Anthony had been due to visit the Yugoslav President, Marshal Tito, who was sending messages: 'Please bring your bride.' I was pleased, as I had never been to Yugoslavia, only to be told there was no question of my going – I would be in the way at all-male dinners and so on. So it was the last straw to get a jaunty letter from Anthony in Yugoslavia announcing that 'the super excitement of the day has been the sudden discovery of a Mrs Tito!! Nobody knew she existed until the invitations to the evening's reception on our arrival. He might have told me before I left. She is a major in the Yugoslav army. Nobody knows when they were married or anything about his romance, and I didn't like to ask questions.' I was furious with him for not discovering the existence of Jovanka Tito beforehand. We newly-wed brides could have had a delightful time drinking slivovitz together. It was the first of many frustrations about foreign trips.

I was allowed as far as Paris, however. The Foreign Secretary in those days travelled on cramped commercial flights with one secretary. I suppose the theory was that naturally the relevant embassy

---

* Lord Waverley, formerly Sir John Anderson, Home Secretary in Churchill's wartime Coalition, had married Clarissa's old acquaintance Ava Wigram. He was elevated to the peerage in 1952.

would be full of experts. If he went to Paris there were outriders and sirens, with other cars veering out of the way into the gutter; in England the ancient official car had a little bell which it rang futilely, hoping – and failing – to get a through passage. It had no heating, and one would travel wrapped up in rugs and arrive frozen in evening dress for some function.

On one Paris trip for talks on the EDC (European Defence Community) I sat next to an American who was different. We clicked, and had great fun. This was Dean Acheson, Secretary of State in President Truman's Administration, with whom many years later, with his wife Alice, we would regularly exchange holiday visits between Barbados and Antigua. After they had both retired, Dean and Anthony would write to each other with their thoughts on current affairs. One of Dean's last letters was a draft he had written on yellow legal paper – he died before sending it.

The Harveys had succeeded the Coopers at the embassy and the atmosphere changed completely. Oliver Harvey had been Anthony's Private Secretary in the 1930s, and later during the war. One night when we were staying there the Windsors came to dinner, it being the Duke's birthday. We had been told that the Duchess could not drink gin, only vodka. We were all standing about before the meal in the Salon Jaune, when she let out a yell and said it was GIN! I was next to the Duke at dinner and he only wanted to hear about House of Commons gossip. He was a wistful man.

*   *   *

Clarissa recorded in her diary events as witnessed from Carlton Gardens and the flow of political life as reported to her daily by her husband. Foreign affairs were at the centre of the political agenda, as Britain struggled to adjust to post-war military and economic realities and to reassess its imperial role and its place in Europe.

The future of the Suez Canal base in Egypt caused bitter division in the Conservative Party. The emergence of Egyptian nationalism had led to the abrogation of the 1936 Anglo-Egyptian treaty, followed by anti-British riots and guerrilla attacks on the base. In July 1952, in a bloodless coup, a group of military officers overthrew King Farouk and established a government headed by General Mohammed Neguib with Colonel Gamal Abdel Nasser his charismatic deputy. Eden decided to work with the new government and negotiations on the terms of a phased withdrawal from the Suez Canal base occupied much of his time.

Eden acknowledged that Britain in the straitened post-war circumstances could no longer sustain its extended imperial commitments, and was sympathetic to nationalist aspirations and calls for self-determination. He believed the unwieldy Suez Canal base no longer served a useful military purpose in the nuclear age. It was 'an outdated commitment'. This was not the view of a vociferous section of mainly Conservative backbenchers – the 'Suez Group' – who resisted any British withdrawal, which they described as a 'scuttle' from Empire. Charles Waterhouse was their leading figure, with Clarissa's friend, Julian Amery, in support. Churchill reluctantly supported Eden but privately shared the rebels' anxieties about imperial 'scuttle' and supported them behind the scenes.

*   *   *

DIARY – 17 FEBRUARY 1953

Charles Waterhouse put down a private motion question – he went to see Anthony earlier on in a great stew. Anthony said, 'If you don't like my foreign policy, by which I am going to stick, then I can go.' 'Oh no, my dear fellow,' says Charles Waterhouse. 'You can't do that. We'd never win another election without you.' Later he told Anthony that he, Anthony, had swung the Foreign Affairs Committee and the House entirely through his personal popularity.

DIARY — 18 FEBRUARY

Dined at the Berrys'.* Anthony came in afterwards very sweet, from a successful dinner at the Carlton Club, with his tie all undone, and talked to everyone about Suez. Nigel Birch & James Stuart were there agreeing with him. Michael Berry very quiet and not agreeing, Anthony didn't like Pam Berry, who spoke ill of everyone. 'Does she speak like that of us?' he asked. 'Yes,' I said.

Though not usually allowed by Anthony to accompany him on trips abroad, I sailed in February 1953 across the Atlantic for a meeting at the United Nations. Only a month before, General Eisenhower, whom Anthony knew as Allied Supreme Commander during the war, had been inaugurated as President. John Foster Dulles, a dour Presbyterian New York lawyer, was his newly appointed Secretary of State.

Nicko Henderson was on board but I was still in such a haze that I was not even aware of my friend being there. Randolph was lurking also. This was my first opportunity to observe Mr and Mrs Butler.† I am oversensitive to appearances and tones of voice, so that Rab's famous brilliance passed me by on this occasion. Sydney, his wife, on the other hand, was a straightforward school prefect, bullying the new girl, and she kept that up throughout the entire visit. For busy politicians, going to the cinema played a large part on these therapeutic days of rest on liners. *An American in Paris*, the film with Leslie Caron, was particularly appreciated by Winthrop Aldrich, US Ambassador to Britain, who, I noticed, saw it more than once.

---

* Michael Berry was Chairman and Editor-in-Chief of the *Telegraph* and his wife, Lady Pamela Berry, the political hostess and daughter of F. E. Smith (Lord Birkenhead).
† Rab Butler was then Chancellor of the Exchequer.

DIARY — 4 MARCH

We arrived in New York and at 11.15 we went upstairs for the press conference. Evelyn [Shuckburgh, Head of Anthony's Private Office] had rung us at 9 o'clock to say that Stalin had had a stroke and was not expected to last another 48 hours. Anthony very moved by the significance of this, quoted Shakespeare and dwelt pessimistically on the probable future.

On the promenade deck the photography began. I smiled & said 'good morning' and some of the reporters said, 'Good morning, *dear*.'(!) We and the Butlers sat on 4 chairs — television & movies going on all the time, blinding lights in our faces.

Anthony and I flew on to Washington immediately. On the plane we looked at the US press clippings about our impending visit. They all mentioned Anthony in the headlines and much was made of his having said some weeks back that if Stalin were to die, a very dangerous situation would arise for the world.

Our Washington arrival was a mad rush by pressmen to photograph Anthony, then Anthony and Dulles, who'd come to meet him. Then Anthony on the radio and so on.

A dull day, but spring. The willows were out along the Potomac. The Lutyens embassy was cool and rather grand, and all the staff were on the steps clapping. I found cables waiting for me from Valentine Lawford and Rudi Bing, and an invitation from Mamie Eisenhower to visit her at the White House.

Anthony went off to see Eisenhower and found him extremely friendly and pleased to see him — worried mostly about the Middle East — while Dulles was moaning all the time, saying he'd no idea his job would be so difficult and how awful it was having to make momentous decisions in five minutes. On his way out Anthony met Mamie in the corridor who said, 'Come and see my new bedroom' and Ike said to Mamie, 'That's the first time you've ever asked a foreigner into your bedroom.'

DIARY — 5 MARCH

Anthony's speech was thought to be too vague – they wanted him to talk about the blockade of China and things like that. This is the worst of the FO – they will never let him make a meaty speech, out of fear. He says the chairman introduced them and said how they all knew Mr Eden. Then there was Mr Butler whom they didn't know, but who they understood might with luck one day become Prime Minister, and who had the dubious compliment of being backed by Lord Beaverbrook.

Anthony wanted me to visit Annapolis, so the next day I started early. Anthony's ancestor Sir Robert Eden had lived there as Governor of Maryland until the War of Independence. He was sympathetic to the rebels and one of the last governors to leave. Later, when he went back to see his estates, he sickened and died of a fever in 1784, which is why he is buried in Annapolis and not in County Durham. Anthony joked that otherwise he might now be the Senator from Maryland!

DIARY — 6 MARCH, ANNAPOLIS

Endless suburbs all looking like a *New Yorker* cover. At the Governor's house a posse of photographers waiting & a Union Jack flying. The Governor a big boiled brash maniacal Irishman. We set off on a very high-powered tour to see Robert Eden's picture, and all the time flashlights flashing, ending at the churchyard to lay a wreath on Robert Eden's tomb. The wreath was wired to a tripod so all I had to do was touch it & appear to lay it while the photographs were taken. The arms carved on the tomb were very beautifully done. I would have liked to have a copy, should we ever need to use them.

I asked rather plaintively if we could go & look at some of the older houses – the point of my visit, personally. The Governor seemed rather surprised by this but conceded. Lunch was fish-cakes and chiffon sponge. Iced water – no cocktail.

I returned to the White House for tea with Mrs Eisenhower. We were shown into a room where Mamie was waiting uncomfortably behind a tea urn, all of us in cocktail dresses. The first ten minutes were impossible because she did the tea herself and had to ask eight of us eight times what each lady wanted. After this she relaxed some-what. I noted: 'Like all celebrities, I find her much smaller than expected. Very dignified and grand atmosphere, which she combines with grimaces and wisecracks.'

Afterwards she wisely suggested I might like to look at the White House rooms. Upstairs was absolutely charming – American toile de Jouy, enchantingly pretty chintzes, very good colours in all the rooms. It just showed what an Office of Works can do. As we left, Mrs Eisenhower put her arm round me and said, 'Well, anyway, it wasn't stuffy, was it?'

DIARY — 7 MARCH

Dinner at the embassy. Sitting next to [Roger] Makins [British Ambassador to Washington] & Senator Wiley, Head of the Foreign Affairs Committee – a homespun type who was very isolationist but has been softened by marrying a secretary of General Dill [the popular wartime British Chief of the General Staff]. She came over during the war and hails from Epping.

Get on fine with the Senator who makes wisecracks, digs me in the ribs, and roars with laughter and says he will send me a real Wisconsin cheese. His wife is very stately, dressed in white diamanté from top to toe. She melted before the Senator, however, and said that the other night he had woken her up, shouting 'To hell with protocol' in his sleep.

Back to the Waldorf Hotel in New York. We had been invited for drinks with my old friend, Nin Ryan,* who had an apartment on the Hudson, followed by dinner with Clare Boothe Luce and Henry Luce.† I was paralysed by Mr Luce as I wanted to tell him what I thought of *Time* magazine. Meanwhile poor Anthony was being lectured by Mrs Luce on how to solve the Trieste problem.

When we returned to the hotel the atmosphere was spoilt by a telegram from Winston raising more difficulties about Egypt. This put Anthony in a hopeless mood of tension. I felt very lonely looking out at the town lit up.

DIARY — 10 MARCH

At the Waldorf, electrified by everything one touches. Endless frustration over the slowness of the room service. Anthony very tetchy about everything – from having his trousers, pressed upwards. I ring Garbo – get straight through to her. She's in bed today. Wants to lunch Thursday, but no doubt she will stand me up at the last minute. After lunch Anthony announces now that he feels very well and is in good form.

It was on this trip that I first met the Jebbs, in New York, where Gladwyn was Ambassador to the UN. Gladwyn was very sure of his superiority and Cynthia showed her talent for hostessing.

When we dined with them I sat between Lester Pearson, the

---

* Nin Ryan (1901–95): Mrs John Barry Ryan was daughter of banker Otto Kahn, who funded the Metropolitan Opera.
† Henry Luce was the publisher of Time Life Inc. Clare Boothe Luce was a magazine editor, playwright, journalist, politician and diplomat, who became Eisenhower's Ambassador to Italy 1953–6.

Canadian Foreign Minister, and Trygvie Lie, the UN Secretary General. There had been some hanky-panky about sitting on my right and left. Afterwards we learned that Lie had gone into the dining room beforehand and altered the place cards so that he should be on my right. Extraordinary, as everyone, including Pearson, had already seen the correct table plan in the front hall. Afterwards we talked to Fleur Cowles* and her husband. Anthony was very excited and animated.

DIARY — 12–13 MARCH

To the UN to hear Anthony's statement. Amused by both Lie & Pearson who sit behind a wooden coffin smirking at me in the middle of the proceedings. Gromyko & the Russians have the stiff, remote manner of prisoners. A tour of the UN building with Lie. I enjoy using my lorgnettes for the first time.

The next day I lunched with Greta. I was late but found her standing with an umbrella in the rain on the pavement. We went off to Maud Chez Elle, a very good French restaurant. Well, there she was, the same, but unmagical now, dressed in a plush greatcoat, full of what Cecil used to call cock-teasing, planning to holiday in Corsica with us. I said Mr Eden likes to play tennis. Oh, then she will play tennis with him: 'I think I can give him some sort of a work-out.'

So, far from skulking in the streets unrecognised, she insisted that we shop at Altmans. Walking down the aisles to the shoe department, all the sales girls called out 'Good afternoon, Miss Garrbow', and she took it as her due. In the shoe department I discovered her feet, contrary to the press, were of a normal size.

---

* Fleur Cowles: writer, painter, founder and editor of stylish, innovative but shortlived *Flair* magazine in 1950, married to Gardner Cowles, whose publishing empire included *Look* magazine.

That evening Anthony gave a speech at the Foreign Policy Association dinner – a nationwide hook-up. Afterwards we had drinks at Helen Ogden Reid's* where everyone sat cross-legged on the floor and asked Anthony questions in a very serious manner.

*   *   *

In the meetings with Eisenhower and Dulles, Eden had discussed American backing for the proposals for withdrawal from the Canal base. But the Americans, while offering assistance in the Anglo-Egyptian negotiations, were wary of taking any joint action that might appear to support colonialism, or that might alienate their relations with other Arabs in the region. They agreed their aim was the establishment of a Middle East defence organisation to fill the vacuum left by British withdrawal from the base – a 'Northern Tier' of alliances, which would form a bulwark against Russian incursion into the region.

*   *   *

DIARY — 17 MARCH

Back in Britain we find that the Americans had refused to join the Egypt discussions unless invited by the Egyptians, who of course will do nothing of the kind. Winston is sending a 'My dear friend' message to Eisenhower saying, 'If you won't be with us, at least don't be against us.'

It was not the last time this sentiment was expressed about the Americans.

---

* Owner and President of the *New York Herald Tribune*.

CHAPTER 10

CARLTON GARDENS

After we had returned to England, suddenly there was an unexpected personal bombshell, which changed everything. Throughout these trips Anthony had been troubled by intermittent pains. His doctor seemed overawed by the importance of the Foreign Secretary's life, supplied him with pain-killing injections and never got him examined – and then it was too late. It turned out to be his gall-bladder. Horace Evans, the Queen's physician, thankfully appeared and an emergency operation took place. What should have been a simple operation – which Anthony, being basically very strong, would have taken in his stride – became a major crisis, requiring yet another operation to try to repair the damage of the first. At one point Anthony was very near death. My friend Ann Fleming wrote to Diana Cooper, 'Anthony was over three hours on the operating table, I went to the clinic to be with Clarissa, a grim day for her – sixteen doctors and Winston tampering with the bulletins.'

Evans then said the greatest expert on botched gall-bladder operations, an American – Dr Richard Cattell – happened to be visiting London. He saw Anthony and pronounced the only hope of saving his life was yet another operation – a major repair job. My uncle said it should be done in England – after all he had had his appendix out on the kitchen table. The expert said there was a better chance of survival if he could do it in Boston with his own team. So in early June a dying Anthony was transported to the New England Baptist Hospital for his third operation, which lasted eight hours.

As Foreign Secretary, Anthony had been due to give the new Queen a dinner for the Coronation in June, and I had spent a lot of time borrowing silver objects for the table and choosing the menu. I went to the Coronation ceremony alone, Anthony being in hospital, and my Aunt Clemmie had to take over the dinner, and naturally changed everything.

If I had to invigilate anywhere in the States, Boston in the summer was about the most sympathetic. I made friends with several Bostonians, and Isaiah Berlin put me in touch with McGeorge Bundy,* Arthur Schlesinger† and William James, the nephew of Henry James. There were unexpected meetings with refugees like the Lobkowitzes – last seen as lodgers at the Vansittarts' during the war. Rudi Bing, then Director of the Metropolitan Opera House, came up from New York. Once, dining in an Italian restaurant with a friend from England, we were confused by seeing all the Italian waiters sporting bright green bowler hats – I never knew what for, but there were a lot of Irish in Boston.

This was democratic America, yet it was a town more stratified than anything in England. A rich industrialist gave a dinner for me in a house in a Georgian square exactly like one in London, and the guests were a whole different raft of people. My Bostonian friends of the 'old' class were consumed with mirth and wanted to know every detail. In London that kind of snobbery no longer existed.

When Anthony was finally on his feet again Richard Cattell had

---

* McGeorge Bundy (1919–96): worked at the Council on Foreign Relations; from 1961 he was National Security Adviser to President Kennedy and President Johnson.
† Arthur Schlesinger Jr (1917-2007): American liberal thinker, historian and Pulitzer Prize-winning writer; served as Special Assistant to President Kennedy.

us to a dinner of steak and ice cream at his house, then telling him he should be on a strict diet for the rest of his life – and comforted him by saying he would be able to lead a reasonably active life and possibly do something like a bit of sailing. Three months later Anthony was back at the Foreign Office, working from 8 a.m. until 1 a.m. the following morning, seven days a week – whereas Cattell sadly died before Anthony did, having performed three more major operations on him over the years, the last being done by his successor, Dr Braasch.

The intensity of this crisis after only a short period of marriage bound us together in a situation of emotional dependence. You cannot nurse a dying man surrounded by publicity in Boston, Massachusetts, without a very tight bond being forged. If a patient is willing himself to live, it makes the role of nurse-wife that much easier. His obsessive job might otherwise have made our life together politically humdrum for much longer.

*   *   *

While they were away, Churchill had a stroke during an official dinner with the Italian Prime Minister, Alcide de Gasperi, on 23 June. It was kept quiet at the time and Churchill, against all the odds, recovered, though there were doubts among the colleagues about his ability to carry on. Clarissa learned of it during Eden's convalescence in Newport, Rhode Island.

*   *   *

DIARY – JULY, NEWPORT

Roger Makins had rung me up with the news on Wednesday. Jock Colville [Churchill's Private Secretary] wrote to me on the 26th. He said Winston made a short speech at the de Gasperi dinner. As he was leaving the dining room he suddenly lost control of his legs, and his speech became inarticulate and slurred. The guests were got rid of as quickly as possible and Winston got to bed. Next morning his left arm was paralysed and he could walk only with difficulty. Nevertheless, he took a Cabinet (Wednesday, that was).

From other letters – from Rab and Oliver Lyttelton – it appears that they got Winston to Chartwell. He says he will continue as Prime Minister for one reason alone – to give Anthony time to convalesce completely before taking over from him. He has told Rab and Bobbety this, and they say they agree.

Should he have to resign the Palace would ask Bobbety to form a caretaker government for six months. The doctors give Winston a 50:50 chance of recovery.

A day or two later came letters from Walter Monckton and Jim Thomas, both of which contained pleas to try and return as soon as possible – with typical masculine circumvention, not specifying exactly why. Anthony tried to play for time, because he doesn't want to have to fly home. A day or two later again came another message from Jim, and a charming letter from Oliver Lyttelton; both continuing to say: if possible return home before the House rises – or, anyway, be here a little in August.

We take it they were first of all afraid Winston would die before we returned, and then, when the danger of that lessened, of possible plots. Jock wrote again to say Winston had improved miraculously and it now looked likely that he could hang on until the autumn.

DIARY – 7 JULY

Letter from Jim, saying the immediate necessity of our return was less pressing, but we should come as soon as possible. It would seem that what they all feared was Winston's sudden demise with Anthony out of the country.

*   *   *

The Edens returned to London briefly in July and spent the weekend at Chequers. The issue of Churchill's resignation and the succession was hovering and unresolved, and Eden was unwilling to press his case. His undevious style and fondness for Churchill prevented him from confronting the Prime Minister. But the colleagues were increasingly concerned about the leader's ability to continue. Churchill prevaricated continuously for nearly two years.

*   *   *

DIARY — 27 JULY, WEEKEND AT CHEQUERS

Winston appears on the lawn in a siren suit & Stetson with a nurse and shins unaided up the bank. Anthony is handed a long, careful but deeply agitated letter from Harry Crookshank about Winston saying that they've only just managed to scrape through to the end of the session.

Winston's line clearly would be, if pressed right now, we must wait until the autumn and see how Anthony is. He keeps on teasing — 'What! Can't you drink? I can.' Anthony finally said, 'Winston, you are very rarely ill and when you do you choose your illnesses very carefully.' 'Anthony must get his strength back,' he said to me.

At Sunday lunch Anthony was very outspoken to Winston about his Russian get-together, Aunt Clemmie agreeing with Anthony. Also defending Ike, of whom Winston says, 'He is a nice man, but a fool.'

The Salisburys don't come till Sunday teatime. Bobbety & Anthony talk, Bobbety saying he is prepared to speak to Winston but they'd better sleep on it. Agrees the present position cannot go on. Says Anthony will get well and Winston won't.

Bobbety skirted the question with Winston who was evasive, & talked frankly with Jock saying the position could not be held. Jock made a face, then said that Winston talks of staying until the Queen returns from the Australia tour next May. Bobbety said to Jock this was very unfair on the Queen, supposing anything happened while she was away. It's one of her few prerogatives to appoint the PM and supposing the new PM wanted the dissolution of Parliament it is one of her few prerogatives to call this. Jock agreed. Bobbety says there's nothing for Anthony to do but he will try & rally the colleagues in Anthony's absence. Says he's never known a more dangerous situation.

*

We finally escaped for our holiday. Mountbatten had offered his flagship *Surprise* for the first stage of the convalescence. He was Commander-in-Chief of the Mediterranean Fleet at the time. I was surprised to find that the ships of this fleet were not battleship-grey, but beige. We stayed briefly with friends Bill and Babe Paley,* who were at a house at Antibes. My stepson Nicholas was very taken by Babe.

I heard that Garbo was in the vicinity, but Anthony would have none of that and only wanted to see Annabella – a small blonde star of the French screen very famous at that time. However, after we had embarked on *Surprise* and weighed anchor, a speedboat came racing towards us with a figure standing up, frantically waving – this was Greta, too late to say goodbye.

---

* Bill Paley: head of the American CBS network. Barbara 'Babe' Paley – one of the three beautiful Cushing sisters all of whom married well. She was fashion editor for *Vogue* and became a fashion icon and, with her lavish entertaining, leader of New York Society.

Bridget Parsons, who came with us, was my friend. I have never had women friends with whom I exchanged confidences, except perhaps now in old age and retrospectively. My friendship with Bridget was based on her being exceptionally intelligent and knowledgeable and, being older, more sophisticated. She was also extremely beautiful and had been loved by many, but either through fastidiousness or lack of passion seemed never to have responded.

The first stop was Malta and Gozo, headquarters of the Mediterranean Fleet.

DIARY — AUGUST, MALTA

We arrive off Gozo on Sunday morning. The island looked as if it was made of sandstone chips, the sea bluer and cleaner than anything seen up to now. No sooner anchored than the Admiral's barge came charging through choppy seas round the point and they all swarmed on board *Surprise*. Lord Mountbatten, in a heavily patterned shirt and slacks, Lady (Edwina) Mountbatten trim and withered. Everything very matey. 'We shall arrive in picnic clothes,' Lord Mountbatten had said in a letter to put us at our ease. With a dental surgeon commander in tow, who looked at my wisdom tooth, said it was septic, and wanted to take it out that evening. Lord Mountbatten very overbearing about our plans: tells us what, and what not to see, until Lady Mountbatten intervened.

We pack off for our bathe and picnic. Lord Mountbatten tries to press-gang everyone into wearing masks, which I am in fear of, having inflamed my ear with salt water. Anthony absolutely refuses to look under the water, even through a glass box from a lilo, and says crossly 'Hell, I want to rest' when I say 'Come and look at Lord Mountbatten on the bottom of the ocean'. During the meal on the barge I was struck by Lady

Mountbatten's gaiety and simplicity. They neither of them put on any side.

After lunch I had to rush away with Lady Mountbatten to the Royal Naval Hospital. She talked about Winston a bit; neither of them seems to know the truth, but she is obviously being very very careful of what she says.

Surgeon-Rear-Admiral to meet me. Injected 20 minutes later; operated on one hour later. I was there three days. Anthony came in every day – upset the first day, because Lady Mountbatten had brought me roses and he had forgotten. The next day he came with lovely climbing roses and lemon verbena, and a handful of the lovely waxy North African jasmine flowers in his handkerchief.

Apparently, while I was incarcerated, they had the Mountbattens at every single meal, but even Bridget Parsons was won over by their friendliness and niceness. She had been in a state of almost neurotic rebellion about meeting them for days beforehand.

I was impressed by Edwina Mountbatten's perfect manners, good sense and kindness. Years later when they were lunching with us in Wiltshire, she was the only visitor ever to have gone to the kitchen afterwards and complimented the cook.

DIARY – 31 AUGUST

Bag from London brought letters from Jim Thomas, Bobbety and Evelyn Shuckburgh. All said Winston is improving daily and has quite decided now not to leave. He plans to try and force Anthony to leave the Foreign Office, become Lord President and Leader of the House, and also answer all Foreign Office questions in the House. Bobbety says this is a thoroughly bad plan. He urges Anthony to return home by 20 September to be on the spot. One would assume from this that he plans a showdown, and wants Anthony there.

When we got to Palermo on the way to Athens, there on the quay, very soberly dressed in a suit, I was surprised to see my friend Fulco Verdura waiting to show us around – including his family palazzo. After an idyllic picnic in the shadows of the temple at Agrigento (since, I am told, ruined by being built around) we sailed on, changed boats at Athens and did the Greek Islands – except that the *meltemi* was raging and at one point the boat was even forced to stop at an island we hadn't wanted to go to. I understood why Ulysses had such trouble getting home. My favourite island was Rhodes. Mussolini had banished all the goats, so the island was verdant and on one white beach I saw for the first time Pancratium, the sea daffodil, springing up in the sand.

We were thankfully without letters during the cruise, but on our return to Athens, found an accumulated postbag:

DIARY – 23 SEPTEMBER

1. Jim hopeful – says Winston is determined to continue, but if he finds he cannot make public speeches or answer questions in the House, he will go at once. Winston was playing croquet with the aid of a stool.

2. Bobbety: a very strong letter saying he had, the day before (6 September), sent in his resignation to Winston on the grounds that, having reached the age of sixty, he felt he should give way to a younger man – most of the Cabinet being over seventy, he says, and keeping out the younger men will ruin the Conservative Party.

We returned from Greece on 2 October. Although very thin, Anthony sprang back into the old life.

*   *   *

During Anthony's absence, Winston had on 11 May made a major speech declaring his determination to work for a summit of the Big Four leaders to discuss ways to bring about an 'easement' of Cold War tensions. Churchill offered to meet the new Russian Premier, Georgi Malenkov. Neither Eden nor the majority of the Cabinet favoured this initiative: with scant evidence of change in the Russian leadership they feared that Churchill's faltering command of detail would lead to unwise concessions. The Americans opposed it. Eisenhower was not prepared to risk his reputation on a fruitless meeting. They also judged that Churchill's style of 'summitry', effective in wartime conferences, was now inappropriate in the Cold War context.

*   *   *

DIARY — 2 OCTOBER

Bobbety and Anthony dine with Winston at No. 10 – Rab also. Winston adamant about his meeting with Malenkov, which he wants to do alone with Malenkov, if necessary in Switzerland. Bobbety and Anthony argue with him. At one point he says, 'Now I begin to understand what Chamberlain felt like,' i.e. trying to do what the people wanted in working for peace at any price.

Bobbety gets very angry and says this is too much. Winston is still determined. Anthony depressed as he says in the old days, after that sort of struggle, one knew that something must have sunk in, whereas now one doesn't know if he will remember.

DIARY — 6 OCTOBER

Winston *did* remember and was much mollified on subsequent meetings. I met Oliver Lyttelton in Fortnum's, where he was having a package of pre-cooked foods made up from under the glass dome. He said, 'The trouble about Winston is that the art of being a politician lies not in doing the right things, but in persuading the others that what you do is right.'

We lunched at Downing Street. Winston seemed much better – almost as he used to be. He drank two glasses of champagne, two glasses of brandy, and took an aspirin in the middle of lunch.

The next day was the Annual Party Conference at Margate.

DIARY — 8 OCTOBER

When we enter the Conference hall Anthony gets a good ovation. Bobbety makes a quite excellent speech – clear, intelligent and right. After praising Julian Amery's diatribe about keeping the Suez Canal, he proceeds to demolish it. Anthony rises and does very well – by far the best speech he has made, delivered with great punch, all on the right lines: Nato, EDC, the Canal, Four Powers; good applause.

Jim says someone overheard a delegate say 'Well, they got away with it' about Anthony and Bobbety's defence of the agreement with Egypt. The Party absolutely blimpish at core. Mark [Chapman-Walker – Communications Director at Conservative Central Office] says the press were ecstatic. Evening papers are good, the *Standard* saying the speech was delivered without any sign of strain and punctuated by wild applause.

*   *   *

While Churchill persisted in seeing signs of hope for a Malenkov meeting, the Americans now hardened their opposition.

*   *   *

DIARY — 17 OCTOBER

Dulles arrived on the 15th and he, Anthony and Bobbety dined with Winston that night. Dulles was very good with Winston, and said that the US wished to work with Britain in complete partnership, that he and Eisenhower were prepared to accept Anthony and Winston's lead in foreign affairs, i.e. as regards Persia and Egypt, but that if Winston persisted in his efforts for a Big Four or Big Two talk before the EDC was through, Britain would lose America, and American public opinion would be dead against her.

Winston was furious. Dulles did not become excited, but merely repeated his words firmly, adding that after the EDC in January the Americans would welcome Winston as a mediator between the US and Russia. 'Me as a mediator!' growled Winston, more annoyed than ever.

*   *   *

Eden now faced fierce opposition at home over his decision to support Sudanese demands for self-determination. The Suez Group, backed by Churchill, saw this as another 'scuttle'. Churchill told Eden in a cruel jibe that he had not known before that Munich was situated on the Nile. During the Canal base negotiations Eden had persuaded the Egyptians to give up their claim to union with the Sudan, which cleared the main obstacle to self-determination, and elections in Sudan duly took place. But the outcome was initially a disappointment for Eden.

*   *   *

DIARY — 30 NOVEMBER

We opened our papers in the morning to learn that the pro-Egyptian party had won hands down in the Sudan election. In his bath, Anthony said, 'Now I can resign – they will all be baying for my blood.' I did not pay much attention, as he frequently said he was going to resign.

This time, however, he went to the office and quietly wrote a letter to Winston sending in his resignation. Anthony went to see Winston who said he fully understood his feelings but that in fact the decision on the Sudan was not his responsibility alone, but endorsed by the Cabinet and Winston himself. Anthony said yes but Winston had never wanted it and therefore Anthony must take full responsibility. Winston said he was sick of the whole job and hated every minute of it, but felt he must remain while there was a chance of furthering peace.

Winston's seventy-ninth. The birthday party was different this year. We were all asked in after dinner. I sat with Duff on a sofa in the furthest room, and did not budge. We were soon joined by Anthony, Judy Montagu, Antony Head, and Brendan [Bracken]. Afterwards we returned to the cake, where Anthony had to propose Winston's health. Winston listened with a vague smile and was about to reply when Diana [Churchill], with her usual desperate bravado, struck up 'Happy Birthday to you'. 'Be quiet!' said Winston, who was still trying to speak, but it was no use and he had to subside while we sang the silly song.

DIARY – 11 DECEMBER

The government are concerned about the rebels, i.e. the Tory blimps who don't want us to scuttle down the Suez Canal. Winston rang up at 10.30 p.m. and said, 'Stand by for an important document that I'm sending round.' Anthony went to sleep.

I was woken by Anthony the next morning with the important document. It was a plan to send troops and aeroplanes to Khartoum on a trumped-up pretext of keeping order, and virtually to reoccupy southern Sudan. In the end, Winston promised to do nothing while Anthony was away. Anthony was due in Paris for talks on European defence, but the problem of the Canal base – and the Suez rebels at home – could not be forgotten.

DIARY – 13–16 DECEMBER, PARIS

At lunch with Monty [Field Marshal Montgomery] I said across the table to Anthony, 'Why don't you ask the Field Marshal to go and talk to your rebels?' Whereupon it was arranged that he would ask Waterhouse to lunch on the Thursday and go for him hammer and tongs. Monty is dead against staying in Egypt and wanting his bases in Libya, Syria, Cyprus and Turkey.

We spent Christmas at Rose Bower after Anthony returned from a major conference with the Americans and French in Bermuda, which he said achieved nothing.

I was increasingly aware of the awkwardness of the situation both for me and Anthony, given that Winston was my uncle. There was now increasing pressure on him to retire, but Anthony as his successor was not prepared either to plot or put pressure.

It was at his point that, much as I had always admired my uncle, I had to side with my husband in any divergence of opinion or interest. As it turned out, there were to be many.

My uncle had hoped to appease Anthony's growing frustration by allocating him Dorneywood as a weekend retreat, Lord Courtauld Thompson having recently died and bequeathed his house for the use of government ministers. I believe other ministers and their wives have subsequently enjoyed Dorneywood enormously. It was impossible for us. It was too hurried. Lord Courtauld Thompson's hairbrushes had not even been removed from his bedroom. The old servants were still there, and grumpy at the invasion of private secretaries and government boxes arriving daily during the weekend.

The house was dingy and dark; there was nothing to do. The woods were full of rabbits dying of myxomatosis, and the now obligatory swimming pool and tennis court were unheard of in those days.

Whenever we could, we retired to my cottage in Wiltshire instead. This was up a long lane, which meant that the detective and our old manservant had to commute from the village pub on mopeds, and the other cottage nearby was outraged when a hut was built for the police. It did mean, however, that at last the telephone company had to install a telephone – plus a scrambler, of course. I loved those weekends at the cottage – I did the cooking and Anthony shot a few pheasants on the farmer's fields. In the summer, roses, sweet peas, lobster, strawberries and cream, Meursault, complete peace and enclosure from the world. It beat Dorneywood, our sop from my uncle, any day.

*   *   *

For Eden 1954 was a year of major diplomatic success on several fronts – some call it his annus mirabilis. *In February the Berlin Conference of Foreign Ministers of Russia, America, France and Britain achieved little of substance but the ground was laid for negotiation on the German question and future European defence, the independence of Austria, which was still occupied by Russian troops, and measures for easing international tension. All these, as well as the problem of the rival claims of Italians and Yugoslavs to the port of Trieste, were resolved by the end of the year. The most important outcome of Berlin was the decision to hold a five-power conference including China to discuss the volatile situation in Indo-China – due to start in April.*

At the beginning of March, Clarissa discovered that she was pregnant. As always when Eden was away she spent time at the Bower and saw friends.

Meanwhile Churchill began to discuss the date of his departure. Since his stroke, in the inner circles of government there had been a growing feeling that Churchill could no longer continue, and that Eden should take over. Eden, whether because of temperament or loyalty, would not press the issue, despite his growing frustration with Churchill's prevarication.

*   *   *

DIARY — 10 MARCH 1954

While I was in a nursing home after a miscarriage Winston sent for Anthony and told him he wanted to go after the Queen's return from her tour in May – or, at the latest, after Harold's Rent Bill in July.

Harold [Macmillan] had advised Winston against taking a dukedom on the grounds that Randolph would be such an awful marquess. Winston thanked Anthony for not having jogged his elbow and for having allowed him to play his hand on retirement as he wished to.

DIARY — 19 MARCH

Anthony worked out a last-ditch plan for Egyptian settlement this week, to try and make the Americans come in with us in getting civilian firms to run the base after the soldiers have been evacuated. This would get round the stumbling block of technicians' uniforms, and civilians would not be open to outrages in the way that the military are. Winston very glum about this plan.

Meanwhile, [President] Neguib announces that he does not subscribe to the availability clause that Nasser agreed to a few weeks ago – that the base should become available if Turkey is attacked – and says he is not interested any more in getting a settlement. Everything plays against poor Anthony. Sir Ralph Assheton [one of the Suez Group] boasted to Anthony that the rebels 'have all the press with them', which looks sadly true.

The Egyptians start shooting our soldiers again, too.

Anthony is still convinced that the general temper of the country is for him, and also that the ratio of rebels to those who want agreement with Egypt among backbenchers is 250 to 50 – though of course Anthony himself now says that agreement is no longer possible in view of the increasingly bad behaviour of the Egyptians, both in the Canal zone and in the Sudan.

DIARY – 21 MARCH

Winthrop [Aldrich – US Ambassador to Britain] rang Anthony up last night to say that Eisenhower accepted Anthony's suggestion about the US and us each putting in civilian contractors. It is Anthony's personal prestige that has done it, says Winthrop. Anthony now thinks that the rebels will dislike the new idea more than anything.

*   *   *

The Canal base negotiations were completed in October 1954. The phased evacuation of troops would be completed by June 1956, British civilian technicians would maintain the base for a defined period and the British had the right to return if Turkey or an Arab state was attacked. The British military headquarters shifted to Cyprus.

Alongside this, Eden had been working on a wider plan for the defence of the Middle East which would tie into alliance the states bordering the Soviet Union. This became in 1955 the Baghdad Pact, which with Turkey and Iraq, and later Pakistan and Iran, had a frontier extending from the Mediterranean to the Himalayas. The Americans stood aloof, with Dulles protesting that the British had failed to consult sufficiently with them and – ever suspicious of colonialism – he construed it as a device to perpetuate British influence in the region.

A more immediate problem was the war in Indo-China where for eight years the Communist nationalist Vietminh had been fighting for independence from French colonial rule. With the French nearing defeat, the Five Power Foreign Ministers Conference met at Geneva to broker a solution to the area's future.

Uncertainty persisted at home over the succession. In discussions with the Cabinet colleagues Churchill put off his retirement date until July at the earliest.

It was in these uncertain circumstances that Eden embarked on what was considered one of his greatest diplomatic achievements.

*   *   *

DIPLOMACY

The backdrop to the Geneva Conference was an escalating crisis in Indo-China as the Vietminh mounted the final bloody siege of the French fortress of Dien Bien Phu.

At preliminary meetings of the Allies in Paris, Dulles, backed by Eisenhower, urged immediate Western intervention in the form of air strikes to save the French and stop the expansion of Communist China's influence in the region. The use of nuclear weapons was even being canvassed by US hawks. When unilateral intervention was blocked by domestic opposition, Dulles called on Britain to support united action.

Despite his considerable pressure, Churchill, Eden and the Cabinet came out firmly against British support for any military action that might precipitate conflict with China. The Times thought this the most dangerous situation since 1945. Eden believed that war with China was more dangerous than the threat of some Communist advances in the countries of Indo-China. His job was to negotiate a political way out of the crisis and he hoped through the conference to broker a peace and stabilise the region after the inevitable French defeat.

Eden's flat rejection of intervention put considerable strain on the Anglo-American alliance. His relations with the fiercely anti-Communist Dulles were tense. Dulles was furious at the British rejection of force, and also at Eden's refusal to discuss the then unclear proposals for a Far

East defence pact, which Eden supported (and which eventually became
SEATO), until after the conference had convened. Dulles was anyway
a very reluctant participant in a meeting that involved China, since
the US government refused to recognise its Communist government and
powerful domestic pressure groups were adamantly opposed to any joint
negotiations. As it was, he hardly spoke to the Chinese at all.

*   *   *

DIARY — 24 APRIL 1954, PRE-CONFERENCE MEETING IN PARIS
French in a panic about Indo-China. Dulles tells Anthony in
the afternoon that the French have asked for help and that the
Americans want to go in but won't unless we agree. Anthony
says he won't agree and if they go in it will mean fighting
China & setting off a Third World War. Admiral Arthur
Radford [US Chairman of the Joint Chiefs of Staff] has arrived
and is spoiling for a fight with China.

Anthony cables to Winston the position, who meanwhile
wanted to come over after receiving yesterday's cable. Anthony
dissuaded him & also flies back to London himself to spend the
night at Chequers.

Cabinet called for the morning to back up his decision on
not going in on Indo-China. Winston on the open line said,
'Well if we do, perhaps we can make a bargain with the Americans to help us in Egypt in return.'

The Geneva Conference opened on 26 April at the Palais des Nations.
As it lasted several months, it was therefore something I could
observe at first hand. We started living in the Beau Rivage Hotel,
Anthony's old haunt from League of Nations days. When Paul-
Henri Spaak, the Belgian Foreign Minster, came to dinner, Anthony
had been told that the Chinese had some new device across the lake
for eavesdropping, so Spaak and Anthony had to talk while banging

their hands on the dining-room table – which of course they were always forgetting to do. Intelligence and Anthony's own staff were getting very jumpy about general security. Evelyn Shuckburgh twice interrupted other meetings with a warning to speak lower as this time the Chinese were on the floor above and might be eavesdropping. It appeared that the hotel had been re-wallpapered recently and it was thought there had been Communist workmen putting devices under the paper. This was obviously going to be dangerous, as well as ludicrous, and a nice banker who owned the *Journal de Genève* came forward and volunteered to lend the British delegation a lovely eighteenth-century house on the lake, Le Reposoir.

DIARY — 27 APRIL

I went with Mrs Dulles & Mme Bidault [wife of the French Foreign Minister Georges Bidault] to the conference. She waved cards & got us in to the chamber itself, decorated with ugly progressive gold and black frescos by Sert.

We sat in the hall and watched the delegates arrive. Each husband in turn stopped dead in his tracks at the sight of his wife, and laughed helplessly.

Molotov [Soviet Foreign Minister] appeared surrounded by hatchet-faced henchmen. His skin is like the best-quality transparent wax.

Immediately behind the Russians come the 200 Chinese delegates, so close that they trip over themselves, all looking about 14, small, delicate, dressed in loose blue uniforms. Impossible to know which is Chou En-lai [China's Foreign Minister].

Molotov had revealed traces of a sense of humour. When Anthony went to see him in the morning to arrange on behalf of the others who should be chairman at the conference Molotov, who had a bad cold, said to Anthony, 'Why don't you and I seize power?' They decided that it should be themselves, alternating with a third party from a minor country. 'After all, it can't be America or China,' said Molotov. Dulles and Bidault were very tepid about this arrangement.

Anthony and I were naively impressed by the fact that Chou En-lai had brought a lot of Ming china with him, which was ranged on shelves in his sitting room. This, and the fact that he spoke fluent French (having worked in the Renault factory in his youth), made him seem a sympathetic character. It was only years later, when I read Jung Chang's book on Mao, that I learned he was, if anything, more awful than Mao himself. Mao gave the orders, but Chou actually carried them out. While Chou and Anthony would chat informally to each other in French, naturally the iron rule was that all negotiating took place with all participants speaking their native language and then being expertly interpreted so that there should be no possible misunderstanding.

DIARY — 28 APRIL

Lunch with Dulles at the Hôtel du Rhône. Sticky meal. Mme Bidault rattled on. Before lunch – '*J'ai horreur du sherry – c'est une faiblesse anglaise.*' We gave her sherry yesterday, incidentally. Infuriating lunch in an overheated room. Dulles incredibly slow, vain, jealous – a question of what should be done to get restricted sessions & get on with the conference. Anthony suggested asking Molotov's help in this. Dulles says Anthony oughtn't to become a go-between for the Allies & Russia in spite of the fact that he is chairman and therefore it is his job.

DIARY — 1 MAY

We have moved into Le Reposoir. Wake in the morning to a pretty scene – park full of buttercups, a pleached avenue, box shapes, a good view of the lake. The first swallows dipping about.

This evening we embarked on what seemed a harmless, though deadly dinner with the Dulleses at the Perle au Lac. Mr Dulles tells me about tree surgery, which he practises.

Bedell Smith [US Deputy Under-Secretary of State] just arrived, tired from flying and not well. I find him unusual to talk to. When the ladies retired, Anthony was apparently set upon by Dulles and the iniquitous China lobby man, Walter Robertson [Assistant Secretary of State]. They want Britain to give 'moral' support if they go into Indo-China. Anthony refused and had the official Robertson arguing with him.

Nin Ryan told me that Anthony had been getting a wonderful French press. They say he is running the conference and is wise and trying to save the peace of the world. Anthony certainly fought hard tonight to prevent the Americans starting a war. He says at the Russian lunch yesterday it was clear the Russians & Chinese are terrified of the Americans' bellicosity.

Dulles has been sore for three days – he said to Anthony yesterday that he felt isolated and that Britain had let the US down etc. etc. Yet he admitted that he had no plan for Korea or what to do next in the conference. Dulles said to Anthony, 'Well I hope you treat Bedell Smith better than you've treated me.'

*　　*　　*

Dulles left the conference on 3 May and was replaced by the more sympathetic General Walter Bedell Smith, whom Eden liked and trusted. Eden's parting words to Dulles as they stood on the hotel steps were: 'The trouble with you, Foster, is that you want World War Three.'

*　　*　　*

By now, Evelyn seemed over-burdened so I took on the housekeeping at Le Reposoir, and when Evelyn left my old friend Tony Rumbold replaced him. At the first meal Tony said, '*Fraises des bois –*

Smiles all round. The arrival of General Bedell Smith (left) at Geneva, replacing Dulles, was welcome. With French Foreign Minister Georges Bidault and AE.

AE joking with Chou En-lai with the Ming porcelain in the background.

Coming back from a function, hence the bouquet.

Opening a bazaar. What on earth shall I buy?

In Paris with AE on a diplomatic trip, nabbed by French TV.

On the steps of St George's Chapel after the Garter ceremony. A real flush: Monty looking away, Clemmie encased in tulle, Winston with his handful of ostrich plumes. At the rear, the Edens.

Leaving for a conference with something to read.

A few days' holiday on the Würtersee before rushing back to England for another crisis.

Waiting for Winston.

A serious talk after dinner at the Embassy in Cairo. Nasser with British
Ambassador Sir Ralph Stevenson and AE – both unfortunately in black ties.
Nasser defiantly surmounts the sartorial faux pas.

Rangoon, the Great Pagoda which I visit with Mrs Aung San. Socks on.

I escape from the SEATO Conference in Bangkok. At Bayu with the ex-French Cultural Attaché.

Krishna Menon and President Nehru are in high spirits meeting us
at night at Delhi airport.

In the Far East, leaving yet another reception.

Arriving at the farewell dinner for Winston at No. 10.

Winston congratulates his successor.

they are in season – why aren't we having any?' He was dead right, we should have been. I ordered some at once. He was a welcome addition and always got the point.

DIARY – 5 MAY

Anthony had Bidault to dinner last night. He announced that in the French talks with the Russians, no date had been fixed. Moreover they have no representative from Laos or Cambodia here, without whom the talks cannot take place. Anthony very cross.

Molotov came to dinner. It seems typical of me that I should be upstairs in bed reading the newspapers meanwhile, which anyone in the world could be doing, instead of seeing Molotov. They had an hilarious evening which went on quite late with screams of laughter and talk on all subjects, Molotov speaking of the conference as someone completely detached & agreeing with Anthony on all points and making no difficulties about anything.

He said he sees the world now as stable except for two restless powers – China & America. He sees Britain and Russia in analogous positions regarding the conference. Neither wants an extension of war and both have these belligerent allies.

DIARY – 12 MAY

Bobbety writes to say Winthrop [Aldrich] is back from America & very worried because Foster said he had been double-crossed, not by Anthony, but by Winston and Selwyn [Lloyd] in the House – and that the President agrees with the lobby in the US who want the US to enter the Indo-China war alone.

DIARY – 14 MAY

The Americans are just continuing with their plans for a South-east Asia pact exactly as they want it, irrespective of what Bedell Smith & Anthony have decided here as regards timing & details. Anthony very angry & anti-American over these dictatorial methods.

I had returned from the conference on 15 May, and Anthony made frequent visits back to London. When he was away I visited Rose Bower, met old friends and saw some plays. The pace of life at Carlton Gardens had left me little time to see my friends. I didn't have a life with them any more. Life was so full and I was so busy thinking about Anthony and looking after him and being sure that everything was just right for him. They used to come in for drinks sometimes. But I thought, the last thing he wants to see, when he comes up to dinner, is a lot of my friends lolling around on the sofas.

DIARY — 5 JUNE

Anthony home from Geneva for the weekend. Cabinet sat in the morning followed by lunch with Winston. Anthony said to Patrick [Buchan-Hepburn, Chief Whip] something about summer holidays and Patrick said, 'Holidays, my foot.' Did Anthony realise the mess that every single minister and all departments were in? It would take months of work sorting it all out and putting it in order.

Anthony followed up his talk with Winston by a letter saying the middle of July. Back came an answer saying that owing to the unsettled international situation, he might have to stay till after the autumn. This presumably is Beaverbrook working on him while Clemmie is away.

DIARY — 10 JUNE

Anthony flew back to discuss plans with Winston. We went to

Chequers for one night. Winston seemed brighter than usual. He told Anthony the end of July was still the date unless something happened to delay it. In the middle of a perfectly normal dinner *en famille* Winston suddenly stood up & said 'The Queen', so we all had to jump to our feet.

DIARY – 21 JUNE

Anthony returned from Geneva again yesterday, Patrick came last night full of gloom. Said last weekend Winston was in a vicious mood about going – 'Nobody is going to push me etc.' – and finally taking Patrick's arm, he said, 'Besides, there may be a war by August.' September is the new deadline.

*   *   *

During a break in the conference Churchill and Eden travelled to Washington on 24 June to meet Eisenhower. Progress was made on several issues relating to the Geneva talks: Dulles and Eden reached accord on setting up study groups for a South-East Asia Defence Pact, and on a peace settlement in Indo-China in which Vietnam would be partitioned and the independence of Laos and Cambodia guaranteed. In this new spirit of co-operation, Dulles was persuaded to return to the conference, which had been in danger of breaking up with no agreement.

On Europe, Eisenhower supported rearming West Germany as part of a European defence organisation. In Eden's parallel negotiations with Egypt the US would back the principle of international freedom of traffic in the Suez Canal.

However, to the dismay of Dulles and Eden, Eisenhower agreed in principle to a meeting with the Russians, though he would change his mind several times after that. This thin straw fired Churchill to renewed efforts to ease Cold War tensions through a top-level face-to-face meeting of leaders – and the postponement of his retirement.

*   *   *

DIARY — 8 JULY

On the boat coming home from the American trip, Winston announced he was going to send a message to Malenkov [Soviet Premier] suggesting a meeting in Moscow. This he wanted to do without telling the Cabinet. After a day-long wrangle in which Winston threatened to throw Jock [Colville] & Christopher [Soames] out of the porthole, Winston agreed (a) not to mention Moscow and (b) to send a message to Rab for the Cabinet.

On arriving home on 26 July, Rab & Harold were called first – Harold outspoken that he didn't like the idea. I suggested to Anthony the moment I heard of it that he ought to have no part in this projected meeting. It will forever be flung back at him long after Winston is gone. Anyway it is a matter of principle. He doesn't believe in it, therefore he should not do it. Let him at least not diverge from the Americans when it is not strictly necessary, i.e. when he doesn't even believe in the point of disagreement.

The next day a message for Winston came from Eisenhower beginning 'You certainly haven't let the grass grow under your feet' & continuing in the same rather resentful strain.

The Cabinet greeted the idea with anxiety and were openly furious about not having been consulted, Bobbety being particularly outspoken in this. Winston very much the old lion at bay – at one point saying that he thought that a message sent by him and the Foreign Secretary needn't have Cabinet approval. Whereupon Anthony was forced to point out it hadn't been sent jointly and what was more, he himself had been very much against it going at all. Everyone adamant it should not be Moscow. Anthony pleased with his compromise idea that the Russians should be asked to meet us in Bern. This compromise is cabled to Eisenhower who sends back a mild reply.

DIARY — 11 JULY

Lovely weekend at Rose Bower with arches of old-fashioned roses particularly lovely – the papery crimson purple grey Tour de Malakoff and the incredibly abundant Filipes. Strawberries from the barrel, *fraises des bois*, blackcurrants and the first peas and beans. Anthony was happy & worked in the garden. We wondered whether or not to spend part of our holiday there after all.

Rather awful drinks on Saturday. Juliet Duff brought the Robert Sherwoods* and Diana Cooper [and the drink I had concocted was disgusting].

* * *

Progress improved at Geneva. When the French government fell in mid June the new Prime Minister, Pierre Mendès-France (who also became Foreign Secretary), pledged to reach a settlement on Indo-China within a month.

At face-to-face meetings, Eden had managed to coax Chou En-lai out of his initial uncompromising aloofness to a more conciliatory approach to the issues of Vietnam, Laos and Cambodia.

* * *

We returned to Geneva on 12 July. The conference had gone on so long that even M. Pictet's hospitality ran out of steam and our delegates moved to a less commodious house – Les Ormeaux – which I found a bit dusty but bearable.

---

* Robert Sherwood (1896–1955): successful American playwright and screen-writer (*Idiot's Delight*, *The Best Years of our Lives*). Member of original Algonquin Round Table with Dorothy Parker.

DIARY — 13 JULY

Comings and goings all morning – the last being Molotov whom I went down to meet. He looks as waxen as ever. Anthony had migraine for the first time since his illness. Tony Rumbold woke us up at 7.30 by having a noisy bath. Re-pack again and join the others for lunch. Krishna Menon [Indian delegate to the UN in 1952] there. Very ill suited to Anthony who is mistrustful & uneasy about his very feminine brilliance combined with continual digs at the British.

We have to leave him in mid-sentence to catch the aeroplane Mendès-France is taking us to Paris in. Very small aeroplane full of people sitting on camp stools, which was disquieting. Mendès-France a pale squat little man.

Paris hot & sunny. What a relief to get away from Geneva. Jebbs on the runway. I am swept away to Cynthia's car. Go to Bagatelle* to see the roses – not pretty, many hideous terracotta, scentless new varieties & lots of polyanthus. The curator gave us sprigs of orange blossom.

Anthony goes to dine at the Matignon with Dulles & Mendès-France. Anthony comes back very late – 1.30. He says Mendès-France was terrific with Dulles – very different from Bidault. Wiped the floor with him. Stood by all his guns, aided by Anthony. Dulles got very cross and cornered.

DIARY — 14 JULY, PARIS

Rumbles of tanks all the morning [because of 14 July celebrations]. I stay in bed & then start the usual wait to leave. Lunch at 12 and then don't leave until 4.30. Back again in Mendès-France's plane. I wondered whether it was not infra dig

---

* Bagatelle was a late eighteenth-century house at one time owned by Sir Richard Wallace, whose possessions at Hertford House eventually became the Wallace Collection.

for Anthony to be travelling on Mendès-France's plane instead of his own.

Tony [Rumbold] has lost the key to one of Anthony's ministerial boxes. He is liable to an enormous fine and all the keys of all the boxes have to be changed.

DIARY — 19 JULY

Met Chou En-lai today – much ruddier and more shiny than I expected. Had an almost identical conversation to that which I had with Molotov. Apparently Mrs Molotov was here for several days – a closely guarded secret from the world. She went around surrounded by ambassadresses and had a special aeroplane sent to fetch her because the one provided wasn't comfortable enough.

DIARY — 20 JULY

Letter from Oliver Lyttelton saying the situation at home was the most dangerous and tricky he'd ever known, and that the Cabinet couldn't go back on the Russian meeting now, or they would 'look like a bunch of stone-heads led by a reactionary marquess who had let his gun off before September 1st and shot the dove of peace in a turnip field'.

Comings and goings all day. The Three finally met at our villa at 9.30. Delay caused by the Cambodians who are rather in the US pocket. However the armistice was signed not at midnight but at 1 a.m., no one having had time to study the terms.

Next day we flew home for good after the plenary session, which was a very depressing affair in which Vietnam and Cambodia were full of complaints about the armistice they had just signed. Anthony, who was in the chair, was very withering to the Cambodians. As he declared the session over, Molotov said he had not realised it was over and he had a few remarks to make. He then spoke for half an hour, which had to be translated, whereupon the same happened with the six other countries. Halfway through, Bedell Smith got impatient and suggested that the session be closed before everyone started disagreeing again.

I had an American next to me in the conference centre who shook with over-simulated laughter when Molotov praised Anthony, and wrote notes down in Chinese. He was typical of an extreme, but substantial, wing of the US State Department, whose historical ties with China and refusal to recognise the Communist government formed a powerful lobby in US politics, which had influenced Dulles.

It seemed to me that every country made a propaganda speech except us, who were unprepared. Our plane was over two hours late and came down too quickly at Heathrow for the pressurisation, and one was left feeling deaf.

DIARY — 22 JULY

Garden Party at Buckingham Palace. This counts as my 'presentation', though in fact I am not actually formally* presented. Anthony had an audience with the Queen afterwards. She told him Winston seemed less truculent about going now.

Dinner at Downing Street. Bedell Smith en route to Washington. The Aldriches and us. Winston and Aldrich not hearing a word, Mrs Aldrich screaming. Bedell intoning endlessly about his aeroplane, the *Dewdrop*. Before dinner Bedell had told Winston he oughtn't to meet the Russians, and they weren't at all the Uncle Joe [Stalin] sort of set-up.

After the Americans had left, Anthony got home, dead tired, having left me behind at No. 10 by mistake. In the middle of the

---

* Clarissa had not been formally presented to the King when she was a débutante in 1938.

night he woke up, and me too, and wrote a Minute to Winston saying while he has always disagreed with the idea, if Winston wishes to go ahead [with meeting the Russians] he can, provided it is not Moscow. He cannot, however, support him on the issue in the Cabinet tomorrow.

DIARY — 23 JULY

A dreadful Cabinet. Winston got into a scrap with Bobbety almost immediately. Winston saying that last night he had thought that he and the Foreign Secretary were agreed, but now he appeared to have changed his mind. He then looked round the table and said, 'Well, does anyone want to say anything at all?' whereupon everyone — with the usual exceptions (Rab, Walter Monckton and Lord Woolton) — did say something: to wit, that they were all against Winston. Oliver said afterwards that Winston could not have played his hand worse. No one wanted to speak up, but he had more or less forced them.

DIARY — 25 JULY

Dead silence from Winston over the whole weekend — unheard of for him. He always rings Anthony up about something or other. Anthony spends the weekend in bed, sleeping.

DIARY — 26 JULY

Winston gave in at the Cabinet and agreed not to send his note to Russia. Winston said that 15 September was still his date, but Anthony hears that he told Madam Pandit* that he wouldn't go until he dropped down dead.

*

---

* Vijaya Lakshmi Pandit: Indian diplomat and politician, sister of India's Prime Minister Jawaharlal Nehru, she was High Commissioner to London 1955–61 and became the first woman President of the United Nations Assembly.

That summer we hoped at last to get a holiday on the Würthersee in Austria – the only summer holiday I had with Anthony in office. Unfortunately, after a few days he discovered an easy way to telephone London – via the military telephone – which was disastrous, as he spent all day ringing them. He became worried about Mendès-France and the EDC modifications. A cable came saying Mendès-France was going to England to see Winston for two hours at Chartwell.

DIARY – 27 AUGUST

Hurried home on the 23rd in order that Anthony could join in the talks between Winston and Mendès-France at Chartwell. Mendès-France was tired – less ebullient and shorter-tempered than at Geneva.

Next day Harold [Macmillan] came round before lunch to see Anthony, as he had been summoned to Chartwell. He came to the flat in the evening in a great stew. Winston said he feels better all the time and he has no intention of retiring until a fortnight before the General Election. Poor Anthony absolutely stunned.

DIARY – 19 SEPTEMBER

The Big Four* had a meeting to urge Winston to reconstruct the Cabinet. Mark Chapman-Walker, on hearing of the new developments, is in despair. He says the Party is disintegrating and that they will surely lose the election, and that Anthony ought to resign to save the Party.

The *News Chronicle* gallup shows the loss of place clearly.

Harold and Rab are utterly frantic. They have woken up to reality at last. Harold, at 62, sees his last chance of a career going to naught, and Rab sees the Party getting so low that he will

---

* The Big Four were the key Cabinet figures – Eden, Bobbety Salisbury, Rab Butler, Harold Macmillan.

have a long wait before his Premiership. They thought of suggesting to Winston that he leave on his 80th birthday. Rab talked of it to Winston, but it was no go – as one could have foreseen.

Randolph came to see me and to my surprise did not defend Winston's decision at all. He was very chastened and ashamed. This did not last long.

*   *   *

Eden had left Geneva with his reputation enhanced, the ground laid for increased stability in the Far East and the threat of a Third World War averted. He now turned his attention to the European Defence Community (EDC).

Proposals had been discussed since 1950. The EDC involving France and West Germany would strengthen European defence and enable the rearmament of West Germany within a supranational framework. Eden would not commit Britain to it, but assured his close association with it, just as he generally encouraged movements towards federation in Europe. He continued to see Britain's role as a bridge between America, Europe and the Commonwealth.

After two years of dithering and pressing the British and Americans for stronger guarantees, the French on 30 August refused to ratify the treaty.

Eden immediately came up with a revised proposal – he got the idea in his bath one night – a non-federal mutual defence pact based on the 1948 Brussels Treaty, which would end the Allied occupation of West Germany, grant it sovereignty and full membership of NATO, and establish a Western European Union.

He decided to go on a whirlwind tour of European capitals to canvass support. Dulles followed Eden doggedly on his own visit to Bonn, which caused suspicion, unfounded as it proved, that the Americans might destabilise the delicate negotiations. (The level of trust between Eden and Dulles had not yet improved.)

A Nine Power Conference was arranged in London on 28 September

at which Eden, to everyone's surprise, finally conceded what he had
refused in the earlier EDC plan – that Britain would maintain four
divisions in Europe and the Tactical Air Force in virtual perpetuity.
Relations between Eden and Dulles were on this issue more harmonious.
Only the French had lingering doubts.

*   *   *

DIARY – 3 OCTOBER

All went smoothly at first; then on the fourth day Mendès-
France produced a series of fantastic objections and demands.
The last day they worked at a concession. After the signing
René [*Massigli, French Ambassador to Britain*] said to Anthony,
speaking of Mendès-France,* 'C'est comme Poincaré.'† *'C'est*
pire,' Anthony replied. Mendès-France said to Anthony, *'Par-*
donnez-moi mes faiblesses.'

Adenauer said to Anthony, 'By your trip [*to the four capitals*
after the EDC collapsed] and your handling of this conference,
you have saved Europe.'

The idea of using the Brussels treaty was entirely
Anthony's – not the Foreign Office's or any other member of
the government. He thought of it one night and told me of it
in the morning. Putting the four divisions and the air force into
the continent was also entirely Anthony's idea. When told,
Winston could not understand the principle and raised objections. The Cabinet approved the idea for the first time – thereby
overruling Winston.

---

* At Massigli's farewell dinner at the end of 1954, René explained to Clarissa that
'Mendès-France's three masters are de Gaulle, Léon Blum and Poincaré', and that
'he has the latter's inability to know when to call a halt in negotiations. He always
presses too far & infuriates his opponent.'
† Raymond Poincaré (1860–1934): French statesman – five times French Prime
Minister and President during the First World War.

DIARY — 7 OCTOBER, CONSERVATIVE ANNUAL CONFERENCE, BLACKPOOL

Long tiring slow train last night. Blackpool – enchanting frontage of luxurious neon lights, the best I've ever seen. We become perhaps a little too cross at the hotel on seeing the bedroom, and I insist on sleeping in the one destined for Winston.

Enormous hall, big enough for no overflow meetings. A mistake was made in the telegram sent about the number of the hymn to be sung, and we had an extraordinary one in praise of St Paul.

Anthony's speech was not one of his best: he sounded tired and flat and slow, and the whole was not well worded or stimulating. Julian Amery found himself on our side and we duly congratulated him.

Over an hour's drive to Bury through blasted country and interminable towns of long low-built streets, hundreds of belching factory chimneys in valleys, fog everywhere, everything green and grey. The trees have already lost their rotted summer leaves and are all twisted stunted things. Anthony does not understand the horror of it, having been brought up among the coal mines of County Durham.

DIARY — 8 OCTOBER

First, Anthony's interview with Winston, which took place at 6.30. The *News Chronicle* poll came out this morning. Half the people want Winston to go; if he went, 13 per cent more would vote Conservative. The editorial says he should go. Winston was naturally in his 'back to the wall' mood and started by saying it was an excellent government and they would win the next election easily.

I went to the conference hall in the morning to hear Rab. He made an excellent speech, and got a great ovation – more at the end of the speech than at the beginning. Down in the lounge, to give my Bradford people drinks. Constituency people arrive, and Anthony appears surprisingly soon (in fact because his talk with Winston came to an abrupt end).

After the Mayor's dinner, Clemmie and I are roped in to look at the illuminations with the Mayor and Mayoress. There are seven miles of lights, and the general vista is rather wonderful, and the atmosphere very gay. As we rose up in the Tower, I suddenly realised it was like the Eiffel Tower in that the lift had glass doors and gaps through which one saw down. I got vertigo, and disgraced myself by being unable to look out at the view. Got to the agents' ball at about 11.30, shoved into a box, floodlit, and announced.

DIARY – 9 OCTOBER

Set off at 2.30. Crowds all gathered along the route to cheer for Winston. 'Anthony Eden! Mr Eden!' they shout. I lead the procession on to the platform. I thought Winston's physical condition much better than last year at Margate. He looked brighter and pinker and spoke more strongly and less slowly. The property-owning democracy bit was interesting. Anthony had good reports in the papers of his Bury speech. They particularly noted his theme on home affairs, and took it as a sign that he was thinking of changing jobs.

Dinner with the Churchills on their train back to London – a prelude to the famous talk between Anthony and Winston. Clemmie, Jock and Christopher and I retire after the meal and make conversation, most of it made before, while the two of them talk. Anthony said his piece about the timing again. Winston, after a lot of pauses, said he now saw the force of that argument, and that he promises to get out in good time.

DIARY — 11 OCTOBER

A newspaper strike, so *The Times* editorial does not appear.
Anthony spends the day in bed and goes to Kent to dine with
his Squadron in the evening. [He was Honorary Commodore
of 500 (County Kent) RAF.]

The State visit of the Emperor of Ethiopia, Haile Selassie, followed.
Anthony had single-handedly backed Ethiopia against Mussolini in
the Abyssinia crisis at the League of Nations in 1935, so he held a
particular place in the hearts of the Ethiopians. There is still an
Anthony Eden Avenue in Addis, not as grand as its title, however.

There was a dinner at Buckingham Palace for the Emperor, where
the table was laden with flowers in flame and yellow and silver-gilt
objects – much admired by all. Anthony disappeared early on, but
eventually rescued me for a brief conversation with Princess Alice,*
who was always tremendously lively, her conversation punctuated
by laughter. When she was the Chancellor of the University of the
West Indies, even when aged ninety she would stand for hours in
heavy Chancellor's robes in the tropical heat.

Next day, an impressive ceremony in the Guildhall Library, where
the Emperor had on his brand-new Garter and a hat with lion's tails
instead of feathers. The enormous elephant's tusks, which were the
Emperor's present to the City of London, were let fall with a resound-
ing crash just as they were about to be borne in.

DIARY — 15 OCTOBER

We trail to the Mansion House for an interminable lunch.
Winston gets rather fidgety & very impatient as he wants a
Cabinet on Qemoy. Attlee goes to sleep & his lighted cigar falls

---

* Princess Alice, Countess of Athlone (1883–1981), was the granddaughter of
Queen Victoria.

onto the table cloth. Adeane [Private Secretary to the Queen] upsets a glass of royal blue liqueur all over the place. We listened for ten minutes to the Emperor speaking in Aramaic.

Then a dinner at the Ethiopian Embassy. Wonderful black footmen in red plush knee breeches & emerald plush swallow tail coats – pretty flowers & very good food. Another speech in Aramaic from the Emperor – to which the Queen interposes a 'thank you' occasionally. Afterwards Betty Salisbury said to Katharine Scarbrough, 'Didn't the Queen do that *wonderfully* & without anything written down.'

I managed to escape to the Old Vic to see the first night of *Love's Labour's Lost* with Ann and Ian Fleming and Alan Pryce-Jones. Cecil had done the scenery in topiary; the clothes were mainly black and white, but these were overlit. Afterwards we went round to see the stars – Ann Todd, Paul Rogers, etc. I couldn't enjoy Cecil's supper party afterwards because I wanted to go home early to be fit for the Garter tomorrow. Ian said he'd drop me home, so I left.

Anthony had been appointed Knight of the Garter – a rare honour for a Cabinet Minister when still in office. He had been offered it by the King after the war, but turned it down then as Churchill had refused it, so Anthony thought it inappropriate. It was awarded in recognition of his achievements on the international stage.

To the Palace in the morning, returning with the Garter and all the trappings. We were both very excited and the news was on the ticker tape immediately. The Queen shook him by the hand and said how pleased she was, and how she had wanted this for a long time. When we left there were lots of photographers there saying, 'Just one more, please, SIR Anthony.'

As the knights have reached a certain eminence in life, they tend to be fairly advanced in years. On formal occasions they wear satin breeches and silk stockings and, for some reason, the garter itself is difficult to tie on to the calf. The velvet robes are extremely heavy, decorated with bows on the shoulders and with the chain of the Order round the neck, terminating in 'The George' – an enamelled figure of St George. Some Georges are very old – it is the luck of the draw, as you get handed one for life. Being only twenty-six of them (including the Sovereign) at any one time, the new K G inherits the one from the last Knight who died. This outfit is completed by a flat medieval-style velvet cap decorated with a swaying white ostrich plume.

On the day of Anthony's installation four months later, weighed down as they were, most of the Knights managed the cobbled walk from the castle to St George's Chapel. Only Lord Stanhope had to go by car. It was a toss-up as to whom one sat next to at lunch in the Waterloo Chamber after the service. We went every year. After the Labour Party got in (1964) I was fascinated to see the Queen and Prime Minister Harold Wilson having such an enjoyable time together. Once I was next to Gerry Wellington – he who had designed Gerald Berner's folly at Faringdon. I thought he would be amused if I told him that I had discovered that the Knights were really a super witch's coven, twenty-six in number, because that was the equivalent of two covens. Far from being intrigued, he was furious. He also told me that the Garter was now 'too full of field marshals who did their own washing up'.

At another lunch I was between two Service Chiefs – Templer and Mountbatten. I was hardly able to say a word as Gerald Templer, Chief of the Imperial General Staff, spent the meal berating and teasing Dickie Mountbatten, First Sea Lord, for his behaviour during Suez.

CHAPTER 12

ABROAD

Anthony had to go to Paris immediately after his Garter ceremony for the concluding stages of the WEU (Western European Union) talks. There was the usual scrum at the airport and
Anthony was swept off without me. At cocktails at the US embassy
with Ambassador Douglas Dillon there was no '*Lady* Eden'. Foster
arrived at the end and praised Anthony, but Anthony told me that
Dulles had said, 'Is it true they've made you Prime Minister?' –
another of Foster's heavy jokes.

Cynthia and I went to the Comédie Française, arriving half an
hour late, as instructed, to be told it had started half an hour ago. It
was intolerably hot and long, with Madame de Margerie (wife of
French diplomat Roland de Margerie) scrunching sweets in cel-
lophane wrappings at the back of the box. But the unknown Molière –
Les Amants Magnifiques, which was simply a court masque – was
really enchanting to look at.

As usual we were staying at the British Embassy. In the morning
Anthony had thought he would not be able to go to the Galerie
Charpentier because the Saar talks (the only obstacle left at the
conference) were snarled up. I was talking to Grace Radziwill in the
Salon Vert when Anthony was suddenly free. So he and I, and Grace
and Tony Rumbold, walked down to the Charpentier to see the

exhibition of modern paintings. It was shut, but we got it opened. We had hoped to buy some of the paintings, but Anthony did not like any of those I had selected and – as so often – there was no time to settle on any others and I was glad he did not want any of the three Segonzacs.

During this visit Daisy Fellowes gave a lunch for me – Cynthia, Grace, Diana Cooper, Nancy Mitford, Gérard van der Kemp (Curator-in-Chief of the Château de Versailles), Fulco, Charles Mendl and so on. It was a lovely house, perfect of its kind. I noticed the way the ruched blinds are half drawn and lit in daylight. Lots of jokes and the most wonderful food in years: hot oysters, a large fish in flames (sticks of flaming charcoal under it), a turkey stained pink and stuffed with foie gras mixed with cream, and *coeur à la crème* with raspberries. At the end one did not feel in the least full. Immediately after this I was bidden to tea at the Hôtel Matignon given by Mme Mendès-France. I always found her charming and soft.

The dinner given by our embassy was not stylish. I began to think that dinners at Carlton Gardens were better done than anyone else's. Adenauer was there looking remarkably well – much fatter than when I had seen him last year. Mendès-France was next to me. He gave nothing away, either in character or information – except that he would reconstruct his government in a few days and cease to be Foreign Secretary. Afterwards, he and Adenauer disappeared immediately to continue struggling over the Saar question. I thought, here I am now, lying in bed at 1.30 in the morning, while below me on the next floor the shape of Europe for the coming decade is being decided.

Next day I had lunch with Mme Mendès-France in the charming Pavillon d'Amour at the end of the Matignon gardens, which were very autumnal, before returning to London.

DIARY – 25 OCTOBER

Off to the Italian embassy. I am between Manlio Brosio [Italian

Ambassador] and Peter Ustinov [actor, writer and comedian] at one of three round tables. Anthony at the Duke of Edinburgh's table with Vivien Leigh. Ustinov amusing. Interesting grand Italian food – never tasted that before.

After, saved from talking by Ustinov's imitations. Bed at 2 a.m. It had been an awful day. Ronnie Tree for a drink, and Anthony in and out trying to get his Garter on right.

DIARY – 5 DECEMBER

After the opening of Parliament on 30th there was a presentation to Winston in the West Hall – curiously unemotional both on the part of Winston and the assembled company. Winston's speech good, containing many phrases that will become old tags, e.g. about the lion and his roar.

One painful moment when the curtain concealing Sutherland portrait was drawn back and Winston turned to look at it with loathing, and he then said, 'This is a remarkable example of modern art,' whereupon the blimpish Tories let out a yell of laughter & Sutherland blushed.

On the 1st, we went to Anglo-German football in Wembley, which was great fun but too long. Again wintry sun in which we basked, wrapped up in rugs. When we stood for the anthems and the band played 'Deutschland über Alles', the Duke of Athlone muttered into his moustache, 'Such a pity this, all William's fault.' *

Anthony returned from more defence talks in Paris on 19 December and immediately fell ill. This put him out of action for the next day.

---

* Earl of Athlone (1874–1957): Kaiser Wilhelm II, the German monarch during the First World War, was his cousin by marriage. The Kaiser was a first cousin of his wife, Princess Alice, granddaughter of Queen Victoria.

Winston said on the telephone, 'We don't have time to have our meeting before Christmas now.' Anthony replied that he would be up the following day. Winston then agreed, in view of the impossibility of his Big Three meeting now, to reconsider dates and call a meeting for the day after with whoever Anthony wished. Anthony chose Bobbety, James Stuart, Harold, Harry Crookshank, Rab and Lord Woolton.

At the meeting next day there were more arguments about election dates, this being their veiled way of discussing when Winston should go.

Meanwhile Winston's message to Eisenhower asking for a Big Three meeting next year had been turned down categorically by Eisenhower.

Just before Christmas we gave a farewell dinner for the Massiglis, whom we were both very sorry to lose. They had been *en poste* in London since 1944 and we had both independently enjoyed their friendship and hospitality. The French were apt to leave their diplomats for much longer than we ever did. After Christmas at Rose Bower, we made a rare visit to Dorneywood, where Dag Hammarskjöld, General Secretary of the United Nations, came to lunch. Very Scandinavian.

Winston sulked and was standoffish with Anthony over the Christmas holiday and for some days after, but then his mood changed. Jock Colville told Tony Rumbold that he had suggested to Winston that he should go to Marrakesh for the holidays, but Winston had replied, 'No, if I'm going to be a dog in the manger, I'd better stay in the manger.'

DIARY – 26 JANUARY 1955

Rab to dinner. How self-important all politicians are. He said he has never believed before that Winston is going, but now he does. Winston said to him last night – he will be gone after the

Budget. Rab thinks the doctors may have warned him that he cannot take another session of the House.

Rab then dictated to Anthony what his Cabinet should be. Anthony played him along, which I suppose is his method of getting Rab to help. I find Rab curiously unnatural.

During the Commonwealth Conference that month there were the usual meetings, and dinners at No. 10 and at Buckingham Palace. Some leaders expressed anxiety about the uncertainty of Winston's retirement plans. Nehru was worried about the South-East Asia Treaty Organisation (SEATO),* which India as a 'non-aligned' nation had refused to join. Krishna Menon, his right-hand man and confidant, was looking splendid with his stick, white pants and smarmed-back hair.

Anthony was due to leave on 19 February for the inaugural SEATO Conference to be held in Bangkok where the member states gathered to discuss the defence of the Far East region.

DIARY — 2 FEBRUARY

Yesterday Anthony went to Winston and said, 'I don't know what to do about my journey – what are your plans?' Winston replied that he was going at Easter but wanted no one to know, and would like Anthony to say it was the summer so that he could tell the Queen quietly and have no fuss.

After the Commonwealth Conference we had gone to the Mountbattens at Broadlands for the weekend. Nehru and Madam Pandit were the only other guests. It was not a very exhilarating atmos-

---

* An organisation established under Western auspices as a South-East Asia version of NATO to provide collective security and contain Communism in the region, with headquarters in Bangkok. Members: United States, Britain, France, Australia, New Zealand, Pakistan, the Philippines and Thailand.

phere. I had expected a feeling of intimacy between the Mount-battens or at any rate between Edwina and Nehru. Instead, she seemed embarrassed and at a loss as to what to say to them or they to her. After tea we went up to our rooms – which were too cold, the bathwater was cold and there was no water by the bed. There were lots of menservants running around in navy-blue battledress with all their medal ribbons.

We were swept off after dinner to look at a film of Nehru's panda and India's Independence Day. The next day Dickie, all got up in suede riding boots, carried Anthony off to plant a beech tree, while I had a walk by the river and saw greenhouse walls with peaches on them. Dinner that night was the stickiest of all. It seemed as if every-one was holding back. The talk was of dialects, then Nehru showed us an Indian doll that wagged its head and wobbled its hips, and seemed pleased by it.

Anthony and Nehru had no talk at all, in spite of all the papers saying they were locked in consultation over Formosa. The trouble with the whole weekend was that one couldn't be frank with anyone, plus Dickie and Edwina were so pathologically anti-American.

DIARY – 14 FEBRUARY

Sir Horace [Evans – Anthony's doctor] came before dinner at my request, festooned with stars and orders on his way to some public dinner. He wouldn't hear of Anthony not being well enough to become PM, naturally.

Anthony went to dinner at No. 10 with Winston and Rab. Rab kept on saying to Anthony what a historic dinner it was. Dates were finally gone into. Winston haggled about being allowed to hear the Budget but Rab was firm about it and he gave in. Winston is going to Florence & Venice & intends to be back in good time for Anthony's installation as Knight of the Garter at St George's Chapel. This *really* looks like it.

Anthony has thought for a year now that we will run into trouble with our trade. Rab has never agreed and gone on making optimistic back-patting speeches. Now apparently the blizzard has started & everyone is alarmed. Anthony wonders if a snap election immediately after taking over may not be the best chance. He feels sure we will lose if we wait till the autumn.

On 17 February we had the visit of the Shah of Persia to cope with. While we were waiting in the hall two people came in. First, a man looking like the Shah, and his wife, so we bowed and curtsied but on closer inspection they proved to be Zahedi (the Ambassador) and a lady-in-waiting. Queen Soraya was very quiet and solemn. I did not enjoy the evening; the Shah was unforthcoming on every subject. After dinner I shovelled all the available men alongside the Queen, who became slightly more animated. I talked with Attlee, whose speech had become most indistinct.

The next day we lunched at Buckingham Palace. Queen Soraya seemed still ungracious and was possibly very shy. Many of the same people as the previous night appeared plus Harold Nicolson and Vita Sackville-West — Harold had served at the Tehran Legation in the 1920s. When I was talking to Winston afterwards, I mentioned that Queen Soraya had been told she couldn't have a child and was barren. Winston said, 'No seed of any sort is infertile. It is the method of communication that is sometimes at fault.' We were given a huge modern Persian carpet. We would rather have had a prayer mat two foot wide than this huge modern horror — one never did get given antiques.

*

Almost immediately we were off to the SEATO Conference in Bangkok. Anthony needed several advisers, so a lumbering propeller-driven plane called an Argonaut was allowed. I was therefore able to go too.

We believed that before our departure my uncle had, at their meeting on 14 February, finally committed to a firm date for his retirement. So, with the situation apparently stabilised, we set off on 19 February.

The first stop was Rome. We stayed in the huge, hideous embassy that had been occupied by the Nazis, with a twisting hill approach lined with palms and cacti like a very first-class hotel. Anthony had always disliked the building. He said the Gestapo had tortured people in the cellars. After the war we could have chosen any palazzo in Rome – the French snapped up the Farnese, the prettiest. We were fond of both Ashley and Virginia Clarke. The Ambassadress had always preferred dogs to children, hence the two huge brindle bulldogs, one of whom she disconcertingly called 'my son'. I made a lightning tour round the city, which I had never seen before – temples, arches and palaces all floodlit.

Flying over Alexandria to Cairo I saw the bright green of the huge Nile valley ending in the pink of the desert. We had to circle round because, as usual, the reception committee had not assembled below. Soft flaky desert and a very hot evening. There was a placard saying 'Welcome to Egypt' but was it for us?

DIARY – 20 FEBRUARY

Dinner at the embassy is late. Come into the drawing room to find Nasser already there. Great impression of health and strength. Terrifically broad and blooming. Very brown face and black hair.

I am not next to him at dinner, unfortunately, being between Sir Ralph Stevenson and a general called Amir, and Nasser next to Lady Stephenson to whom he talks merrily all through, shouting across to the General, 'We are talking about your son and mine.' 'Yours is the best,' the General quickly says with a smirk. The General is thirty-five, has never been out of Egypt, is rather inscrutable and very polite with very indifferent English.

Anthony came up late having had what he thought was a good talk with Nasser, except regarding the Turco-Iraq pact [which became the Baghdad Pact], upon which Nasser was very bitter.

It turned out that Nasser had been deeply offended by the whole evening. He had come to the embassy, not Anthony to him. He had on the wrong clothes – as it was the Egyptian President coming to dinner, the men had changed into black ties. 'What elegance,' he said afterwards. 'It was made to look as if we were beggars and they were Princes.' Finally, he was offended by Anthony speaking to him in Arabic.

DIARY – 21 FEBRUARY

Fly over Pyramids which from the air are very disappointing because they are suburban. They bear the same relationship to the landscape as gasworks on the edge of a town. Fly several hours over Saudi Arabian desert. Changes surprising: white sand, then dunes and wadis to red sand, each change suddenly in a straight frontier.

Land at Bahrain immediately after lunch and taken off to the Sheikh, who is waiting to meet us in front of a small white barn with rugs laid down on the sand from the car to the door. Inside, more rugs and ranged round the wall numerous armchairs & sofas from Maples. We all seat ourselves and half an inch of coffee is handed round followed by half an inch of tea with condensed milk, followed by a dosing of rosewater into my lap – my silk dress ruined.

The Sheikh & Anthony exchange flowery remarks through the interpreter & then we leave them alone so that Anthony can tick him off for something or other.

Think of what Bahrain is like today.

We only touched down for the night at Karachi, Pakistan's capital, and were escorted from the plane to the Governor-General's house by a smart young ADC. Ever polite, Anthony made conversation by asking for the latest news on the Test cricket. 'I'm afraid polo's my game, sir,' came the reply. We dined that night with Mohammed Ali, the Prime Minister. Too many courses and the pudding was made of sweetened carrots covered in gold leaf. The Prime Minister did a lot of shouting and eating simultaneously.

At Calcutta to refuel, there was only time to pile into a car and drive to the outskirts of the city and back, past row upon row of shacks with many kids and goats and little grey cows. On the way back we saw charming but derelict nineteenth-century gentlemen's villas with lakes, and also Warren Hastings's house and, of course, the Eden gardens. When George Eden, Lord Auckland, was Governor there in the 1830s his two sisters accompanied him. Emily was the author of *Letters from India* and *Up the Country* – excellent – also *The Semi-Detached Couple* and a sequel, all written in a pseudo Jane Austen style. It was she who planned the gardens and her watercolours are still in the museum there.

Finally we got to Bangkok, where we were greeted by a prince with tuberose garlands. After I had been for a few days in Bangkok, where they seemed to be busy filling in the canals with concrete, and I had sat next to every high commissioner present at banquets, I asked the Thai authorities if it might be possible for me to pay a brief visit to Cambodia. Ever polite, they said yes – but then they thought all the wives should go too. So at 6 a.m. a gaggle of bored Philippines and Malaysians in tight skirts and high heels, plus Janet Dulles, assembled to board an old Dakota. Janet read her paperback over dramatic jungle, rivers and mountains to Siem Reap.

We landed on a red dust airstrip in the jungle in a mist and were met by lots of disgruntled ambassadresses brought from the capital, Phnom Penh, to meet their ministers' wives.

Angkor Wat was approached on a causeway across the water with children splashing in it. Lonely and intact in those days with its serried rows of statues it gave an impression of blackness looming up. A great smell of bats. I liked being right on top with a view over the forest.

Then driven back to the huge hotel in the jungle run by White Russians and full of French big game hunters in camouflage dress talking about whatever they had shot. We were shown into separate suites to freshen up. Mrs Dulles emerged from her room and said with animation, 'How did they know that Pears was my favourite soap?'

At lunch we were incongruously given chicken *à l'estragon* in the middle of the jungle. No nap afterwards because of the noise of the Cambodian battalions practising bugling.

After the other wives had departed again for Bangkok I set off with a bearded man who turned out to be the ex-French cultural attaché and who had settled there. He was an ideal companion – knowledgeable and discreet. We visited a temple with banyan trees twisting round the arches and monkeys chattering, then on to Bayu temple. As evening came I stood at Bayu on the upper platform watching the avenue of huge serene faces carved into the rock gleaming at all angles in the sunset.

At dinner at the Frenchman's that night the Cambodian Governor of the district became very relaxed and told me the US was no good. Money needed, not propaganda – 'Why doesn't Anthony help to get this going?' A bell tolled in the middle of the night and made all the animals in the forest chatter and howl. They stopped the second the bell stopped – rather uncanny. Then the Cambodian bugles started.

The French ex-consul and his wife and the Cambodian Governor came to see me off. The plane was late, since they hadn't been able to find the airstrip. I had a great rush straight from Bangkok airport to the PM's wife's lunch at 12.30, then had to wait till 1.30, because the Philippine wives were changing their clothes after shopping. I would have liked to change mine after my journey. Finally they came mincing and twittering in, a bunch of tartan butterflies. When I returned to the embassy I found the men at lunch eating meatloaf, so I joined them for coffee.

Afterwards I dragged myself off to the chief site of Bangkok, the Emerald Buddha, set in an enclosed courtyard with temples dominated by the palace, which looked like a minor casino in a French provincial town. Extraordinary offerings in front of the Buddha consisted of two alabaster weeping cherubs, two grandfather clocks and two cheap cheval mirrors. John Rayner, on Malcolm MacDonald's staff in Singapore and attending the conference (MacDonald was Commissioner General for South-East Asia), insisted that the Bangkok temples 'were far superior to Angkor Wat – which everyone went to see'. This was obviously going to be the clever opinion in future.

Dinner that night was at the PM's – the house saturated by green floodlights, fountains changing colour in the garden, the band labelled 'SEATO' soaring away. Flashlights went off without ceasing the entire evening. Afterwards the usual Siamese dances, about which Dulles complained to me. I agreed with Foster that the dances were always the same. But would he have said that also about *Swan Lake* perhaps?

We then reversed our direction and headed homewards, taking Malcolm MacDonald in our plane as far as Singapore. His residence there was very Camberley – rather sad that it could look so unMalayan. Built by a rich Scotsman, it had perfect lawns and bedding-out, and was surrounded by other villas the same.

We flew up to Kuala Lumpur where Anthony wanted to see how the war was progressing. British troops were under constant attack from Malayan Communist insurgents fighting a jungle war of independence. Each time I go to KL there is a ferocious thunderstorm. In spite of this, it was thought I should pay a call on the local Sultana. She had very sunken jaws, with rimless pince-nez, and was swathed in beautiful white chiffon. I was led into a throne room through a hall full of toy cars 'from Selfridges' and offered striped blancmange. I love the eccentricities of the East.

Anthony spent a day visiting the troops and came back very happy and red as a lobster. At the reception and dinner for us that night the Chief Secretary was very pessimistic about the situation. He said no one knew who was a Communist, that Chinese boys disappeared to China to be trained without their parents knowing, and the Malays to Indonesia with whom they have racial and social ties. During the entire visit an enormous armoured car bristling with Malays and tommy guns came everywhere to protect us.

We were feeling very hot the next day so Anthony, Tony Rumbold and I were driven six miles out in the jungle to a pool with rather murky water. The troops encircled the water and watched, bayonets fixed. Just as we finished bathing a tropical storm broke out. We sheltered under a small thatched lean-to to have our picnic, getting wetter and wetter. The chocolate biscuits melted; what a curious choice for a tropical picnic anyway.

After standing dripping for ages we dashed for the cars, soaked through. As Anthony splashed along in dripping shorts, hair over his eyes and a towel round his shoulders, all the Malayan sentries guarding us came to attention and he had to salute back. We were helpless with laughter.

Glad to be out of Kuala Lumpur, we flew over solid jungle to Rangoon – drier and with a breeze blowing. Under an awning Mrs Aung San was waiting, very shy and soft-spoken and apparently a great figure there. Her husband, Aung San, was the man who led the Burmese to independence. I was taken off to the Great Pagoda, whose gold point one could see for miles in the town – a mêlée of children, puppies, figures lying about. I bought some paper parasols but the steward on the Argonaut complained they were full of flies.

Simon, Anthony's eldest son, had joined the RAF and was killed a month before his twenty-first birthday, almost as soon as he arrived in Burma in the last days of the war. Anthony said the death of a child is the worst death to endure. He had never been able to see his grave. He had given instructions that news of Simon's death should not be mentioned by the press as he had not wanted it to influence the vote in the 1945 General Election.

DIARY – 2 MARCH

Anthony and I left to visit Simon's grave. I got some badly wilting flowers for him. Drive through mango forests for a long time. The cemetery is mournful, very arid and many bodies are still being moved there from temporary mountain cemeteries, so there are mounds of earth everywhere. The graves are distressing too, just a leaden plaque in the earth.

Poor Simon's is a temporary cross made of tin with the names of his crew on it too, as they could not distinguish the bodies. Anthony very moved.

Leaving for India that evening we flew over the mountains where Simon's plane had crashed in the monsoon. When I visited Burma some years later Simon's grave had been moved to a war cemetery in the suburbs of Rangoon and a depressed Burmese guardian said the lead plaques were being stolen all the time. It was horrifying and I was glad Anthony never saw this.

Arriving in Delhi at night we had a very warm welcome from Nehru standing on the tarmac and stayed with him at his official residence. He was a shy host, but we should have remembered his kindness and good manners. The house was 'dry' – following Indian official protocol. On opening what we thought was a wardrobe in our bedroom there was a complete bar containing every sort of drink. The next day, while Anthony and Nehru talked, Mrs Gandhi, his daughter, was delegated to take me sightseeing. She was a reluctant hostess. I liked Nehru – he had a dimension to him that other public figures did not usually have.

Years later, when we were briefly at Chequers after Anthony had resigned, Nehru rang up from London to ask if he could come down to say goodbye to his old colleague. He arrived bearing all sorts of gifts – a gesture of genuine friendship.

DIARY – 3 MARCH, DELHI

We woke to find men in scarlet turbans with porridge, fishballs and goodness knows what, and from our terrace a view of an English garden, lawns, hollyhocks, roses, sweet peas, also kumquat in fruit & flower.

Dinner at the Viceroy's palace, now the President's house. Everything exactly as it was in the old days. We walk up the flights of huge stairs which are lined by guards in scarlet and gold – all presenting arms. Indians playing safe with the meal – mulligatawny soup, fish cakes and a crème brûlée. Nothing to drink.

I sat between Nehru and the Chinese Ambassador who speaks no English and doesn't wish to converse through his interpreter. Nehru speaks at dinner. He is very nice about Anthony and about British relations with India. Anthony

Downing Street

Climbing the steps to a function, as usual. AE with his detective.

AE speaking for Charles Curran at Uxbridge during the election of May, 1955.

Election triumph.

The village fête at Ellesborough (nearby Chequers), the vicar on my right.

At Winchester, AE and the Queen are laughing at something on the left, and Prince Philip and I are laughing at the Queen laughing. The two Generals don't see the joke.

Her Majesty and Prince Philip talk with the Prime Minister and Lady Eden and

Geneva Summit 1955

With Mamie Eisenhower and Mme Faure ('Ah, voilà les photographes!'). Mamie and I are wearing gloves for Mamie's boat trip on Lake Geneva.

Opening 'Sixty Years of Film' exhibition.

Line-up at Balmoral. With the Queen, AE and Prince Philip.

A weekend at Broadlands. Dickie (Mountbatten) and Edwina chat
to each other while AE concentrates on official papers.

The Russians arrive to stay. Khrushchev (left) and Bulganin at Chequers.

With Rudi Bing, founder of the
Edinburgh Festival, at Chequers.

All passion spent. Max Beaverbrook
and AE are reconciled at last and pose
carefully at Chequers.

Winston at Chequers: his usual pose.

AE and his old mate, Bob Menzies, the Australian Prime Minister, at Chequers during the Commonwealth Conference.

Albert Schweitzer and AE at No. 10. Nobel prize-winner Schweitzer was a great cultivator of Prime Ministers.

The Suez Crisis

Iraq's Prince Faisal, with the Prince Regent behind, bids farewell to AE. News broke of Nasser's nationalisation of the Suez Canal during a dinner in their honour.

French Premier Guy Mollet shaking hands with AE on the steps at No 10. Looking on are Foreign Ministers Christian Pineau and Selwyn Lloyd (left).

Relaxing at Chequers in mid-crisis. Chairs courtesy of the Chequers Trust.

Making the best of it. AE with John Foster Dulles.

The cast of Suez – the head men. (From left) CIGS General Sir Gerald Templer, Air Marshal Sir William Dickson, AE back to camera, General Sir Charles Keightley and First Sea Lord Mountbatten.

replies very well. Both of them are really in the same world position – floating neutrals, Nehru conditioned by his difficulties with the East and Anthony by his dependence upon America.

Anthony also addressed the members of Congress after our tea there – also well done. I liked the Vice-President, Sir Sarvepalli Radhakrishnan, an excellent speaker, philosopher and Fellow of All Souls.

We were touched & impressed by our welcome here which was significant and genuine. Warm goodbyes from Nehru who clasps my hands with fervour. This is the only country I want to come back to.

And so I did, again and again.

Arriving in Baghdad, I liked the oil lamps as a flare-path at the airport and the Arab horsemen guarding the approaches. We stayed briefly at the embassy for Anthony to consult with Michael Wright, the Ambassador, whom I remembered as First Secretary at the Paris embassy before the war and as a rather sedate senior participant in Fitz's night-club forays. From the Baghdad embassy I can only remember noticing the horrible colour of the Tigris river, and the fact that if you wanted anything done to your clothes a man in a turban, instead of a woman, appeared to help. The muezzin calling from a dozen minarets meant no sleep that night.

We went to dinner with the King, a small, polite and intelligent boy. I had Nuri es-Said,* the Prime Minister, the other side of me – clever and interesting, and a great friend of Anthony's, but difficult to get to grips with because he was so deaf. The King gave me a

---

* Prime Minister of Iraq since 1930, a conservative pro-Western Arab and ally of Britain. He resisted the growing influence of Arab nationalism in the region.

cornflower for Winston in an envelope – the Harrow connection. Later they were both killed in the most brutal way imaginable. When General Abdul Kassem overthrew the regime in a military coup in 1958, the King and all his household were murdered, and Nuri was captured and shot. His and the Crown Prince's bodies were then dragged through the streets.

When we arrived back in England, poor Anthony found himself on the roundabout yet again.

DIARY – 8 MARCH, LONDON

Harold Macmillan came to lunch full of advice – they all are – about Cabinet making. We dine at Downing Street. Winston dressed in red velvet with brocade jacket and red slippers. He seems in top form with lots of jokes about his going. They now plan to go to Syracuse and the Salisburys are going too. Betty is dragging Bobbety along. The Moncktons travelled all the way to Taormina to try out the hotel for Winston.

DIARY – 10 MARCH

I go to Downing Street in the afternoon to look it over. Clemmie very animated and domesticated showing me around. I am a little disappointed in the upstairs or bedroom floor. It is so very shabby and dirty. Also there are so many spare rooms.

DIARY – 11 MARCH

Come back from the Ideal Home Exhibition to find poor Anthony in full crisis. Eisenhower is sending a message to say would Winston meet him in Paris in May to save the Paris Agreement [setting up the WEU]. Anthony says anyway the visit wouldn't help in the least even if he is substituted for Winston.

DIARY — 12 MARCH

In the middle of lunch at Dorneywood a messenger comes from Chequers with a letter from Winston. He says Eisenhower's message has changed everything and he isn't retiring, that it is momentous etc. etc. Anthony justifiably nettled.

Anthony meanwhile rings Ivone Kirkpatrick who says he hears from Montague Brown that Clemmie and Christopher are battling with Winston at Chequers.*

---

* Ivone Kirkpatrick: Permanent Under-Secretary at the Foreign Office; Anthony Montague Browne: Churchill's Secretary; Christopher Soames: Churchill's PPS and son-in-law, married to his daughter Mary.

CHAPTER 13

DOWNING STREET

C̲hurchill's resignation date remained uncertain until the end. Frustration among Anthony and his Cabinet colleagues was reaching breaking point.

On 8 March during lunch at Downing Street, Churchill told Eden alone that he intended definitely to resign on 5 April. Then came a telegram from Eisenhower suggesting that he, Churchill and Adenauer, the German Chancellor, should meet in Paris in early May when Eisenhower might consider plans for a meeting with the new Russian regime.

Churchill seized on this new opportunity and withdrew his 5 April resignation offer. In Cabinet that day, Eden made clear his view that the telegram presaged no change in relations with Russia.

*   *   *

DIARY — 14 MARCH

Anthony came back for the Cabinet followed shortly after by Bobbety. It sounded awful. Winston completely unmoving. Finally Anthony burst out on a rather personal note, it seems, saying this was the second time Winston had given a date and all arrangements had been made and then he had broken his word. Bobbety said, when he was kept 'after school' Winston said he hoped Bobbety was still coming on the holiday in Sicily with him. Bobbety said that would be very nice. Winston then said, 'It isn't against your principles to fly on holiday with a Prime Minister?' – showing that he does not intend to give in.

*　　*　　*

When discussion that day had turned to a possible June meeting with the Russians, Eden had turned to Churchill to ask slowly, 'Does that mean, Prime Minister, that the arrangements you have made with me are at an end?' His Cabinet colleagues (with the exception of Harold Macmillan) knew nothing of the new date. Lord Salisbury asked for clarification, but Churchill avoided a reply. Eden was vindicated when a further telegram arrived that very day stating that neither Eisenhower nor Dulles would participate in a Four Power meeting with the Russians.

The colleagues were in uproar.

*　　*　　*

DIARY — 15 MARCH

Rab spoke to [David] Eccles last night and Anthony saw Lloyd George today. That would make Rab, Harold Macmillan, Bobbety, Harry [Crookshank], Lloyd George, Eccles who would certainly resign, possibly more.

Cabinet: Winston has given in. He's now going as arranged before.

*　　*　　*

But it dragged on. When Churchill heard that Marshal Bulganin, the new Russian President, had spoken positively about a Four Power summit, he told the Queen at his audience at Buckingham Palace on 29 March that he was once again thinking of putting off his resignation.

*　　*　　*

Anthony had come back late for lunch. Rab came pale-faced, said that he had been fetched to No. 10 at 9.45 by a distraught Jock. My uncle announced that the international situation was so bad that he couldn't resign after all.

Ironically, this was the day of our dinner party for the Churchills with my friend Alex Korda, Nin Ryan, Anna Hägglöf and the Chauvels. My aunt rang up to say she had bad arthritis again and couldn't come; Lady Korda couldn't come because of her agoraphobia. Winston rang to say he had been delayed at Buckingham Palace and would be late. Anthony interpreted this pessimistically. However, at dinner Winston turned round and said to me, 'How did you like Downing Street?' I said I was sorry that my visit got into the press. 'Oh well,' he replied and then went on to discuss the bedrooms. Later he talked of being in Venice in June.

* * *

The next day, 30 March, Churchill informed the Queen that he intended to resign in five days' time. At 6.30 p.m. he called Eden and Butler to the Cabinet Room to tell them that he was definitely going and Anthony would succeed him. This had been the tenth and final time he had said he would resign.

* * *

DIARY — 30 MARCH

Everything all right again. Winston said we had been so nice to him last night. Dinner at the Aldriches for General Gruenther [Supreme Allied Commander US forces in Europe]. Winston says to me, Anthony has been wise, far-seeing, always kept to his principles and is, in addition, a very charming character. A wonderful Latour 1929. Senator Cooper drank it in one gulp — like vodka.

*   *   *

Arrangements went ahead for Churchill's departure, including hosting a dinner for the Queen and the Duke of Edinburgh at No. 10 on 4 April.

*   *   *

DIARY — 5 APRIL

Last night was Winston's dinner for the Queen.

I sat between Harold Macmillan & Oliver Lyttelton. Oliver said Anthony would have trouble with Harold at the Foreign Office. He was one minute a member of the Whig aristocracy and the next a simple crofter's son. He would be full of spectacular ideas, out of hand, whereas at the Treasury the dead weight of officialdom would absorb him. Rab on the other hand ought to be got away from the Treasury officials and would be good as gold at the Foreign Office.

Afterwards Randolph comes up, huge, pale, sweating, and says, 'I suppose you know I'm against the new regime.' I say, I guessed so, as he still had the integrity to keep away from me when he was vilifying Anthony, but that I was sad that he placed our friendship lower than the pleasure he derived from a cheap campaign in clubs.

The handover was on 6 April.

DIARY — 6 APRIL

Queen sends for Anthony at 11 a.m. A warm spring day. He says they sat around talking of this and that until he thought she wasn't going to ask him to form a government at all. So he said, 'Well, ma'am' and she said, 'I suppose I ought to be asking you to form a government.' (!)

After lunch we go off to the House. The new Mrs Herbert

Morrison [second wife of the Shadow Foreign Secretary] is full of chatter to me.

The Peers' Gallery very full. Floor of the House packed. When Anthony comes in they all cheer and someone shouted, 'If you do it louder you may get a job.' Attlee makes a good speech about Winston and Anthony. Then Walter Elliot gets up and says Anthony must be the only man who was tipped when young to be Prime Minister who has in fact done so. Everyone laughs nastily as Walter was such a one.

Anthony gets up and the House is very quiet. He speaks without notes and really does it perfectly. Sounds reflective & true. Fleur Cowles, Fulke & Raimund come round for drinks. Anthony sticks his head round the door and is trapped. Mrs Cowles maintained that she had told Nasser where he got off & wrote all Selwyn's speeches for him at UNO. Not a good word for Mr Nutting [Minister of State at the Foreign Office] though.

We spent Easter at Chequers. I never liked Chequers. It had been spoilt by Sir Reginald Blomfield in 1909, though there were still some traces of the beautiful original brown/black panelling in the Private Secretary's office and the so-called Prime Minister's wife's room was pleasant – the panelling, which was not original, was painted white. The glory of the place, however, was the peerless park; the lie of the land and the perfect planning was a joy to look on from the windows. Neville Chamberlain, I believe, was the last, perhaps the only, Prime Minister who was an arborealist. I was distressed when the Chequers Trust started felling what I thought was an unnecessary number of trees. I found out that in my aunt's day, she always ordered the food, chose the chintzes and did the garden. I had at first misunderstood the situation.

*

This is curious for us. One does feel rather dizzy & insecure as if on a high peak. There seems to be nothing but clouds and space all round us.

Anthony opens his new red box [previously, at the FO they were black]. Nothing but two papers at the bottom, one about a plaque for Queen Mary and the other about the Primrose League. We think of Harold and his bursting boxes of papers and of all the activity at the Foreign Office this weekend with everything going on.

Winston had a dream: he went to sleep one afternoon. When he woke up he said to Jock, 'I have had a dream and everything is settled. Feel completely calm about it now' – and from then on he never wavered.

Another version, which is Betty's, says he woke up and said – 'he was ineffectual and weak', and Jock said: 'but you have always maintained the opposite' – and Winston replied 'I don't mean Anthony, I mean Melbourne'.

We were asked to stay at Windsor.

Anthony made his broadcast yesterday. The Queen told him that Prince Charles insisted on staying up to hear it, but was presumably none the wiser. The evening is broken by a comic film after dinner. Much amusement over the sealyhams getting fleas.

Next day, service in the private chapel. We slept in a very Victorian room, originally George IV, full of pictures of Prince Leopold. After lunch sit in a huge bay window to be stared at by a large crowd while two rival bands play below.

Then we all pile into two station wagons with the corgis &

sealyhams and the royal children and go to Frogmore, a pretty Georgian house furnished in charming early Victorian fashion with a well-clipped garden full of narcissi, cherries & a serpentine lake, also the Mausoleums. The Queen Mother kindly shows me Queen Victoria's Mausoleum – good of its sort, Byzantine with enormous over-life-size marble effigies.

It is decided we have a picnic. Excitement, everyone fetches chairs. Anthony sits on a cushion. When he moves to help someone, the Prince sits on it. The Queen tells him to move, he refuses, she tells him again, because it is the Prime Minister's cushion and he is tired. The Prince says, 'I'm tired too. I've been running about' and he doesn't budge. When he refuses to eat his food because he hasn't washed his hands, the Queen Mother says, 'Oh I do understand the feeling. Put some water in a saucer for him.' Prince Philip is meanwhile going around the lake in a flat-bottomed punt.

After dinner, tour the castle looking at roomfuls of van Dycks, Holbeins, Rubens. Then, too late, come to 200 Leonardo drawings. Lord Plunket [the Queen's Equerry] is very knowledgeable.

*   *   *

Almost immediately after taking office, Eden decided on the General Election date in May. With Budget Day in the offing, he deferred any major Cabinet changes, though Macmillan was promoted to the Foreign Office.

*   *   *

DIARY – 19 APRIL, BUDGET DAY

Rab came to lunch yesterday – very énervé. Harold continues 'viewy'. [After a Cabinet one day Winston had said wearily to Anthony, 'Harold is very viewy.'] Still large crowds outside

No. 10. They even clap me. I have my chauffeur now but not my car, yet. The House of Commons very nasty now the election has been announced.

DIARY — 27 APRIL, DOWNING STREET

Winston has decided to return prematurely from Sicily, driven back by boredom and bad weather. Harold is so exhausted by two weeks at the Foreign Office that he has gone to the country.

I left No. 1 Carlton Gardens as clean as I could manage for the Macmillans. I was glad to be at No. 10. I never liked Carlton Gardens with its pitch-dark hall and sunless rooms. But Anthony didn't like the large mansard bedrooms with their sloping ceilings, on the top floor at No. 10, and the fact that the main first-floor rooms were full of government furniture and pictures.

Mrs Donnan, my secretary, and I had slaved for three days while the furniture very very slowly came in. I succumbed long before she did. In the early weeks I had people in once or twice – Anthony's old friends, the Palmellas, now at the Portuguese embassy, the Mountbattens, Ivan Moffat, David Brooke (Fulke Warwick's elder son), the Flemings etc. It raised my spirits.

I thought No. 10 a lovely house to live in. The jerry-built façade gave way at the rear to a well-proportioned rectangular building. I was told it had been the Bavarian embassy, bought by Walpole.

Nothing could be more beautiful than the situation of the building. My sitting room had a wondrous view of St James's Park and, from another angle, Horse Guards. From our bedroom windows at night we could look straight on to Wren's façade, floodlit and beyond, Nelson and the Duke of York – pale, cobwebby figures on their pedestals in the dimmer light. To the left the classical frontage of Carlton House Terrace in the street lights. By day the lovely plane trees of St James's Park, shaded with blue. In Horse Guards itself there seemed to be a perpetual parade. The Pakistani police in flowing Scottish plaid, bagpipes whining, and a goat with gold-tipped horns, or the Arab Legion in white ducks, singing as they formed fours.

There were three Walpole reception rooms on the first floor: the White Drawing Room, the Red Room, and the yellow Pillared Room; then a small square ante-room and finally the large Soane dining room. The White Room had been used by my aunt as her own sitting room and had comfortable sofas and a desk, so I used it in the same way. I was delighted to find two Turners in my room. The Red Room had odds and ends of furniture allegedly belonging to Clive of India. The ante-room we used as a dining room, with adjacent kitchen. The Soane room was for the official sixty-seater banquets, with the antisocial U-shaped table.

I had hoped, for a relatively small sum of money, to be allowed to emulate the French official residencies by decorating and furnishing them in their correct period – that of Walpole and Soane. Some flock damask wallpaper and one or two Kent side tables would have been all that was needed for the two state rooms. I visited Houghton, Walpole's house in Norfolk, now lived in by my family's friends the Cholmondeleys, to get an idea of the colours and feel of the period, and I visited the Soane Museum in Lincoln's Inn Fields to get an idea of the eccentric colours Soane would have used in the state dining room.

Then came the Credit Squeeze and that was the end of that project. It would have been an economy, because no subsequent wives could have objected to the décor. After that, Downing Street sank into the marsh on which Mr Downing the speculator built it, and the rebuild it needed changed it for good and laid it open to the fluctuating tastes of various inhabitants – the usual English compromise.

The garden was pleasant, with a magnolia and cherries and narcissus and dicentra in the flower beds. We did not use the garden much – though I filled it with regale lilies – because it was overlooked by three government offices.

At No. 10 I decided the entertaining should be less the usual official stuff – different caterers, different florists. At one banquet Dulles turned to his neighbour and said, 'I bet you £5 I know what we're going to eat.' He lost his bet.

Within a few weeks we were launched into a General Election. This was a new experience for me. We had a hectic schedule, often fitting in four or five towns on a single day. Everywhere I had my first astonishing experience of large crowds with people lining the routes and almost no heckling at meetings. Nottingham on the first day, where only one small voice asked about the cost of living, then we piled into cars followed by the press to Newark and Doncaster, where we were greeted by more enthusiastic crowds and given tea and biscuits in a judge's front drive.

Next day, we set off in a small and uncomfortable car – Anthony having changed us from the Humber Pullman and the local MP's Rolls-Royce of yesterday – to catch the train from Sheffield, passing through beautiful country after Gloucester along the banks of the Severn. At Cardiff the meeting of 6,000 people was in a huge stadium. The hotel was freezing cold. There was at that time a fiendish system in some hotels of shilling-in-the-slot electric fires, which didn't help after a long day.

Through the Cotswolds – Cheltenham and Stroud, where the whole town came out and every street was jammed – then the Vale of Evesham with the Malvern Hills large and blue on the horizon, and more and more trees everywhere. By nightfall we finally arrived at Anthony's constituency, Warwick, rather frayed, with just time for a bath and a snack of food, and off to the adoption meeting, again a wild success with two overflow meetings and great enthusiasm. As a result, Anthony began to feel that things would be all right.

The next day at Atherton, a mining and hat-making town, the audience was full of cloth caps all of whom listened enthusiastically. Anthony got presented with an Eden hat – a black Homburg that had been named after him in the 1930s, when he always wore one. On to Wolverton and Bletchley, and still no heckling. People had been waving and cheering along the entire route.

Then we moved on to four or five meetings in London – Woolwich and Battersea and so on – with large crowds of factory workers everywhere in spite of drenching rain. One heckler was screaming 'Scoundrel' and 'Traitor', and he was set upon by infuriated spectators. At the next place, parading banners, which said 'Phoney Tony'. Anthony was always very jovial with the hecklers. The police were told the Socialists would try to break up some meetings – Anthony said he betted not and it was perfectly quiet.

DIARY — 17 MAY, 10TH DAY, GLASGOW

Attlee had been the day before and St Andrew's Hall was two-thirds full. For Anthony, the hall was jam-packed and there were three overflow meetings of several hundred each. Anthony spoke for nearly an hour to a rapt audience. One woman shouted just as he was about to begin, 'A full house' and everyone laughed. After 20 minutes or so of prepared stuff for the benefit of the press, Anthony launched out impromptu.

Glasgow was a turning point. I thought it an important occasion because it was the first time Anthony spoke as leader and branched right off into his own brand of Conservatism – first in the manner in which he spoke of such things as slum clearance, beating the Socialists at their own game. Second, about the colonies and how we must allow them self-government and retain their friendship. Third, when he said slanging matches would do no one any good – a crack at the old Conservatives who are continually calling Attlee and Bevan names. The audience applauded thunderously at this.

The next day there were several open meetings. Most remarkable were the people who all hung out of the windows waving, and lorry drivers out of their lorries, and factory workers lined the road. During our peregrinations the car came to a halt in a strange district and we were surrounded by men staring curiously at us. I asked where we were and was told 'the Gorbals'. I had a frisson of apprehension – then they recognised the person in the car and, smiling, they banged on the bonnet and the windows. Extraordinary. They were all going to vote Labour, but they supported *Anthony*.

At this point I thought I should interfere. Anthony wrote in his memoirs, 'My wife immensely eased the burden of the campaign. While she has no love of politics, or perhaps because of this, she was a firm, if sympathetic critic. More important still, she understood how to limit the strain by reducing the number of personal engagements outside the meeting halls, and so on the whole I got through in better physical shape than I had expected.'

DIARY – 21 MAY, 14TH DAY

After 3 days of hell with far too many people buzzing round him with expert advice, Anthony ignores them all and speaks for 15 minutes on TV without any cutaways or props or distractions of any sort. He is a complete success, thus proving that none of the experts knows anything yet about the technique of television.*

---

* This was 'by common consent the greatest *tour de force* among the television broadcasts', according to historian David Butler in his study of the election: 'Without any tricks or visual devices he talked directly to the viewers for a quarter of an hour, speaking in a genuinely extempore fashion . . . He won universal praise for the way in which he managed to convey a sense of calmness, optimism, decency and compassion.' (David Butler, *The British General Election of 1955*, Macmillan, 1955, p. 61.)

Back to the Midlands and a meeting in the Rag Market in Birmingham. Anthony was sure it would be rowdy. So were the officials, who packed the platform and arranged a protective front in the audience. It was the first time the Conservatives had had a meeting in the Rag Market in living memory, and the first time any party other than Labour had had one since Joseph Chamberlain. The Rag Market was an open – not a ticket – meeting. Anthony had an audience of 12,000. There was a trickle of rather feeble, but good-natured, heckling.

Before the result at Warwick and Leamington, the Opposition, while not expecting to win, were certain Anthony's majority would be slashed. They were openly ungracious at the result.

Even a year later, in July 1956 when Anthony visited Lancashire, during a solid hour's drive the route was still lined with waving people everywhere and flowers were being thrown into the car.

*   *   *

The General Election result was a Conservative victory and a personal triumph for Eden. Fighting on a platform of the strong economy, the creation of a property-owning democracy and Eden's reputation in foreign affairs, 'Working for Peace' (as the poster proclaimed) – the Conservatives increased their overall majority from seventeen to sixty – the first government to increase their majority in nearly a hundred years. Eden's own majority at Warwick and Leamington went up by a then massive 4,000, and he achieved a higher popularity rating after a hundred days in office – 68 per cent – than any other post-war prime minister.

*   *   *

After the election, one of our first visitors was the German Chancellor, Konrad Adenauer, who came on 17 June for three days on the way back from America and told Anthony that Eisenhower wasn't looking forward at all to the forthcoming Geneva Summit. Ike certainly fulfilled this warning.

Then Nehru came to Chequers in July on his way back from Russia. Anthony went to the airport to meet him and while I was having a bath a huge Navy helicopter came swirling down, making the most infernal noise. This was the practice landing in case Nehru needed it. Nehru, Mrs Indira Gandhi and Madam Pandit, Nehru's sister and Indian High Commissioner to Britain, arrived tired but very happy. Nehru was completely relaxed with us by then. The Attlees came to lunch but Nehru didn't seem to have anything to say to Attlee during their visit. He was in even better spirits next day and gave me his ivory-tipped baton made of sandalwood, which he always carried, when I admired it. Krishna Menon, who was usually a malign influence – accentuated by his wild eyes and wild hair – seemed less tortured and offered me some fans of sandalwood.

Nehru told Anthony he thought the Russians really did not want war now because they were full of internal projects they would like to carry out. Mrs Gandhi said she never had a bath during the whole Russia trip. There was always only one bathroom, and her father used it.

*   *   *

At the Four Power Summit Conference in Geneva in July, European leaders and President Eisenhower met the new Russian leaders, Marshal Nikolai Bulganin and Nikita Khrushchev. The discussion focused on German unification, European security and disarmament in the nuclear age.

Eisenhower was indeed a reluctant participant. When he proposed an 'open skies' plan for mutual aerial inspections of military facilities as a device for easing the arms race, not unexpectedly the Russians did not respond.

The British had gone ahead with the Baghdad Pact. Turkey and Iraq signed in April followed by Pakistan and Iran. But Dulles would not commit the US. He argued that the prominent presence of Iraq – as leader

*of the conservative Arab nations, and still in Britain's sphere of influence
and, moreover, without a border with the Soviet Union – would antagonise
other Arab states.*

As Foreign Secretary, Harold Macmillan accompanied Eden.

*   *   *

DIARY – 16 JULY

We arrived on Saturday, a company of Swiss drawn to attention,
and the two thousand press behind a wire fence. We stay at Le
Reposoir, which seems very much the same: same old chef, and
the same shifty major domo as we had last year. Two Pictet
servants who were vetted by Security turn out to have been in
prison.

Sunday Anthony goes to lunch with Eisenhower. The latter
refuses to go out at all on the grounds that if he does he would
have to go also to the Russians. He has also arranged that the
heads [of government] should meet one half of the day, and the
Foreign Secretaries the other half, which is exasperating for
Anthony.

Another feature of the Conference will be the buffet which
takes place every day at 7 p.m. and is when everyone is meant
to be able to get people in corners. Harold Macmillan says these
are the prices we pay for getting Eisenhower here at all, as he
didn't want to come.

DIARY – 17 JULY

Conference opened yesterday. The Consul lent me a car to visit
Madame Faure [wife of the French Prime Minister] who obliges
us to be photographed for half an hour. '*Ah, je vois* Paris Match,
comme toujours. Bonjour' and so on. Why Mendès-France finds
her more attractive than his heavenly wife is amazing. Mamie is
rather nervous but she tells me: 'When I was in Ayrshire I

bought a ready-made tweed suit and I've had a just wonderful time in that suit.'*

After this, Dorothy [Macmillan] and I decide to go to Coppet to see Madame de Staël's house. Dorothy is so eager, I can't make out what she likes or is interested in. Coppet was frowsty and tattered, but very pretty. Then to the Eisenhower 'palace' for a bathe. A pretty 18th-century house in American sur-roundings – too many flowers, and a tea-house with herbaceous borders round it. The bathing is lovely but we are surrounded by FBI men, a flagpole, and a police boat.

Anthony comes fuming back to *Le Reposoir* with a headache. The FO had blundered, the French behaving badly. I sat on the balcony tonight and looked at the lights on the lake, and thought how magical it all seemed when I first came here again after the war. It seemed luxurious and glamorous. At night the jet fountain seems in its floodlight like a trembling spire of stone.

DIARY – 20 JULY

The Russians come to dine with Anthony. Dorothy and I stay before dinner to see them. Khrushchev looks frightening, pale and bullet-headed, like a Russian peasant. Bulganin looks like a professor and was full of chit-chat. Molotov looked more jaundiced and more bourgeois than ever, with his pince-nez.

The evening went well. Bulganin asked Anthony to Moscow, so Anthony said Bulganin ought to come to London for a change, and he said he would like to. He told Anthony the present regime simply could not agree to the unification of Germany. The Russian people would say 'Stalin would never have done that.'

Anthony had breakfast with Ike this morning. He thinks he is

---

* The Eisenhowers had been granted a grace-and-favour flat at Culzean Castle and often visited Scotland privately.

bored by the conference. Anyway, he misses all the negotiating points.

I had a break when my friend John de Bendern, formerly Duff Cooper's Private Secretary at the Paris embassy, turned up with Bob Boothby to take me for lunch and we drove to near Lausanne, where the de Benderns were living in a small bungalow. It was nice to see John again – he had great charm. Terrible stories about Randolph's behaviour to waiters in a Geneva restaurant. On the way home Bob and I insisted on stopping at John's father's aviary. John was in a muck sweat of fear lest he should be recognised. His father hadn't seen him or spoken to him since his remarriage to a sweet Spanish girl. The father was a mystery figure to me – born de Hirsch, he changed his name to de Forrest, then to de Bendern.

After a lot of ringing the bell we got into a large, utterly hideous, Tudoresque house, with masses of woodwork and brick. A strange woman with white eyelashes and blue eyebrows led us up some stinking stairs, with plates of animal food on each step. Every room of the house had been converted into an aviary, with tree branches painted white. Funnels of wire netting led from the windows into huge enclosures outside, where the birds flew around. Little rafts floated in a lake for those birds who were free. Donkeys wandered around – and cats, and kittens, and foxes. The stench was overwhelming. John's father lived in another, larger house nearby.

On our way out we met a man in white ducks and said, '*Bonjour*'. John said this was his brother, Alaric. He seemed terror-stricken at the idea of meeting us. He eventually joined us, jittering and looking at his watch all the time and saying 'I must fly'. A man of over fifty, living in terror of his father, who used him as chauffeur and birdman.

Mamie Eisenhower had organised a lake trip for the wives. We embarked on a sumptuous launch and had to face several hundred cameramen who were ranked in tiers on the quay: 'Look this way – that way – wave.' Madame Faure was again in her element. Boats with cameras pursued us all the way and Madame Faure ran from side to side shouting *'Vous êtes journalistes?'* excitedly, which they palpably were.

Mamie rang up next day to say that Ike wanted to see just us for drinks. I liked Mamie. She was perfectly natural, no side whatsoever. I was very disappointed by Eisenhower, finding him charmless. I had imagined someone live and dapper, with strength and repose; instead he seemed heavy, hearty and bland. I felt he had been negotiating out of his depth. Dulles was a more weighty character, though Ike was probably obstinate and proud, which, as he was President, was more significant.

DIARY – 22 JULY

Anthony dined with the Russians. First there was a scrimmage with hundreds of photographers who had crashed the grounds and who manhandled Anthony and the Russians. One shoved Anthony from behind and said, 'Get out of the way.' Anthony said, 'If *you* don't get out of the way yourself I'll hit you on the jaw.' No one knew who they were, or how they had got in – the Russians had been so mad keen to show they are unguarded.

Anthony had a good evening. Bulganin's visit to England was fixed for next spring. The Foreign Ministers had met and failed to resolve the deadlock. Anthony suggested a restricted session. The Russians said 'No'. Ike, as usual, missed the Western point, and agreed. So Faure tagged along with him.

Bulganin said to Anthony, 'What do you think of Molotov? We think he's alright, but he's getting old now and we wonder if we oughtn't to replace him.'

DIARY — 23 JULY

Last day. Both the Americans and the Russians had compromised in the end. Anthony said Harold, when a minor point was conceded to him, jumped up and down and wrung his hands like a boxer.

Dorothy and I go to the closing session of the conference. Mrs Dulles was there. When the French saw us they flew to the telephone to tell Madame Faure, who arrived, hatless, about 10 minutes later. The Russians distinguished themselves by making the old aggressive propaganda speech — not only about China but also about Germany.

Ike made a very good reply. He was pretty rueful when we saw him on going out. No wonder. Now the Russians will have undone all the good that might have been created by this conference, and Ike will never set foot abroad again. Anthony went round to see the Russians after dinner to talk about the troubles in Indo-China.

The Russians are perfectly amenable about this. Then they ask if there are no ways in which the two European powers — we and Russia — can get together. They suggest Fleet visits and exchanges of Military Missions. Anthony is fairly cold, because of the speech this afternoon.

*   *   *

Though there were few tangible results, there was much talk of a new 'Geneva Spirit' of international co-operation and it was generally thought that the conference contributed to a relaxation of Cold War tensions between the Great Powers. Eden concluded that it had reduced the risk of war.

A further outcome was the Russians' acceptance of Eden's invitation to visit Britain the following year.

*   *   *

In July we went to a regimental Greenjacket bicentenary in Winchester, headquarters of Anthony's old regiment, the 60th Rifles. Anthony was in his element.

The crowds all over the town cheered him. He kept his car well behind the Queen's. Charming parade – all the officers in their bottle-greens with black braiding looked very foreign, and the old uniforms were covered with astrakhan and froggings.

I disgraced myself by feeling faint even before the Queen had arrived. We were sitting with our backs to the sun and it burnt on my neck. Anthony wouldn't let me leave. I managed to shunt myself nearer to the dais. There were six Americans there, including Stewart Alsop, brother of *Washington Post* journalist, Joe Alsop – all that remained of the US volunteers who joined the Greenjackets before America entered the war. They were terrifically American, with their cameras and loose button-down shirts. The bottle-green officers looked a bit blankly at them.

At the Deanery, where Anthony was to have his audience with the Queen to tell her that Bulganin and company were coming to England, I lay in a room trying to recover. When the Queen finally arrived she and Anthony had the audience next door. The wall was very thin. Anthony was telling her the menu he had had at Ike's – there was a lot of merriment. She was rather taken aback about Bulganin. The Duke when told took it better because, unlike Tito, he would not be their personal guest.

DIARY – 27 JULY

Anthony announced in the House about the Russian visit. I had to leave to join Mrs Chamberlain's tea. Mrs Chamberlain* said that Mr Baldwin† at No. 10 slept in the ante-room, which

---

* Anne Chamberlain, widow of Prime Minister Neville Chamberlain.
† Stanley Baldwin, Conservative Prime Minister 1924–9, 1935–7.

has no light and no air, and she, Mrs Chamberlain, had 10 servants.

[Sydney] Silverman [left-wing Labour MP] wrote to Anthony tonight to say his was the first foreign affairs speech – from either side of the House – with which he had agreed, for the last 10 years.

DIARY – 28 JULY

Lime Grove for the TV. Anthony is made up in the most ridiculous fashion: thick powder and a black, Groucho Marx moustache. I am assured it will look alright on the screen, but it doesn't. Just another thing they don't understand. Very badly produced, the cutaways grotesquely incompetent. Anthony does a splendid performance and on the wireless at 9.15 it is the best broadcast he has ever done. It shows how unnecessary it is to have notes.

I have included this diary entry because Anthony was usually directed by David Attenborough, Anthony's favourite, and mine too, after I realised he was brilliant with human beings as well as animals. Sadly, he now insists that on one occasion at No. 10, it was I who blacked Anthony's moustache. But I never walked around my own home with a handbag, let alone one containing mascara.

Anthony came home later from a dinner arranged by Brendan Bracken, Winston's right-hand man, to effect a reconciliation with Max Beaverbrook, at Brendan's house in Lord North Street. Beaverbrook had shown perpetual hostility towards Anthony hitherto. This was the test. Afterwards Max said to Brendan, 'It's all right. I'll back him' and he was as good as his word, not only up to the resignation but beyond.

DIARY — 29 JULY

Winston came to lunch. Clemmie couldn't come; she sounded terribly flat and piano on the phone, in pain all the time, and no hope of anyone curing her. Great deterioration in Winston. He eats, though: cold eggs and lobster, steak, and blackcurrant ice.

Anthony tells Winston that Ike hadn't meant to make his speech at Geneva about flying over each other's territories and taking photographs, which so hit the headlines. He was riled by the Russians. 'They got me mad,' he said to Anthony. Khrushchev said to Anthony afterwards, 'Well, we have had a wasted day.' Anthony demurred. 'All right,' said Khrushchev, 'let's call it a photographic day.'

* * *

Meanwhile, a constitutional crisis was brewing over Princess Margaret's wish to marry Group Captain Peter Townsend, handsome equerry to the late King George VI, but a divorced man. The delicate discussions would drag on for several months.

* * *

DIARY — 29 JULY (CONTINUED)

Michael Adeane [Private Secretary to the Queen] came to see Anthony tonight. Princess Margaret had wanted to ask Townsend to Balmoral. The trouble would come because to marry him she could not simply renounce her right to the throne. There would have to be an Act of Parliament and the Queen, as Head of the Church, is obliged to refuse her permission to marry. And it is for Anthony to refuse as Head of the Government, and Anthony himself has been divorced. If Walter Monckton is already Lord Chief Justice by then – guilty party and co-respondent – the situation will be even more bizarre.

DIARY — 24 AUGUST, CHEQUERS

Letter from Adeane saying he had had a talk with the Queen and the Duke of Edinburgh and they all saw things in exactly the same way as Anthony i.e. Princess Margaret would have to renounce her rights to succeed.

DIARY — 2 OCTOBER

Yesterday to Balmoral. On the drive from Aberdeen, the landscape becomes progressively more sinister as we approach the castle — lots of pinewoods in a narrower and narrower valley. Found the Queen and Princess Margaret in the front hall. Everything very free and easy. They are dressed in Royal Stuart Hunting Tartan, but with different shades of cashmere jerseys. Anthony is immediately swept off by the Queen — the Duke of Edinburgh being out stalking — to start the discussions on Princess Margaret.

We have a charming suite of rooms done up in tartan chintz, urine-coloured pitch pine with engravings by Landseer and Winterhalter framed in pine, and the bathroom papered like a pebbled house. Rather a chilly dining room and the usual champagne or hock or burgundy goes round with the turbot.

I was next to the Duke of Edinburgh. I always liked talking to him, he was outspoken and didn't try to be tactful. I enjoyed that.

DIARY — 2 OCTOBER (CONTINUED)

Afterwards a film in the ballroom. It was a French X film about gang warfare with a very loud soundtrack and shots of women with breasts exposed. We have the Principal of the Church of Scotland with us.

To Crathie Church the next day. This is a pleasant surprise, as one doesn't kneel, and though the service takes one and a half hours it is easy sitting down – almost the only time one could sit down during the visit. Lunch off Thistle plates; I have Billy Wallace next to me. He tells me how intelligent and charming and gay Simon Eden was. After lunch the Queen, the Duke of Edinburgh and Anthony all leave in another rush for another consultation.

We then go with Martin Charteris [Assistant Private Secretary to the Queen] for a drive – a rather unreal drive because it is so like a national park. We drive through pinewoods and granite rocks and very high heather and see, at appropriate moments, herds of deer and grouse and capercaillies. Although the woods have a dappled Courbet look I prefer it when we get above the treeline and have the rounded hills.

*   *   *

The outcome of the consultations was that Princess Margaret, who would have had to give up her rights to the succession and her Civil List allowance, decided against marrying Peter Townsend. The press had a field day, with many inferring that the out-of-date 'establishment' was interfering inappropriately in the young Princess's romantic life. Eden, in fact, thought she should be free to make her own choice.

*   *   *

CHAPTER 14

PRESSURES

By October 1955 Eden's honeymoon period was coming to an end. When he became Prime Minister, one of his strongest electoral assets was the economy, which appeared to be booming as wartime controls and restrictions eased (all rationing ended in 1954), the terms of trade shifted in Britain's favour, there was full employment and purchasing freedom was restored which led to a rapid growth in consumer spending.

Butler's pre-election Budget with a 6d cut in income tax had reflected this optimism, but even then there was concern, expressed earlier by Eden, about a growing trade deficit and rising inflation. Within days of the election Eden faced nationwide rail and dock strikes and had declared a state of National Emergency. The dispute was settled but the longer-term inflationary tendencies were not resolved.

By July, with pressure on sterling, Butler had imposed a credit squeeze and reductions in public expenditure; then in October he applied further unpopular measures – purchase tax was extended to previously excluded kitchen items, which earned it the title Pots-and-Pans Budget.

This triggered mounting press criticism of the government's handling of the economy. Eden was chided for uncertain leadership and failing to invigorate his front bench – the only change had been Macmillan's move to the Foreign Office and the retirement of a couple of older colleagues, including Lord Woolton.

Eden's handling of the press had not helped. That August he had appointed William Clark, a former Observer *journalist, as his Press and Public Relations Adviser – a post he kept until November 1956.*

*   *   *

DIARY — 25 AUGUST, CHEQUERS

William Clark for the night. He is so bumptious that I find it terribly embarrassing and do not know where to look. It is like someone with hiccups. I hope I was not too brusque.

Anthony belonged to a generation who did not understand the demands of a modern press – although Winston, who was of an older generation, did. He also had a ruthlessness that Anthony never possessed – to his loss. If the press becomes frustrated they will retaliate, rightly or wrongly.

Mark Chapman-Walker (of Conservative Central Office) later explained to me how in Winston's day, he, Jock and Winston would meet every week and go over the press. Jock and Mark decided what to leak and to whom, including Cabinet proceedings; stories were invented, even. Whereas now the press got no leaks and were correspondingly sour. This was at the bottom of the *Mail*'s hostility. The leader writer complained openly that he no longer got stories from No. 10 and Esmond Harmsworth had told him that Anthony said all the press would be treated en masse.

In other words, Anthony was very bad at press relations. He was used simply to talking periodically to selected lobby correspondents and confidentially to an editor such as William Haley of *The Times*. He had never heard of spins or deliberate leaks.

Anthony's first Party Conference as Prime Minister was at Bournemouth. A very lavish suite had been redecorated in grey and rust especially for us. On our way to the constituency drinks we bumped into Patrick Buchan-Hepburn, Chief Whip, Rab and Harold in the passage, all talking to [my cousin] Randolph, I noticed – a bad sign. Anthony was working on his speech until 1 a.m.

The next morning was the farewell for Lord Woolton as Party Chairman, though he was perhaps best known for his wartime 'Woolton pie'. He was as good as Micawber – the speechless half-minute, stifled with emotion, the turning to his wife, the gestures – poor Maude crying. When her turn came she said, 'I've got nothing to groomble at' and told us it would be their forty-third anniversary on Monday.

They came to lunch with us for Anthony's mass meeting, which got good applause. The heat and glare of the TV lights meant that we could see no further than the first few rows. I thought he delivered the speech excellently and forcefully. The speech got a bad press, nonetheless.

DIARY – 10 OCTOBER

An even worse press, particularly the *Daily Telegraph*, which says outright there is no leadership, and Rab ought to leave the Treasury and pull the home front together. Anthony is very despondent. He wishes he had made an ordinary Cabinet reconstruction now.*

The Conference over, we had an idyllic week at the cottage with lunch on the lawn every day. We went over to lunch with Oliver Lyttelton at Trafalgar House. I hadn't seen it before – an unexpectedly lovely place; the most beautiful ceilings and mantelpieces in every room. Oliver, as always, was delightful and very amusing. They discussed plans for the reconstruction and Oliver thought it

---

* Eden had decided against a major Cabinet reshuffle after the election, but came under increasing pressure to make changes.

well worth waiting for, if Rab and Harold could be switched. He said Rab had more intellectual hubris than anyone he had ever known, and Oliver had known very many clever people. He had dined with him recently and Rab was lolling back, saying, 'Yes, Anthony's doing very well, really; and yes, there are really some quite intelligent people in the Treasury.'

Later that month I flew to Belfast to launch a ship called *Eden*. It was rather small, but I was presented with some large diamond earrings. The chairman of Harland and Wolff, the shipbuilding firm, was much more cheerful than on my last visit about the position of the industry (which had been hit by dock strikes earlier in the year), and all the dockers seemed very chipper and gave me three cheers.

In November there was a party at the American embassy for the Queen, to be informal, we were told. Aldrich said that, to offset the harm done by the Russian visit here next spring, the Queen ought to visit America, but not surprisingly it didn't happen. The royal family were sandwiched between Mr Ford and Mr Rockefeller, I got Mr Firestone, and Mrs Luce insulted Princess Margaret by saying, 'I had no idea you were so small.'

*   *   *

Egypt was again looming. Eden had in autumn 1954 concluded an agreement to the phased withdrawal of troops from the Suez Canal base by June 1956.

Nasser now planned to build the Aswan High Dam, an ambitious project to regenerate Egypt's economy. He turned first to the West for finance. The US backed by Britain began negotiations for a loan through the World Bank.

The announcement in September 1955 that Nasser had secretly negotiated the sale of arms from the Communist bloc (through Czechoslovakia) generated alarm in Western capitals that Russia was expanding its influence in Egypt. Eden at this stage was in favour of seeking a modus vivendi *with Nasser – if he showed willingness to co-operate, then Britain should reciprocate.*

In November, there were more troubling developments.

DIARY – 28 NOVEMBER

On Saturday morning Anthony got the intercepted message from the Russians to the Egyptians giving the terms on which the Russians would build the Aswan Dam for the Egyptians – far better ones than we, or the Americans, or the World Bank, had thought of on our side. Anthony very upset. Says, 'If the Russians get the contract we have lost Africa.'

Meanwhile Alan Lennox Boyd [Secretary of State for the Colonies] is in a state of umbrage because he tried to get Harold on receiving the telegram – or rather, his wife did – and Harold, who was with the Astors at Hever, was very rude to her and said, 'Do you realise I'm just about to go out shooting?' Alan said, 'He spoke to my wife as if she were a housemaid.' Harold, being so out of touch, has not yet received the telegram.

By the time Anthony tried to get him he had already gone shooting and was not returning until 4 p.m. Eventually Anthony, Rab, Alan and Harold all had to go to London Saturday evening to hammer out telegrams to Dulles (that was Harold) and Eisenhower (that was Anthony). Harold then went all the way back to Hever, and the next day to his home at Haywards Heath, where he calmly remained until Monday afternoon.

DIARY – 29 NOVEMBER

Anthony learned tonight that Attlee is retiring. I said to Mrs

Resignation: departure from Tilbury.

Below left: AE at Goldeneye and the private coral cove.

On the deck of RMS *Rangitata* with correspondence.

Arrival at Auckland was very different from the send-off. Good old Commonwealth.

Arriving at the French Embassy in 1960. AE in full rig with the Garter on his calf.

Winston and AE relax at Rose Bower.

OLD FRIENDS SAY GOOD-BYE : Sir Anthony Eden watches from the gate of his thatched cottage as his wife stands by the door of the car for a final word with Sir Winston and Lady Churchill. The cottage stands off the road which runs through the Chalke Valley from Salisbury to Shaftesbury. Although there has been speculation about Sir Anthony's future, it is considered improbable that his health will allow him to return to politics

Fyfield Manor. I am tying up fruit on the right. Belle the blue whippet doing a 'Mountbatten' to the camera.

Manor House, Alvediston. Home for thirty years. Framed by rosa rugosa.

The new conservatory at Alvediston. No plants yet. AE, Ann Fleming and Freddie Ashton.

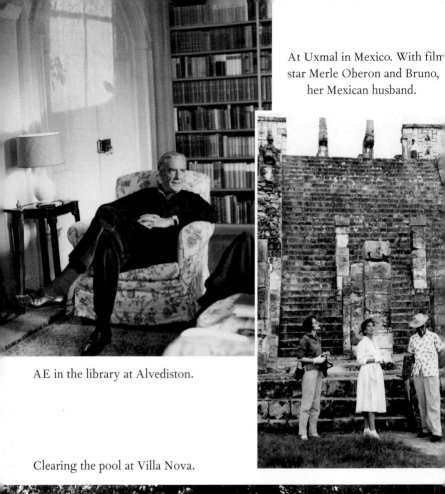

At Uxmal in Mexico. With film star Merle Oberon and Bruno, her Mexican husband.

AE in the library at Alvediston.

Clearing the pool at Villa Nova.

Villa Nova in pouring rain. Hilarity as Prince Philip plants his tree in our garden.

Under the cannon-ball tree with (from left) the film star Claudette Colbert, Laura Canfield, AE and Michael Canfield.

AE, Ham Armstrong, ..., Isaiah Berlin, Aline Berlin, Tony Bower.

Villa Nova. Cecil photographing at his best.

What on earth are *you* doing here? The Emperor Haile Selassie greets AE in Barbados.

Pam Harriman, formerly Churchill, Averell Harriman, C., AE and Douglas Fairbanks Jr at Hobe Sound, the Harrimans' house in Florida, during AE's last two winters there.

In the garden at
Alvediston.

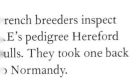

Alvediston. Mrs Thatcher
descends for lunch by
helicopter.

French breeders inspect
E's pedigree Hereford
ulls. They took one back
Normandy.

With my old friend George Weidenfeld.

Ex-Prime Ministers' wives:
(from left) Mary Wilson, Norma Major, Cherie Booth and me.

Attlee today, at the Moderator of Scotland's tea party, that we had passed her on the road from Chequers on Monday afternoon.

'I should think you were going through all the red lights, ringing that bell.'

I replied, 'We were in a hurry to get up.'

'We always went up at 9.30 in the morning.'

Anthony says that when Attlee came to see him he asked for his earldom and said, 'That's the rate for the job.'

DIARY — 27 DECEMBER, CHEQUERS

Rab [whose wife Sydney had died that year] and the children came for Christmas — three rather sad figures who had never left home at Christmas before. Sarah, the child, was taught Bagatelle by Nicholas, and when complimented on her first attempt said it was just a question of using your intelligence and she supposed it ran in the family. Rab talked to me about the scathing reception the new appointments have had in the press, asking what could be done about it. I said that the press had tasted blood and it's going to be a bad time.

Anthony feeling tired and low all the time. Depressed about the press, about Russia and about Jordan. The house looked nice. The handyman had made a huge green bell out of box branches; also very good garlands to twist round the pillars, with swags on the balcony.

Anthony's nephew Fulke came with his son and daughter, and my niece, Sally. Bridget [Parsons] was excellent as usual. She wasn't very taken by Rab, her intended (a joke), and remarked on his forced gaiety unfavourably. She thought the nanny the best of the family.

*   *   *

In December Eden completed his Cabinet reconstruction. It received a lukewarm response in the press as being too late and unimaginative. Macmillan was moved to the Treasury, and Butler to Lord Privy Seal and Leader of the House. The only new faces were Iain Macleod to Minister of Defence and Edward Heath to Chief Whip. Selwyn Lloyd became Foreign Secretary.

The press seized on opinion polls, which showed a decline in Eden's personal popularity from the peak of his election triumph (from a 73 per cent approval rating in April 1955 to 50 per cent by February 1956 and 41 per cent by April 1956) and general dissatisfaction with the government in a succession of disappointing by-election results. At Taunton, the Conservative majority was reduced from 5,542 to 657.*

The Daily Telegraph *was showing increasing hostility to Eden, fuelled by the personal antagonism Lady Pamela Berry, wife of the owner, now felt towards the Eden regime. In January an article in the* Daily Telegraph *heavily criticised Eden's leadership, calling for 'the Smack of Firm Government'.*

*   *   *

DIARY — 23 JANUARY 1956

In the last few weeks we've been through a violent attack by the press. The only interesting part was the *Daily Telegraph* which, by innumerable petty manifestations of sourness or hostility, betrayed the personal nature of the attacks. Trivial fuel was added to the fire by my chance remark to Mrs Hill [the Chequers housekeeper] to the effect that I didn't think the people in the cottage at the end of Lime Avenue need

---

* However, even at his very lowest point, Eden's popularity, according to polls, was still higher (41 per cent) than any subsequent post-war Prime Minster (except Lord Home). Macmillan's approval rating fell to a low of 30 per cent in 1957, Harold Wilson's to 27 per cent (1968), Margaret Thatcher's in April 1990 to 23 per cent.

hang their washing in the middle of it. Mrs Hill immediately rang the Trust's estate manager and said that I wanted the washing removed.

The people told the *Daily Mirror*, who rushed down and photographed and snooped around. Another cottager, on being asked whether I had ordered her washing to be removed, said 'No' and was accused of being intimidated. In the end the *Mirror* didn't print it; but the *Pictorial* did. I felt guilty at my carelessness in doing Anthony harm. It became the subject of jokes and cartoons – some beastly, like in *Punch* – also a few anonymous letters.

Randolph rings up with the tiresome news that the person accused in the *Spectator* of disloyalty to their chief and his colleagues is William Clark. Anthony decides he will leave things for the moment. Clark must have had a good fright, with Randolph bullying and insulting on the telephone.

*   *   *

Eden visited Eisenhower in January for talks over a range of issues, including American proposals for a wider settlement between Arabs and Israelis in the Middle East, and the Egyptian question.

*   *   *

DIARY – 10 FEBRUARY

Anthony pleased with his American trip. He said the reception over there was wonderful in every way and everyone remarked on the sourness of the British press and didn't understand it. Eisenhower was helpful, and clearer-headed than before [his heart attack in September 1955]. He gave Anthony the atomic submarine and the answer to some snags that had developed at Calder Hall, thus saving us 10 years of research and millions of pounds.

*   *   *

Talks were proceeding on the projected loan to Egypt for the Aswan High Dam. A formal offer had been made in December with Eden's support – his view being that if the Russians were to finance the dam it would give them a dangerous foothold in an area vital to Britain's interests. However, the Middle East situation became more volatile, exacerbated in British and French eyes by Nasser's Arab nationalist propaganda throughout the region.

Jordan, under its young King Hussein, was a long-standing British ally with its army, the Arab Legion, British officered and commanded by a British general, Sir John Glubb. In March the young King, faced with nationalist uprisings on the streets of Jordan, abruptly dismissed Glubb. The dismissal was seen as a severe blow to Britain's prestige in the area. Many suspected Nasser's hand in it. The Suez Group used the occasion to revive their attacks on Eden's whole policy of withdrawal from the Canal base.

*   *   *

DIARY — 7 MARCH

The events in Jordan are shattering. Tonight's winding up of the debate was a shambles in spite of the ovation Anthony got at the beginning. Yesterday I saw Mark Chapman-Walker. The only thing people are worried about is Unemployment. They are behind Anthony and think the press campaign unfair.

Later that month we went on the royal train to Coventry for the rededication of the cathedral, which had been all but destroyed in bombing during the war. Each member of the royal family had an entire coach to him- or herself consisting of sitting room, dining room, plus three or four bedrooms and bathrooms. We were given the royal children's. Beforehand I had been to the gala at Covent

Garden and left early for fear of getting to the station after the Queen. At the station we found a rather glum crowd and felt it was a bad omen for the Coventry crowds on the following day.

We woke up in a siding near Coventry, and were told the Queen had had breakfast and was dressed by 9 a.m. When we went along, we found the Duke immersed in an enormous file.

Riding behind the royal car, to our amazement the crowds all cheered Anthony loudly. This was kept up all through the visit. The Duke said to Anthony, 'I never thought you'd get a reception like this.'

DIARY — 4 APRIL

We had Beaverbrook to dine before the Easter holidays. He was more at his ease. Beaverbrook kept asking Anthony questions, the answers to which he already knew. They seemed like traps. Next night we dined at the Hofmannsthals to meet Joe Alsop [journalist on the *Washington Post*] — a replica of the fateful dinner 18 months ago. Too many people, unfortunately, and too much noise. Anthony told Joe a lot and we find it leaked the following week — at least, Anthony thinks it could only have come from him.

The Russians' visit was arranged for April. On the day of their arrival I was going to Norfolk to the wedding at Holkham of Colin Tennant and Ann Coke. A pristine day, washed pale blue, the approach to the house was lovely — an ilex avenue and another in the opposite direction stretching down to the seashore.

I left in good time to drive back to Chequers but it took longer than planned and Tribe (my driver) went on the wrong road out of Luton, so I arrived after 8 p.m. just as Bulganin and Khrushchev were coming down for dinner. Nods and smiles as I rushed upstairs to take off my hat.

*

Dinner next to Khrushchev. He doesn't eat at all. A lot of jovial shouting across the table to Bulganin. He shouted to Anthony, 'You are an island. You depend for your food and everything on your Navy and your ships. Submarines can cut you off in war. We have submarines that can surface and fire rockets inland.'

Anthony replied that England was a porcupine which could send back bombs and rockets to whoever attacked her. Selwyn told me after that Gruenther had been trying to find out if the Russians have rocket-firing submarines for ages.

Anthony told them if anyone attacked the Gulf sheikhdoms, we would fight for the oil. Ugly silence. After dinner I leave them to it.

The Russians got up at 5.45 a.m. There were more talks in the morning — a much cosier atmosphere. Gaitskell, Robens in royal blue, and Griffiths [Labour Opposition leaders] came to lunch.

I get Bulganin this time who makes a great effort and flatters one. With his trimmed beard he looked like a Russian out of Turgenev. Afterwards there is a lot of horseplay on the terrace which I take photographs of. Then the Opposition go off for their talk with the Russians. They overstay their time and have to be asked, and then ordered, to stop.

Next the Russians want to go for a walk. Anthony leaves for Windsor so Rab and I lead off through the daffodils in very slow motion. The Russians disappear on our return and reappear looking very smart in new black suits and clean shirts & different ties ready to meet the Queen. So, goodbye. William Hayter [British Ambassador to Moscow] says that he has learnt for the first time where Bulganin's dacha is. Up to now he hasn't known where he lives.

As soon as they have gone we rush to look at the presents. I have got a sable stole, though it will need remodelling. Poor Anthony has the most appalling conglomeration of writing accoutrements made of brawn coloured marble with ormolu and agate – a sort of proletarian Fabergé with a lamp to match with yellow crepe shade.

Apparently, after their visit to the Queen, the two Russians were very excited in the car going back to Claridge's, saying, 'The Queen said to me . . .' 'No, she said that to me . . .' and so on.

One was never allowed to keep any presents; if we had, they would have had to be valued and paid for. Luckily, we never wanted any of them – though I wouldn't have minded keeping a largish diamond that one of the Gulf sheikhs had given me.

DIARY – 26 APRIL

Yesterday the Russians sent me a camera as an afterthought, with several telescopic lenses & other devices. The Foreign Office value it at £200. I didn't keep it. I went to Jacqmar and bought some material for the wives – satin with embossed blue roses and yellow roses. Today was the last day.

At 11 p.m. the cars and escorts roared up to the Foreign Office for the signing of the communiqués. Afterwards they had a talk. Khrushchev said they would tell Anthony what really happened when the Socialists went to see them in the morning. They asked if they could be invited to Russia and Bulganin and Khrushchev said no. They had come here at the invitation of the government and so they could only ask the government back. Then Gaitskell asked if they might be asked individually. Khrushchev replied it would be very difficult.

*   *   *

During the visit a naval frogman, Commander Crabb, mysteriously van-
ished in Portsmouth Harbour, allegedly while diving in connection with
trials of some underwater apparatus. The Russians sent a note saying his
body had been seen floating in the harbour. When news of his dis-
appearance leaked, a major uproar ensued.

*   *   *

DIARY — 5 MAY

Before the Russians came, Anthony was asked if he would agree
to frogmen exploring the propellers of the Soviet cruiser while
she was in Portsmouth. He said on no account. It now appears
that Intelligence acted on their own without authorisation and
sent a frogman down to Portsmouth, where he registered at a
hotel under his own name. The frogman has since disappeared.
The Russians have been very reticent about it – they say they
saw him surface but will say no more. Anthony wondered why
Khrushchev kept on making jokes about cruisers being so obso-
lete. They must think us perfect fools.

In June, we gave a dinner at No. 10 for former US President Harry
Truman who was on a brief visit. He was very self-assured, very pale
and floury-looking, almost as if made up, with black shaded eyes.
Mrs Truman is a downright little dreadnought and quite attractive.
When I took some of the women up to my bedroom, Vi Attlee
immediately began exclaiming about my bed, and how could I sleep
alone in such a big bed?

The following day we went to a very moving ceremony in
Hyde Park: a parade of VCs on the same spot where they were
first reviewed by Queen Victoria. We stood in the sun for what

seemed a long time waiting for the Queen. Then we saw the glint of the Life Guards' helmets coming through the trees and the royal carriages came slowly across the grass. The Queen came up to the dais followed by the Duke who said, 'Morning all.' At the end the wretched VCs paraded past with eyes right – the halt and the lame tottering by. It was astonishing the huge proportion of them who were Gurkhas. We all cried except the Queen and the Duke.

The Commonwealth Conference started on 27 June. There was the usual dinner at Buckingham Palace. Lady Webb (wife of the New Zealand High Commissioner) was suffering with her back and Mrs Bandaranaike, the Prime Minister of Ceylon, with her knee. The Queen Mother had been dancing till 4 a.m., so wanted to sit down occasionally. I got stuck with Begum Mohammed Ali (the wife of the Pakistan Prime Minister), whose first outing in mixed company it was. She kept on telling me that she worked in the fields, but I think she got her English slightly awry.

Edwina and Dickie were in the receiving line at Buckingham Palace for the first time and, what was more, Worth, the famous dressmaker, had allowed Edwina and me to have the same dresses.

This was the occasion when I sat next to Strydom, Prime Minister of South Africa, at dinner and he was asking me about each member of the royal family until he came to the question, 'And what does the Duke of Gloucester *do*?' Gaitskell was very matey: 'May I call you Clarissa?' and Dora was very friendly indeed.

A few days later Nehru and Sidney Holland, Prime Minister of New Zealand, got their Freedom of the City. The Guildhall was strewn with herbs bought wholesale from the herbalist. Pakistan and Ceylon were too late for the ceremony. Nehru looked very elegant with his white jodhpurs and black jacket with the rosebud and the white hat. His speech was excellent – about compassion and tolerance. Holland's was about beef and cows.

*　　*　　*

This was the last period of normality before the Middle East erupted. Negotiations for the Aswan High Dam loan proceeded but both British and Americans were having doubts. In the US there were domestic pressures, chiefly business lobbies and the Treasury's concern about the stability of the Egyptian economy. After Nasser recognised Communist China in May, Dulles suggested that the project should be allowed to 'wither on the vine' and the British concurred.

Nasser, for his part, had concerns about the degree of Western control over the Egyptian economy which came with the loan, and was still open to Russian offers. But in July he instructed his Foreign Minister, Fawzi, to accept the Western offer.

Dulles responded, in what even his colleagues thought was an abrupt and undiplomatic manner, that the loan was withdrawn. Britain pulled out two days later.

Within two days the Russians denied that they had made any firm offer. Nasser responded by nationalising the Suez Canal Company.

Eden was at a dinner at Downing Street with Iraq's King Faisal and Prime Minister Nuri es-Said, several leading Cabinet ministers and Opposition leader Hugh Gaitskell when the news came through.

CHAPTER 15

SUEZ

DIARY — 27 JULY 1956

Terrible 24 hours. Nasser trying to take over the Suez Canal. Anthony and the Cabinet decide to fight, if necessary alone. The leave of the Home Fleet will be stopped but the Chiefs of Staff say they want *six* weeks to get the troops ready.

Nehru sent a message to say how upset he was and what folly of Nasser etc.

The so-called Suez Crisis lasted for the next four months, with Anthony doggedly attempting to find a diplomatic solution while at the same time not ruling out the use of force as a last resort to regain control of the Canal. My concern throughout was to support Anthony, and I felt that I could only help by bolstering him up without trying to lessen his load or demand that he rested.

* * *

Nasser's nationalisation of the Suez Canal Company shocked the nation. The Conservative Party, Hugh Gaitskell and almost all the press condemned Nasser as another Mussolini or Hitler, demanded firm action to restore the Canal to international control, and railed against any appeasement of the dictator. Snapping at Eden's heels were the Suez

Group, who felt thoroughly vindicated in their opposition to 'scuttling' from the Canal base and pressed for a tough response.

Britain and France, joint shareholders in the Suez Canal Company, agreed that Nasser should not be allowed to get away with his 'grab'. The Canal was the lifeline of oil supplies to Europe on which Britain's economy and prosperity depended. It also carried symbolic power as Britain's link to Empire. Both saw Nasser as a threat to their continuing influence in the Middle East and Africa – already undermined in Arab states by his relentless anti-colonialist propaganda – and to their influence in the world. Nasser's dealings with the Russians raised the further spectre of Russia gaining a foothold in the region.

It was in both British and French interests to humiliate a dictator who, Eden also believed, had reneged on international agreements which he personally had brokered. The treaty Nasser had signed in 1954 reasserted the 1888 Constantinople Convention that the Canal should remain under international control – through international ownership of the Suez Canal Company. But only six weeks after the last British troops had left the Canal base, Nasser nationalised the Company.

With no hope of swift military retaliation, the Cabinet agreed on 2 August to a policy of negotiation – backed by the threat of force.

Eden proceeded to diplomacy. He summoned a conference of the twenty-two maritime nations affected by the action to discuss a solution to the crisis.

Eden sought American support, but found them ambiguous throughout. With Dulles away in Peru, Eisenhower's first emissary was Robert Murphy, whose talks with his old friend Macmillan led him to conclude the British and French were contemplating military action. Harold Macmillan was the most ardent supporter of tough action in the belief that Britain would otherwise lose her place in the world. Alarmed, Dulles hurried over with instructions from Eisenhower to head off military intervention through negotiation, at the same time declaring that 'a way had to be found to make Nasser disgorge' the Canal.

This left Eden, not for the last time, with the impression that the US would not rule out support for force if it came to it, as a last resort. Though Eden preferred to have the Americans on side, he did not insist on US support – only that they should not take positive action against Britain.

Meanwhile, reservists were mobilised and plans for an invasion were being formulated – not only by the Chiefs of Staff.

*   *   *

While we were at Chequers (on 6 August) Winston asked if he could come over from Chartwell for lunch. It turned out he had dictated 'a plan' on the road and the secretary had miraculously managed to type it as they were going along.

Winston now said he wouldn't go abroad while this was on – he was much too interested. He also said, 'I must look up what Napoleon did when he invaded Egypt.' Naturally Anthony had covered everything Winston mentioned in his plan – which turned out to be Harold's anyway. When one thinks of the struggle between Winston and Harold when Winston was Prime Minister and Harold at Defence, with Winston saying, 'I am Minister of Defence – it doesn't exist as an independent job.'

DIARY – 7 AUGUST

Harold sent a Paper in to be circulated to everyone with his ideas on how to arrange the invasion. Anthony stops its circulation. When the Egypt Committee meets in the afternoon – a small Cabinet – Harold starts up about his 'little note'. 'It's not just a little note,' says Anthony, and tells him he has no business to try & circulate Papers without consulting the Prime Minister. Furthermore he saw Winston yesterday & heard all the ideas, and they are based on out-of-date information. There was a silence broken by Bobbety smoothing things over.

When I was sitting in the garden in the evening, Anthony

having gone in to telephone, out comes Harold from No. 11 – all smiles. Anthony comes back to find him in his chair making conversation.

*   *   *

The Conference of Maritime Nations convened in London on 16–23 August. Meanwhile the British with the French prepared plans for military action, code-named 'Musketeer', independent of US support.

*   *   *

Nehru sent Krishna Menon over to England. Krishna hastened to tell Anthony that the Indians had only mixed themselves up in the conference out of love for Anthony. He subsequently proceeded to plug an Egypto-Communist line, then lost his temper and said not enough attention was being paid to him.

Meanwhile the Russian Foreign Minister, Shepilov, told Anthony that Bulganin and Khrushchev had not forgotten what Anthony told them about fighting for Middle East oil.

*   *   *

At the London Conference, eighteen maritime nations agreed principles for the return of the Suez Canal to international control which recognised Egypt's sovereign rights and entrusted its operation to a Board that would insulate it 'from the politics of any one country'. These were to be presented to the Egyptians.

*   *   *

A stalwart throughout was Robert Menzies, the Australian Prime Minster, who had once said, 'The trouble with you and me, Anthony, is that we're just a couple of old Commonwealth sweats.' Now he volunteered to put the London Conference proposals to Nasser.

Menzies therefore went to Cairo on 3 September on the understanding that the British government had American support, and he felt we were entitled to believe that the Americans were determined not to let Nasser get away with it. On this basis Menzies had begun his talks with Nasser. When, the next morning, he opened the newspaper it was to read that Ike had said under no circumstances would force be employed – *he was committed to a peaceful settlement, nothing else*. Bob was very sore and felt that Ike had thrown away the trump card and shot the mission from under him. We realised that the US Ambassador in Cairo, Jefferson Caffery, was doing his best to influence the Egyptians against us, as well as playing to Dulles's anti-colonialism.

Leaving aside the very real subject of Ike's re-election influencing the American reaction,[*] there had always been, in everything the Americans had done since the war, the desire to topple our Empire. Suez and the Middle East cannot be ruled out on that score.

*   *   *

Nasser rejected the proposals and the Cabinet weighed up the next stage. Their objective remained to try to gain a peaceful settlement by negotiation, while not ruling out force. Anglo-French plans for the military armada were now well advanced. The majority of the Cabinet stood firmly behind Eden, but one colleague was wavering.

*   *   *

DIARY – 25 AUGUST

At yesterday's Cabinet meeting, Walter Monckton suddenly burst out with a piece about his disturbedness about any use of force etc. Anthony pointed out that he had agreed with it weeks ago. Today, Anthony received letters from Bobbety, Alan

---

[*] The US presidential election was due to take place on 6 November 1956. Eisenhower was campaigning for re-election as the man of peace.

Lennox Boyd and Alec Home. Alan said he was horrified by Walter's outburst, particularly as nothing has happened since the Cabinet had originally agreed on policy that anyone could not have foreseen.

Bobbety is worried and helpful. Alec is warning that Rab is wobbly to the point of lobbying as a result of which he says he has found seven members of the Cabinet who agreed with him.

Harold came down to Chequers for lunch two days later. He said that Walter had somewhat recovered his poise about the situation but felt old and tired and really wanted to go.

Harold's conversation was littered as usual with historical analogies: 'Of course the situation is really like the Augustan Age' etc. Anthony said this analogy was inaccurate and anyway unfortunate. On another occasion Bobbety had lost his patience in Cabinet and said to Harold, 'I really don't see any resemblance between us and Queen Elizabeth I.'

*   *   *

With the failure of the Menzies mission, Eden decided to take the issue to the UN Security Council. The French reluctantly agreed. Even if the Russians vetoed the resolution (as was expected), Eden and his colleagues believed they might garner moral support if ultimately it was decided to deploy force.

Dulles immediately came up with another proposal – for a Suez Canal Users Association (SCUA), which would establish an international Board to manage the Canal and collect Canal dues, a proportion of which would go to Egypt. Though Eden doubted it would work, he decided to support this latest initiative if it meant keeping in step with the Americans and exploring all diplomatic routes.

The military plan, already delayed, was once again postponed (and renamed 'Musketeer Revise').

*   *   *

I got the impression that Dulles was devising one plan after another to delay any action. I remember Antony Head, Minister for War, then Defence, expressing exasperation at the invention of SCUA, which seemed from the start unlikely to succeed. Indeed, shortly afterwards Dulles announced that it had 'no teeth'. He skewered it.

*   *   *

Dulles had once again taken the pressure off Nasser by declaring, 'There has been talk about the "teeth" being pulled out of [SCUA]. There were never "teeth" in it, if that means the use of force.' He infuriated both British and French, and effectively killed SCUA as a serious solution.

The French, with public opinion behind them, had been committed to military action from the start. They were impatient with the delays due to Eden's insistence on negotiation and doubted that the US had any commitment to a firm solution to the crisis. Foreign Minister Pineau thought the SCUA proposals 'just another Dulles bluff'.

Nasser was a direct threat to French interests. They were joint owners with Britain of the Suez Canal Company and had extensive influence in the region. They were at war in Algeria with rebels fighting for independence, and were convinced Nasser was supporting and inciting the rebels. They, like Eden, were concerned at the threat of Russian incursion in the Middle East, Nasser's rising influence over his Arab neighbours and the vulnerability of Europe's oil supplies. The seizure of the Company provided the pretext to humiliate, if not bring down, Nasser. But they feared that British delay and insistence on negotiations might ultimately lead to abandoning military action.

Unknown to the British, the French had been holding talks with the Israelis on a parallel plan for joint military action and had increased their arms to Israel in August. The Israelis were receptive to the French proposals. During September, provoked by fedayeen raids, they had mounted a series of retaliatory attacks on their Jordanian border, which had ratcheted up tension in the area.

The French talks opened up the opportunity for a preventive war by Israel not against Jordan but against Nasser. Detailed plans for a joint attack were drawn up by the end of September, starting with an Israeli invasion of Sinai (the Israeli's Operation Kadesh). Defence Minister Moshe Dayan later explained to his General Staff: 'We should behave like the cyclist who is riding uphill when a truck chances by and he grabs hold.'

Israel had an interest in toppling Nasser, occupying Sinai and gaining access to the Straits of Tiran, as well as internationalising the Canal. They were the only nation whose ships were denied passage by Egypt – a policy in breach of a UN Resolution and international law – which cast doubt on Nasser's good faith in ensuring international use of the Canal.

On 26 September Eden met Prime Minister Mollet and Pineau who were in a difficult mood and impatient with delays. By now they doubted any peaceful way existed, with Pineau telling the Americans on 5 October that only through Nasser's capitulation could Western standing in the Middle East and Africa be restored.

*　　*　　*

I was able to go to Paris when Anthony went to confer with the French. We left a lovely autumn softness in England for drizzle and fog in Paris. Selwyn was suffering from a cold and sinus so I gave him some earplugs. Chauvel, the French Ambassador, who came with us was reading an Agatha Christie called *Death on the Nile*.

At Le Bourget we were met by Pineau and the Ambassador, Gladwyn Jebb, and his wife Cynthia in a powder-blue Meluzine hat. I had the Borghese bedroom because the embassy was being rewired. The bed had been moved back to the correct place, which was much better. The embassy had been built for Pauline Borghese, the sister of Napoleon, and her bed had remained there and was slept in by some of the British ambassadresses. It was in a crimson damask, but a subsequent ambassador moved it to the ground floor and turned it into a maize colour, which he said was correct.

DIARY – 27 SEPTEMBER

Dinner at the Quai d'Orsay. I find myself next to Pineau at dinner so the conversation (in French) went:

C: My husband was saying in the car that this is like 1936 again.*

P (*very viciously*): Yes, exactly, and I hope it will have a better ending.

C: That's it. If Nasser went most of the way to international control, would that do?

P: Control means something different in France. We want international management.

C: All right, international management, then – would that do?

P: Yes.

C: My husband saw Menon yesterday.

P: Oh did he? That's interesting.

C: Menon said the Indians had really been bringing a lot of pressure to bear on Nasser.

P: Nasser has Russia behind him. Russia is putting in arms and egging him on.

Anthony comes back very late and worried. Mollet good but Pineau is very violent and extreme. Anthony thinks he wants force at all costs and cannot and will not wait and see. Visit ended well. Next day Anthony found the French more reassured and calm.

---

* A reference to Hitler's unopposed occupation of the Rhineland in 1936.

*   *   *

Meanwhile on a visit to Washington Macmillan, the most hawkish of the colleagues, stressed Britain's determination to use force if no diplomatic solution could be found. He reportedly told Dulles that Britain would go on to the end, even if it meant pawning the pictures in the National Gallery: if it came to the worst, they'd 'go down with the bands playing, the guns firing, and the flags flying', he told Eisenhower. Eden meanwhile warned Eisenhower that Nasser was effectively in Russia's hands, just as Mussolini had been in Hitler's, and that Britain could not afford to show weakness.

On his return, Macmillan reported his strong feeling that Eisenhower was determined to stand up to Nasser, and that 'he will lie doggo' until after the election – an optimistic interpretation of Eisenhower's position but one which was seized upon at home as a sign that America would not interfere in Britain's plans. Macmillan, sensing a greater willingness to prolong negotiations, threatened to resign if Britain did not play out her hand to the end.

The diplomatic solutions were fading. With SCUA all but dead after Dulles's 'no teeth' comment, the Anglo-French resolution at the UN Security Council on 6 October was vetoed, as expected, by Russia. A last possibility emerged at the United Nations with agreement between Selwyn Lloyd, Egyptian Foreign Minister Fawzi and Pineau to Six Principles for negotiation, but the operational part of this was also vetoed by Russia in the Security Council the following week and neither British nor French, anticipating Egyptian procrastination, held out much hope of a satisfactory outcome.

Pineau had given an indication to Eden of their talks with the Israelis and asked what his reaction would be to an Israeli attack on Sinai. Eden was non-commital. On 3 October Eden revealed to the Cabinet that the Israelis had come up with an 'offer' to attack Egypt, which could just possibly trigger the delayed 'Musketeer'. The day *before, Dulles had exasperated Eden and his colleagues by repudiating SCUA with his 'no teeth' comment and distancing himself from what he called the problem of colonialism. They were receptive to action independent of America.*

But Eden and the Foreign Office were cautious about involvement with the Israelis. Any joint action would compromise Britain's relations with friendly Arab states in the region. Moreover, the following week the Israelis mounted further fierce retaliatory attacks on the Jordanian border. Since Britain was obliged by treaty to come to Jordan's defence in case of aggression, the prospect loomed that unless the tension could be defused, Britain might be at war with Israel (who were backed by the French) in defence of Jordan (who would be backed by Egypt) – with the possibility of wider conflagration in the region. It was in Britain's interest that Israel be deflected from any full-scale attack on Jordan.

*   *   *

Meanwhile we had our Foreign Secretary, Macmillan's assurance that while the Americans would not back us, they would not be against us. We had to leave at this crucial point for the Conservative Conference at Llandudno.

By train to Wales, where there were groups of women on every platform with sprigs of heather. We got to the estuary through a soft landscape of stone walls and willow trees. At Llandudno we had a rush to change for the constituents' drinks party, where they told us that all the speeches had been good except Enoch Powell's. Then on to the Councillor's dinner, where we were asked to stay back and go in with the Councillor and his wife. Harold then stayed back too and tried to join the procession. Apparently there had been great rivalry because Rab was staging a comeback and making speeches full of metaphors and quotations, which the cleverer journalists adored.

Next day I went off to the conference alone to hear Anthony Nutting make Bobbety's extremely pro-Suez speech for him, he being ill. Nutting delivered it with gusto. This was the last gusto we got out of him.*

In the afternoon Anthony had to speak for over an hour. Rab was in the chair and I noticed he stopped the applause at the beginning by holding up his hand and at the end, after a sidelong glance, by sitting down.

DIARY — 13 OCTOBER

On the Conference train home Anthony talks to Harold about propaganda. Rab's only idea about propaganda is to do it about himself. Harold doesn't bat an eyelid but when I left the carriage he said to Anthony, 'You know Clarissa's quite right, it is always for himself. He was quite nasty about me at the Conference.'

We get out at Watford and all the Cabinet get out too, very jovial, to say goodbye – all these distinguished people shouting and waving when the N U R [the National Union of Railwaymen which had not long ago been on strike] blows the whistle and they all scamper in again.

On arrival at Chequers there was immediate drama – a telegram from Selwyn in New York saying Pineau was being difficult. Anthony got pretty cross with Ivone Kirkpatrick, Permanent Under-Secretary at the Foreign Office, for not knowing about this and Nutting for not being there to help draft a reply.

*   *   *

The conference had provided a touchstone of opinion in the Party, with the imperialist wing (the Suez Group) in vociferous support of government

---

* Anthony Nutting, Minister of State at the Foreign Office, resigned three weeks later opposing the Suez policy.

policy and determined to prevent any backtracking, the Cabinet united and the Party demanding determined action against Nasser, if necessary without the Americans.

The French meanwhile had worked out with the Israelis a detailed plan for a joint offensive, which might be co-ordinated with the latest Anglo-French 'Musketeer'. But the plan seemed workable solely if the British were also on side, since only they could provide air cover for the Israeli advance. The French sent emissaries to Eden at Chequers.

*　　*　　*

DIARY — 14 OCTOBER

A mysterious Frenchman [Albert Gazier, Mollet's confidant] trying to arrive all day — won't say what about. Chauvel doesn't know. Thick mist, which delays him until the afternoon. He comes with a General [General Maurice Challe, Chief of French Air Staff]. They say Israel wants to attack Egypt quite soon, before the presidential election. She will not do it unless we approve. The idea would be that we and the French moved in to keep the Canal working. Nutting comes to lunch to help with the French talks.

DIARY — 15—22 OCTOBER

New trouble on the Israeli-Jordan front. FO being wildly on Jordan's side and Anthony against it in view of Israel's new plans. No sooner arrived at Chequers than news comes that another Frenchman wants to come and see Anthony urgently. He duly arrives with General Keightley. This time it is to say that the Israelis want us to attack the Canal at the same time as they attack Egypt, which is not on. We could only do it after they had begun.

Ben-Gurion goes to Paris next Monday. As a result of all

this Anthony calls a Cabinet to Chequers on the Sunday morning. To my surprise everyone, including Rab and Selwyn, seem to have agreed with the plans.

*　　*　　*

The prospect of any negotiated settlement was looking remote. At the long-delayed armada in Malta, reservists were kicking their heels waiting, while reports came from the military that time was running out for any action before winter. The French, with fewer qualms about intervention, were even more impatient.

Eden and Selwyn Lloyd had discussed in secret with the French in Paris on the 16th what Britain's response would be if the Israelis were to 'break out' and Eden had refused to make any commitment – as he had refused with the French at Chequers. No notes were taken of the meetings and only a close circle was in on discussions.

Eden had informed the Cabinet on Sunday, 18 October, of the growing danger of an Israeli attack on Egypt. They discussed the French plan and the possible British response. The Cabinet members all agreed that steps should be taken to protect the Canal in the event of Israeli attack.

*　　*　　*

DIARY – 23 OCTOBER

Selwyn was packed off to Paris yesterday and returned at 2 a.m. having met Ben-Gurion in a house in the suburbs of Paris [Sèvres]. He reported Ben-Gurion was truculent and denied all the French said and said he had no intention of attacking Egypt first, and so on.

Pineau came here this evening. Anthony went round to Carlton Gardens after dinner. Pineau says the French have now talked Ben-Gurion round and he will attack but only if we do so too, simultaneously. Anthony says no, only afterwards.

*   *   *

The French and Israelis wanted a firmer commitment from Britain. The Israelis, with Ben-Gurion suspicious of the British resolve and unwilling to be cast as the aggressor, were reluctant to proceed with the invasion of Sinai unless the British agreed first to bomb Egyptian airfields to protect Iraeli forces and cities against retaliatory air attack – a timing Eden rejected.

Another meeting was arranged for the next day.

*   *   *

At the second meeting at Sèvres, Selwyn Lloyd absented himself and sent Patrick Dean, Deputy Under-Secretary at the Foreign Office and Head of the Joint Intelligence Committee, and Donald Logan, one of Selwyn's private secretaries, in his place. British instructions were not to negotiate any text, still less sign one, since they had no authority to do so. The Israelis' more high-powered representatives unfortunately, or fatefully, ran rings round us, and our representatives signed in the belief that the document was a record of the meeting – an *ad referendum*, subject to the approval of our government [private information]. We were committed. The French and Israelis popped champagne in relief once Dean and Logan had departed.

Our signed document was technically a secret document and should have been reserved as such. Anthony was shocked that it had been signed against instructions.

*   *   *

On the 25th Eden reported to the Cabinet that an attack by Israel on Egypt was likely. The Cabinet were united in agreeing the policy that, in the event of an Israeli attack, Britain and France should *intervene to stop hostilities and protect the Canal.* The exact details of the separate joint French-Israeli plan were not disclosed to the British.*

*   *   *

DIARY — 29 OCTOBER

A week of increasingly frayed nerves. At the dinner for General Gruenther on 25th all those in the know say what a relief and how Anthony will sleep soundly that night. They had finally laid the plans for war.

Next day it was put through the Cabinet unanimously but for Walter [Monckton] who said he didn't want to stand in the way when he saw he was in a minority of one. Rab had eventually given in. 'I am a realist,' he announced. The rest of the week is mainly wearying because of the Chiefs of Staff – Dickie Mountbatten arguing and arguing until Anthony had to tell him the political side was none of his business. He started on the doorstep the night of the Gruenther dinner and Edwina interrupted him and said, 'You are being very foolish, Dickie,' although she presumably agrees with him. The Chiefs of Staff are very reluctant to have the Israelis as allies.

Dinner today for the Norwegian Prime Minister. The news of the Israeli attack on Egypt comes through in the middle.

*   *   *

With the start of the Israeli attack, the ultimatum to the combatants to withdraw to ten miles each side of the Canal was delivered on the 30th and rejected by Egypt. British planes bombed the Egyptian airfields on the night of 31 October. Meanwhile the invasion fleet had left Malta on

---

* Curiously, both Dayan and Ben-Gurion subsequently called this the 'British Plan'. It was not. It was the proposal the French had outlined to Eden at Chequers on 14 October, which Eden would not commit to at that time.

the 29th, sailing to Port Said, and air squadrons left Britain for Cyprus. The fleet would not arrive until 6 November. On their journey they encountered units of the US Sixth Fleet, with the risk of accidental clashes.

The House of Commons was informed on 30 October and backed the government by 270 to 218 votes. The Labour leader, Hugh Gaitskell, after his initial bellicosity, opposed the use of force without reference to the United Nations. He was furious at not being consulted and launched a ferocious attack on the government.

The action divided the nation, though public opinion moved in favour of Eden and messages of support flowed into Downing Street throughout the crisis. Before the action there had been marginal disapproval of military action (44 per cent to 37 per cent) but at the height of the crisis (November) Eden's approval rating among all voters for his conduct of affairs stood at 52 per cent, Gaitskell's at 44 per cent. Eden's rose to 56 per cent in December 1956, after the action.

*   *   *

Friends were sending me messages of support. Isaiah (Berlin) sent Anthony his admiration and sympathy in circumstances which put 'his courage, honesty and strength of will . . . to a most appalling test . . .' and 'whatever the outcome he has risked his own reputation for what he thinks to be a vital national interest. I think his policy is in essentials absolutely right.' John Sparrow, Warden of All Souls, Oxford, wrote on 9 November of his intense admiration of Anthony's handling of the situation: 'Not even Winston in the darkest hours of the war has had such a burden to bear as he has borne for the last ten days . . . His incredible patience and wonderful firmness are beginning to reap their reward.' Cyril Connolly declared he was '100 per cent behind the PM' and wished he could find more ways of saying so. Others overwhelmingly echoed this approval.

During this time I wrote to Cecil, 'I hope we shall meet soon

when it is a little bit less strained. It is like a bad illness in the house.'
Meanwhile at the Bower, 'everything sounds apocalyptic. Mr Stacey
[the gardener] tells me they have had terrible hailstorms & the hens
are laying unprecedented numbers of eggs.'

From now on there were continuous debates in the House. On 1
November I sat next to Mrs Gaitskell in the Gallery and said to her,
'Don't you dislike the noisy barracking?' She said she disliked the
mounted police charging the crowds outside even more. I always got
on with Dora Gaitskell – she was an interesting person.

Anthony did very well and the second day got a terrific ovation.
Ann Fleming told me that Gaitskell said he, Gaitskell, had made the
best speech of his life. Everyone else found it nauseating. Nutting
was said to be drunk in Boodles – talking against the government
and threatening to resign.

Winston and Clemmie came to lunch on the Saturday. Winston
had had a slight stroke in the south of France. He had said he wanted
to write a letter to his constituents agreeing with the government.
Antony Head and Harold did a draft for him, but the letter was never
sent.

On the fifth day I couldn't face going to the House. Dot Head
said Anthony was cheered more than ever before. When he returned
home, he said that while the morning was good, the afternoon was
awful, and that when he left the Chamber the Opposition front bench
stood up and booed – an organised demonstration. The Speaker, of
course, is meant not to allow booing.

*   *   *

Meanwhile, Eisenhower was not 'lying doggo', contrary to Macmillan's
prediction. With the presidential elections due on 6 November, he was
angry at both the timing and the 'lack of consultation', although,
despite his claim to the contrary, he had been informed of the imminent
Anglo-French action. The US introduced a UN resolution on the 30th

calling on all countries to refrain from the use of force in the Middle East, which France and Britain vetoed. On 1–2 November Dulles tabled a resolution at an emergency session of the UN General Assembly for an immediate ceasefire, which was passed with France and Britain abstaining. Canadian Foreign Minister Lester Pearson came up with a proposal that a United Nations force be sent to the Canal Zone to replace the Anglo-French troops.

Then, with the Anglo-French armada well on its way and the Israelis having achieved their objectives, the British Cabinet discussed the options.

*   *   *

DIARY — 4 NOVEMBER

About 5 o'clock Anthony came into the drawing room with Norman Brook and said the Israelis had announced at the United Nations that they would negotiate with Egypt and all other Arab states immediately. Our paratroop landing had been delayed for 24 hours because reconnaissance had shown possible opposition.

Anthony called a Cabinet. In the middle he adjourned them and kept Bobbety, who had risen from his sickbed for the occasion, Harold and Rab behind and told them if they wouldn't go on he would have to resign. Rab said if he did resign no one else could form a government.

The Cabinet then reassembled and each was asked in turn what they felt about going on. Selwyn, Alec Home, Harold, Alan [Lennox Boyd], Antony Head, Peter [Thorneycroft], Eccles, Duncan [Sandys], James Stuart, Gwilym [Lloyd George] and Hailsham were for going on. Kilmuir, Heathcoat Amory, Macleod, Bobbety, Patrick Buchan-Hepburn were for doing whatever Anthony wanted and Lord Selkirk was unintelligible. Nigel Birch and Monckton said they would go.

Rab wanted to wait another day before deciding.

Just as this was completed a message came through that the report was untrue. Everyone laughed and banged the table with relief, except Birch and Walter Monckton who looked glum. This non-event at least showed where everyone stood.

Pineau arrives yet again and Anthony doesn't have anything to eat till midnight.

*   *   *

A huge Labour-led demonstration had gathered the same afternoon, 4 November, in Trafalgar Square under the banner 'Law not War' to protest against the government's use of force without United Nations sanction.

*   *   *

That afternoon, hearing intermittent roaring and remembering that Aneurin Bevan was having a protest rally in Trafalgar Square, I decided to go and have a look. I let myself out through the garden door on to Horse Guards (a route I always used anyway and kept my car there) and walked up to the square. Bevan was in full flow at the centre, but before I could take in the atmosphere, let alone what he was saying, those on the fringes had recognised me and started to come up with encouraging remarks – 'keep going' etc. So I thought it prudent to retreat again.

By now we had been living in a perpetual state of tension for over three months. The atmosphere was so charged that it became a normal state to be in. Yet when Anthony came up each evening he always seemed calm in voice and manner. He would talk about the troubles in Cabinet.

I didn't feel I knew enough to interfere in any way. I listened sympathetically, and was interested in the details and behaviour of his colleagues. I always assumed Anthony was right because he had so much more experience in foreign affairs.

*   *   *

French and British airborne troops were dropped outside Port Said in the early hours of 5 November.

With the fleet's arrival, bombardment began at dawn on 6 November, Port Said surrendered after some resistance the same day and Anglo-French troops moved rapidly down the Canal.

Pressure was building from the Americans and the UN for an immediate ceasefire.

Chancellor Harold Macmillan had up till then been optimistic about the financial consequences of the action. But selling of sterling was heavy in New York and gold reserves were falling – though even Eden suspected not quite as far as Macmillan claimed at the time. The suspicion persists that Macmillan exaggerated the figures to his own ultimate advantage.

Eden had already been told of a draft resolution in the UN Security Council threatening Britain and France with oil sanctions. On hearing this, Macmillan held up his hands and theatrically exclaimed, 'Oil sanctions! That finishes it!' When the US informed him on 6 November that they would not back an IMF loan to hold the pound unless there was a ceasefire, Macmillan changed from hawk to dove overnight. The Cabinet was left with little option. After discussion, with a few members arguing for going on, a ceasefire was called for midnight that night.

Eisenhower was re-elected on 6 November. However, British relations with him were not immediately repaired. One of Eisenhower's concerns was that all Anglo-French troops should be withdrawn and replaced with a United Nations Emergency Force (UNEF).

*   *   *

DIARY — 7 NOVEMBER

Anthony very tired now. When he comes up for lunch he says

he wants to go and see Eisenhower, who has just got in again. He rings him at lunch – it is incredible now that they have the sub-ocean cable instead of radio – and Eisenhower says 'Fine, fine' but an hour or so later he rings again and says, 'You aren't coming just to argue about the United Nations, are you?' Anthony says 'No'. Then he rings a third time and says he must wait to see the new Congressional leaders first etc. Then Anthony sends him a message about Russian intervention in the Middle East, which crosses with one from Eisenhower that ends by saying, 'Presumably we will withdraw our forces immediately and not wait for the arrival of the UN force.' Anthony very depressed. It looks as if the Dulles regime is going to continue.

The next day Horace Evans came in the morning. He said Anthony's heart and blood pressure were fine but his nervous system was burnt out. It was a question of when and how to go. They finally decided on a month's holiday.

Meanwhile, papers such as the *Observer* carried on their campaign against the government. Its editor and owner, David Astor, wrote to Gaitskell and Frank Cousins, the trade union leader, urging them to call a general strike. They refused.

DIARY – 15 NOVEMBER

Now [Astor] has written to Iain Macleod urging him to overthrow the Government. He said he is using all his money and resources to prove collusion between us and the French and Israelis, and that the reason *The Times* stopped supporting us was because they suspected collusion. I suggest we tell John Astor [Lord Astor owner of *The Times*, an old friend of Anthony's and David Astor's uncle].

*   *   *

The charge of collusion grew out of the suspicion that there had been secret advance co-ordination between the Israelis, French and British which had provided the necessary pretext for Anglo-French military intervention, and that Eden had advance knowledge of the Israeli attack. The further allegation that the British instigated the Israelis to attack Egypt was unfounded. The Israelis and French had since mid-October been contemplating an attack even without the British. Israel had planned her own operation (Kadesh) and both stood to gain substantially from a successful offensive.

Eden, acknowledged even by his detractors to be a man of integrity, held to the agreement made at the Sèvres meetings that the talks were to remain secret. His critics charged him with misleading the nation about the stated pretext for military action.

*   *   *

DIARY — 15 NOVEMBER

After the Young Conservative meeting where Anthony had a terrific reception we had a meeting at No. 10 of Bobbie Allan [Eden's Parliamentary Private Secretary], Horace Evans, Oliver Poole, Norman Brook [Cabinet Secretary] and Ted Heath [Chief Whip] to discuss Anthony's future. In the end it was decided that three weeks in Jamaica, as soon as possible, was the best of the evils. Norman is worried about the collusion witch-hunt and fears Anthony will be accused of running away.

DIARY — 20 NOVEMBER

Harold is playing a funny game. He is frantic at the thought of Anthony going away – Bobby Allan thinks because the time isn't ripe for his own machinations.

In the middle of all this I had to travel to Newcastle with Tony Lambton as I had previously been invited to open the new Conservative headquarters, Eden House, at Gateshead. Two jokes: Tony said to Jakey Astor, 'Jakey, you don't look as if you're looking for your lost conscience'; and Andrew Devonshire to Richard Stanley, a wobbler: 'The Stanleys started running away at Bosworth Field and they've been running ever since.'

Although I did not normally make political speeches – Anthony was not in favour – it was felt that given recent events I should make some remarks, especially to allay concerns in the Party about his health. So I said:*

We had said that we would cease all military action as soon as the Israeli and Egyptian governments accepted an unconditional ceasefire and the international forces arrived. On November 6th, both these governments had in fact promised to do so.

In the light of the undertaking which we had given, HMG could not have refused to conform in also ordering a ceasefire. We had already secured our main objective: to halt hostilities and thereby prevent their wider spread.

Secondly, what seems clear enough to most people is that their action has revealed the extent and the imminence of the plot. Russian tanks, Russian planes, Russian armoured vehicles, Russian ammunition and Russian rockets are reported to have been found in vast quantities. That a most sinister hornets' nest has been uncovered is surely evident from the violent reactions that have come from certain quarters in the last few days.

While dictatorships exist, left ones or right ones, big ones or small ones, we cannot risk a foreign policy that defers conflict or

---

* This was the speech which Clarissa began: 'For the past three months I have felt as if the Suez Canal was flowing through my drawing room.'

principle, that pacifies on principle those who act against the vital interests of our country or of peace itself.

My speech had good coverage. Coming down in the train from Doncaster I took the notice off my reserved compartment and two Americans got in. At the end of the journey they said goodbye, apologised for having barged in, said they didn't know who I was until they saw the photographs in the paper. They wished Anthony good luck and one of them said, 'I guess we've had time to think things over now.'

Anthony worried about the two so-called stalwarts, Harold and Bobbety – Harold because he is so worried about money, and Bobbety because he is so worried about Anglo-American relations.

Anthony rather desperate at leaving, trying to stiffen up telegrams to Selwyn that the Cabinet drafted when he was in bed.

The doctors at this point insisted Anthony should get away. Ann Fleming offered her husband Ian's house in Jamaica for a few weeks' rest, which we accepted. This was thought a mistake, but a spell in Berkshire or somewhere would not have been any good, as Anthony would simply have gone on working.

So off we went to Jamaica. Goldeneye, which could not have been a greater contrast, was perched on its own coral bay. Noël Coward, a neighbour, sent down Frank Cooper's marmalade and Huntley & Palmers biscuits, which was not what we had been looking forward to, exactly. Jamaica is a beautiful island, but sinister. There were strange tom-toms beating in the night – but when I asked Violet, the cook, what was going on she said, 'Sal-va-tion Army.' I was not wholly convinced. Ann told me that when they returned to

Goldeneye they found that the security men had carved 'God bless Sir Anthony' on all the trees.

DIARY — 14 DECEMBER, RETURN FROM JAMAICA

Got several panicky telegrams while we were out there about debates and so on but the government majorities were good.

Returned to find everyone looking at us with thoughtful eyes — evidently the criticism has been rather strong. Letters to me are as good as ever.

The first day Anthony tells the Cabinet that he went away because he was told that it was the only possible way of getting well. He didn't know if he had got well — did they wish him to continue?

Bobbety, Rab, Amory, Patrick, Kilmuir, Eccles, Sandys, Alan, Walter all said yes. Harold and Macleod said only Anthony could decide.

Peter Thorneycroft said Anthony should go, and say he was going to unite the country and the world.

Selwyn had said no then changed his mind when the majority said yes.

It never seemed to me that health was affecting any of Anthony's judgements and this was the opinion of those working for him. I do not remember him being dependent on daily stimulants and I was there with him every day and night. Horace Evans may have prescribed them, but Anthony was not a person who wished to jeopardise his judgement — he even refused to take Sparine, the tranquilliser prescribed, though I made use of them. Later, before and after our return from Jamaica, he was taking the prescribed dose of Drinamyl.

In the course of the next ten days over a rather dismal Christmas at Chequers, Poole and Kilmuir were sounded out again. Both said,

'For God's sake, stay. We would rather have you at half cock than anyone else.' In this undecided frame of mind we returned to London on New Year's Day, with Anthony feeling terribly tired and having pains again. Then, and only then, were the doctors back once more.

To our astonishment we now found Horace Evans adamant. He said Anthony would eventually kill himself, but before that he would collapse, possibly in about six weeks, certainly by Easter. We were dumbfounded and rather shocked. He stuck to his guns in front of Bobbie Allan and Roger Scarbrough, who very kindly came down from Sheffield to advise us as a friend. Roger thought Anthony ought to try and stay, but admitted that the job needed someone who was very well.

The following evening Horace brought in the old surgeon of eighty-five who had made a brief appearance at the London Clinic to advise us to go to Boston three years earlier. He seemed not to make very much sense but was emphatic that to go on could mean danger to the liver.

DIARY — 4 JANUARY 1957

Anthony saw Norman Brook this morning and he felt that three months hence would be no easier than now and probably more difficult. Keightley to lunch with his wife – both really nice.

He seems cheerful after his experiences. He is going to the US in the spring to lecture. This Suez business was his last job. He says he thinks the Dutch and Germans who are clearing the Canal want to go slow to do us down. Even the US, too. The troops hate Gaitskell. Ian Jacob's son in the Navy said the crew came to ask if they could turn Gaitskell off when he was on the wireless.

DIARY — 7 JANUARY

A weekend of tossing and turning. Anthony's pains came back

on top of everything else, or perhaps because of everything else. After dinner Norman and Bobbety came round. Everyone seemed stunned but accepted the inevitable and we went over the bulletin that Horace had produced.

DIARY – 8 JANUARY

Anthony has to go through a Cabinet and listen to Harold prosing for half an hour. This almost puts him against recommending Harold. By train to Sandringham. Many photographers. We arrive into the hall where everyone is looking at the television. Talking to Adeane, Anthony suggested Bobbety, Kilmuir & Winston as advisers to the Queen.

Anthony says he feels the waters sweep on over him now. The moment they know he is to go, they continue making their plans, and the machine grinds on.

DIARY – 9 JANUARY

Dreary journey back to London. A large crowd of photographers at Liverpool Street. Horace & Norman come, and the announcement of resignation is made final.

Anthony then tells Rab, who is completely taken by surprise – Rab says to me afterwards, 'What a shame. He's really quite popular in the country, you know', and Harold, who bursts into floods of crocodile tears. Norman is in real tears. Then the Cabinet. Bobbety reads out a little piece about their long association and his great love & admiration for Anthony but breaks down in the middle. Rab says a piece, so of course Harold has to say a piece too. Anthony then sees the junior ministers who are also very nice – even Nigel Birch. Antony Head comes up to Anthony's bedroom while he changes for the Palace and is very upset and understanding.

Anthony goes to the Palace to give up his seals of office. The Queen says that she has been fortunate in having Anthony.

She thanks him for always being so helpful and making it so nice for her. Anthony refuses an earldom.

After Harold became Prime Minister we stayed briefly at Chequers before embarking for New Zealand. I went up to London, dodging the press at all the main gates at Chequers, and spent an awful day packing up. It was the longest weekend I've ever spent. Dorothy Macmillan came to see me on Saturday. None of the servants wanted to stay. Mrs Skitt gave me a cooking lesson on Sunday morning and cried into the eggs.

DIARY – 13 JANUARY

We were horrified that Harold proposes himself to dinner at Chequers on Monday night. Harold arrives three quarters of an hour late, extremely gracious to both of us. I mistrust him the most when he is like this. He talks of loyalty, the North country, our holiday. 'I'm sure you've had hundreds of letters,' etc. etc. We get information about the changes in driblets.

He sent for Rab and said to him, 'I will offer you anything you like, provided you do not intrigue against me.' Rab went away and came back saying he wanted the Foreign Office. Harold talked him out of that, which would have been a complete denial of Suez. Harold then said to us that of course Rab couldn't have it because we'd got to show Ike & Dulles we meant it, and so on – 'anyway for a few months'!

CHAPTER 16

AFTER

We decided on a trip to New Zealand and eventually on to the Pacific Islands. The RMS *Rangitata* was sailing for Auckland, so we arranged to sail on her. We drove to the docks from Chequers. The Pooles, Leathers, Michael Adeane, Ted Heath, Alec Home, the Waverleys (he was the Chairman of the Port of London Authority), Webbs and so on were there to see us off. Ava Waverley, the skeleton at the feast, said how well Anthony looked and she didn't understand it etc. I refused to answer her letters after this. We found our cabin crammed with flowers.

When the *Rangitata* set slowly off, at each lock the out-of-breath figure of Brendan Bracken appeared – he had arrived late and wanted to give Anthony a box of cigars; finally he caught up. As we went down the Thames all the ships were dressed overall and sending messages of good luck. The boys on the *Worcester* training ship lined the rails to give three cheers and a submarine raced along beside us. Anthony was very unhappy.

Going through the Panama Canal was an anticlimax. A very narrow waterway and no tropical scenery. In the Pacific, the ship stopped briefly offshore at Pitcairn Island, from which whaling boats were launched. I was told the Pitcairn Home Secretary was on one of them. Remembering the stately John Waverley, Home Secretary in 1940, it was therefore a surprise when a ragbag of shoeless figures came aboard with bundles of souvenirs for us. They were all called Christian – the *Bounty* mutineers' descendants.

On our arrival at Auckland there was a fantastic reception. A band playing, a red carpet, vociferous cheering crowds at the Auckland docks and Sid Holland waiting to greet us. We were driven off in the scented air to dinner at the Hollands'.

We had been lent a house at Otekai on the Bay of Islands. Our bay had downs and combes, with groves of pohutukawa trees running right down to the beaches, with deserted sand and rocks covered with oysters – the garden full of hibiscus, bananas, peaches and figs and a magnolia grandiflora as large as an English elm. It was a revelation and a breathtaking combination of everything we liked most in scenery and climate. For several mad days we determined to stay there for ever.

As usual, the Eden family tentacles had reached New Zealand in the past, the town being named after Lord Auckland and the prison on the hill called Mount Eden. New Zealand was rather like America must have been a hundred years ago – but somnolent, because of the climate, and with no one there.

However, I felt sad about everything, even though our mail was still terrific. Then Anthony's sudden high fevers returned.

After some weeks it became clear an emergency operation was inevitable and our dream of the South Pacific, Samoa and Tahiti was over. Sid Holland provided a Sunderland flying boat as far as Vancouver, an horrific trial of discomfort.

So back to Boston and the New England Baptist Hospital for Anthony, and the Ritz Carlton Hotel for me.

We were met at Boston by the British Consul and I found his wife was an old school colleague of mine (and also of Pamela Churchill).

In Boston we got two hundred letters a day on average; almost all went out of their way to mention Suez favourably, ashamed of the part their government had played, though few abused Eisenhower or even Dulles, so they weren't all Democrats.

When John Amies, Winthrop Aldrich's ex-assistant in London, said to me at a luncheon given by my new friends the Coolidges (son of President Coolidge), 'But why didn't you go on?' I replied, 'How could we, when your government instructed Wall Street to sell the pound to the tune of 40 million in one week?' Silence.

*   *   *

Amies was not alone among Americans. When Selwyn Lloyd went to visit the dying Dulles in hospital in November 1956, Dulles had tauntingly asked, 'Selwyn, why did you stop? Why didn't you go through with it and get Nasser down?' Lloyd, astonished, replied, 'Well, Foster, if you had so much as winked at us we might have gone on.' But Dulles replied that he could not have done that.

He maintained that the only difference between them was over method, and deplored that the British had not brought down Nasser. He told others, including Dean Rusk, US Secretary of State to President Kennedy and President Johnson, that he regretted what had happened and how badly the US had handled the affair, and excused himself on the grounds that he was ill (with stomach cancer) at the time. To Christian Pineau he said, 'We were wrong about Suez. You were the ones who were right.'

Richard Nixon, US Vice-President at the time, later regretted that the US, partly because of the timing of the election, had forced the British and French to abandon their efforts to punish Nasser for his expropriation of the Suez Canal and then condemned them for resorting to force in pursuit of their foreign policy objectives. According to Nixon, Eisenhower later said Suez was 'his major foreign policy mistake'.

*   *   *

After Anthony's fourth major operation we finally got back to England. One of the first people to come to lunch was Max Beaverbrook, his chauffeur having arrived two hours before with a small packet of Sanka (decaffeinated) coffee for his personal use. Beaverbrook, once having decided to back Anthony, continued – fuelled partly I suspect by his dislike of Harold. He said to Anthony that all the country was on his side, that he had a terrific position; when he was well he must use it to oust Macmillan, the Socialists and his own rotten ex-Cabinet: 'You are young yet; you must never think of complete retirement' and so on. 'What you did was a fine and courageous thing' etc.

*

Anthony was sixty-one when he retired from politics. He survived for nearly another twenty years and remained energetic, playing tennis, travelling, writing, farming. I was pleased to leave politics, and that we could have a marriage without all the tensions, plottings and shenanigans of political life.

Although we had kept my cottage, Rose Bower, we began to look for a larger house, which Anthony anyway needed to write his memoirs. From Rose Bower, with me at the wheel, we made dozens of expeditions. It had to be Wiltshire or Dorset.

Anthony, with his family roots in County Durham, always said the people in the North were quicker witted and nicer but he could not stand the climate, so it had to be the South. As it turned out, this was a wise decision because we did go to London from time to time and he eventually took up his earldom (Attlee's 'rate for the job') so that he could speak on foreign affairs in the Lords.

Sent by Brendan Bracken to look at a house near Pewsey in Wiltshire one day, I chanced to go down a lane and came upon a red-brick seventeenth-century manor with Georgian windows and an enormous ilex tree. The tree settled it for me and we stayed there eight years. During this time Anthony was writing his memoirs and we needed bedrooms for secretaries and researchers. Gardening was rewarding for me, being on greensand.

The memoirs finished, we found a smaller red-brick Queen Anne manor in – to my joy and Anthony's ruefulness – the very same Wiltshire valley where my cottage was. 'I knew I'd end up in your valley,' said Anthony, but it was easy enough to reach friends from London or Oxford and we had neighbours to suit both of us. The film star Claudette Colbert got hopelessly lost coming from London, Suez stalwart John Sparrow's car broke down coming from Oxford, Mrs Thatcher descended by helicopter and Marcel Ophüls filmed there for *Le Chagrin et la Pitié*, with Anthony the only English politician capable of doing his part in French.

We went to Paris every year, where Anthony would visit the galleries and occasionally buy a painting and always the latest books from the old man in the rue St Honoré. The embassy always put us up and we would have a lunch at the Elysée in President de Gaulle's day, which took place *à quatre*. Afterwards de Gaulle would take Anthony into the garden for a private talk which always ended with him urging Anthony to return to political life. Winston would certainly have got rid of de Gaulle during the war but for Anthony sympathising with the General's awkwardness, and de Gaulle had not forgotten this.

One winter we went to Mexico. Brendan Bracken had business connections there and offered to lend us the company houses and the company aeroplane. Acapulco was then a fishing village and Cuernavaca an inland country town. Settled in a handsome house, Anthony remarked, 'I think there is a woman here I used to know – married to some Mexican.'

The woman turned out to be Merle Oberon – film star and erstwhile wife of Alex Korda. I took Merle to Yucatan. But I thought what tragic figures film stars are – with their small bones, their discontented little faces and their utter, complete egocentricity. She slept badly, she had an allergy, she was always late, and she was followed around by a pallid little husband who called her 'Baby'. Finally, at Uxmal, after hanging about as usual, I jumped into the car and went off. Merle duly appeared, a bit ruffled. Looking back, I remember someone with a rather marvellous face. (I named a whippet after her, as they looked alike.) With little charm, and a lot of will-power, she was not a 'Baby'.

On the excuse that Anthony should avoid colds and flu, we took to going to the West Indies each winter. Thus we visited Mustique, which had just been bought by my friend Colin Tennant. From there we saw on an adjacent island a white spot poised above a deserted long white beach flanked by a coconut grove. We rushed over and bought the small gingerbread house on the island of Bequia – then with no hotel, no roads, no electricity, no water, no telephone and no airstrip. It was paradise. We were the only non-Caribbeans, except a young American who was said to have figured this was the safest place to be if there was an atomic war. Friends could only visit us unannounced from their yachts – including my Uncle Winston on Onassis's boat. We had halcyon winters there and were able to master huge works of literature not possible elsewhere.

For our winters away we then moved to a beautiful plantation house on Barbados, Villa Nova, where it seemed as if the whole world passed through the doors – writers, playboys, politicians, members of the royal family including the Queen. In the garden was a mammoth avocado tree and an even larger mango, which the monkeys usually got before we did. Anthony and Dean Acheson went out with guns to try to frighten them off but came back shocked, having witnessed a monkey funeral procession. One winter when we had a party with the choir of the Seventh Day Adventists from nearby Mount Pleasant singing carols, Dean made a fuss about having to meet Princess Alice, Chancellor of the University of the West Indies; in a matter of minutes the pair of them were in gales of laughter together.

There were also many friends on the island – above all, Anthony's old colleague Ronald Tree, who had built himself a Palladian house of coral stone. When his wife, Marietta, was away in New York, the house would be full of titled English. When she returned it was New York intelligentsia: Adlai Stevenson, Arthur Schlesinger and Hamilton Fish Armstrong. Our favourite neighbour, Claudette Colbert, became a great friend. She had a marvellously stylish house up the coast from Ronnie's, with exquisite food and servants dressed as in the French islands with high twisting turbans. Her father had been chief chef at a New York club where, according to Oliver Lyttelton, he invented Sole Colbert. Nothing to do with Louis XIV's Chief Minister.

Back in England Anthony would speak occasionally in the Lords and every year we visited Stratford – part of his old constituency – where he was President of the RSC, and where friends from the 1920s – Glen Byam Shaw and Angela Baddeley – still were. He had a passion for Shakespeare and whenever he had gone away to a conference or on holiday, he had always taken a small volume of one of the plays with him. He was moved to find that his son Simon had a copy of Hamlet with him when he died.

In the country Anthony had gallantly given gardening over to me, but as he had an unparalleled eye for quality, he started breeding pedigree Hereford cattle (we had just enough acreage to do this). He was always able to pick out a good animal for stud. They all looked the same to me. He became President of the Hereford Herd Book Society. As the pre-name for the herd was Avon, all the bulls were named from characters in Shakespeare. Russian and French breeders would visit. Avon Warwick went to Russia – I always wondered what was his fate. And Avon Priam got a first at the Royal Show.

In spite of two further operations, twenty years passed easily and pleasantly, though Anthony could never forget the fears he had had about Russia and the future of oil – fears which are with us to this day.

By 1976 his strength was failing. As I wrote to Mrs Thatcher, 'His health was gradually robbing him of his zest for life.' During the last two years of his life we spent the winter months at Averell and Pamela Harriman's house in Florida. It was there that the end began, Jim Callaghan arranging for him to be flown back to England so that he could die at home. He was a few months short of his eightieth birthday.

He was buried not in County Durham, where his forebears have lain for centuries, but in the churchyard at Alvediston, his last home. I asked Reynolds Stone to design his tomb in Portland stone and inscribed it with all the offices he held during more than thirty years of service to his country.

SELECT BIBLIOGRAPHY

Dean Achesom: *Present at the Creation: My Years at the State Department* Hamish Hamilton 1970

Stephen E. Ambrose: *Eisenhower: The President* Vol. 2, *1952–1969* George Allen & Unwin 1984

Mark Amory: *Lord Berners: The Last Eccentric* Chatto & Windus 1998

——(ed.): *The Letters of Ann Fleming* Collins Harvill 1985

——(ed.) *The Letters of Evelyn Waugh* Weidenfeld & Nicolson 1983

Cecil Beaton: *The Years Between: Diaries 1939–44* Weidenfeld & Nicolson 1965

——*The Happy Years: Diaries 1944–48* Weidenfeld & Nicolson 1972

——*The Strenuous Years: Diaries 1948–55* Weidenfeld & Nicolson 1973

Anthony Beevor and Artemis Cooper: *Paris after the Liberation 1945–1949* Penguin Books 2004

David Ben-Gurion: *Israel: Years of Challenge* Anthony Blond 1964

Isaiah Berlin (ed. Henry Hardy): *Flourishing: Letters 1928–1946*, Chatto & Windus 2004

Gerald Berners: *Far From the Madding War* Constable 1941

Peter G. Boyle (ed.): *The Eden–Eisenhower Correspondence, 1955–1957* University of North Carolina Press 2005

Richard Buckle (ed.): *Self-Portrait with Friends: The Selected Diaries of Cecil Beaton 1926–1974* Weidenfeld & Nicolson 1979

David Butler: *The British General Electron of 1955* Macmillan 1955

Lord Butler: *The Art of the Possible* Hamish Hamilton 1971

James Cable: *The Geneva Conference of 1954 on Indochina* Macmillan 2000

David Carlton: *Anthony Eden: A Biography* Allen Lane 1981

Peter Catterall (ed.): *The Macmillan Diaries: The Cabinet Years* 1950–1957 Macmillan 2003

John Spencer Churchill: *Crowded Canvas: The Memoirs of John Spencer Churchill* Odhams Press 1961

William Clark: *From Three Worlds: Memoirs* Sidgwick & Jackson 1986

John Colville: *The Fringes of Power: Downing Street Diaries 1939–1955* Hodder & Stoughton 1985

Hannah Cranborne (ed.): *David Cecil: A Portrait by His Friends* Dovecote Press 1990

Michael Davie (ed.): *The Diaries of Evelyn Waugh* Weidenfeld & Nicolson 1976

Moshe Dayan: *Story of My Life* Weidenfeld & Nicolson 1976

Charles Drazin: *Korda: Britain's Only Movie Mogul* Sidgwick & Jackson 2002

David Dutton: *Anthony Eden: A Life and Reputation* Arnold/Hodder Headline 1997

Anthony Eden: *The Eden Memoirs: Full Circle* Cassell 1960

——*The Eden Memoirs: Facing the Dictators* Cassell 1962

——*The Eden Memoirs: The Reckoning* Cassell 1965

——*Another World: 1897–1917* Allen Lane 1976

Timothy Eden: *The Tribulations of a Baronet* Macmillan 1933

Dwight D. Eisenhower: *The Papers of Dwight David Eisenhower. The Presidency: The Middle Way* Johns Hopkins University Press 1996

Herman Finer: *Dulles over Suez: The Theory and Practice of his Diplomacy* Quadrangle Books 1964

Martin Gilbert: *Never Despair: Winston S. Churchill 1945–1965* Heinemann 1988

——*Churchill: A Life* Minerva 1991

Cynthia Gladwyn (ed. Miles Jebb): *The Diaries of Cynthia Gladwyn* Constable 1995

Victoria Glendinning: *Elizabeth Bowen: Portrait of a Writer* Weidenfeld & Nicolson 1977

Nicholas Henderson: *Mandarin: The Diaries of Nicholas Henderson* Weidenfeld & Nicolson 1994

——*The Private Office Revisited* Profile Books 2001

Alistair Horne: *Macmillan 1894–1956*, Vol. 1 of the Official Biography Macmillan 1989

Michael Ignatieff: *Isaiah Berlin: A Life* Chatto & Windus 1998

Michael Korda: *Charmed Lives* Allen Lane 1980

Keith Kyle: *Suez* Weidenfeld & Nicolson, 1991

Jeremy Lewis: *Cyril Connolly: A Life* Jonathan Cape 1997

Selwyn Lloyd: *Suez 1956: A Personal Account* Jonathan Cape 1978

Fitzroy Maclean: *Eastern Approaches* Jonathan Cape 1949

Harold Macmillan: *Tides of Fortune 1945–1955* Macmillan 1971

——*Riding the Storm 1956–1959* Macmillan 1972

Frank McLynn: *Fitzroy Maclean* John Murray 1992

Charlotte Mosley (ed.): *The Letters of Nancy Mitford and Evelyn Waugh* Hodder & Stoughton 1996

John Julius Norwich (ed.): *The Duff Cooper Diaries* Weidenfeld & Nicolson 2005

Anthony Nutting: *No End of a Lesson: The Story of Suez* Constable 1967

James Pope-Hennessy: *London Fabric* B. T. Batsford 1939

Peter Quennell (ed.): *A Lonely Business: A Self-Portrait of James Pope-Hennessy* Weidenfeld & Nicolson 1981

Robert Rhodes James: *Anthony Eden* Weidenfeld & Nicolson 1986

Andrew Roberts: *A History of the English-Speaking Peoples Since 1900* Weidenfeld & Nicolson 2006

Michael Sheldon *Friends of Promise: Cyril Connolly and the World of Horizon* Hamish Hamilton 1989

Avi Shlaim: *Iron Wall: Israel and the Arab World* Allen Lane 2000

Evelyn Shuckburgh (ed. John Charmley): *Descent to Suez: Diaries 1951–1956* Weidenfeld & Nicolson 1986

David Sinclair: *Dynasty: The Astors and Their Times* J. M. Dent 1983

Mary Soames: *Clementine Churchill* Cassell 1979

——*Speaking for Themselves: The Personal Letters of Winston and Clementine Churchill* Doubleday 1998

Francis Steegmuller: *Jean Cocteau: A Biography* Little, Brown 1970

Hugh Thomas: *The Suez Affair* Weidenfeld & Nicolson 1967

Alan Thompson: *The Day before Yesterday* Sidgwick & Jackson 1971

D. R. Thorpe: *Eden: The Life and Times of Anthony Eden First Earl of Avon, 1897–1977* Chatto & Windus 2003

——*Selwyn Lloyd* Jonathan Cape 1989

Hugo Vickers: *Cecil Beaton: The Authorised Biography* Weidenfeld & Nicolson 1985

——*Loving Garbo* Random House 1994

George Weidenfeld: *Remembering My Good Friends* HarperCollins 1995

INDEX